DELIVERANCE FROM DEMONIC POWERS THAT RUN OUR LIVES

SUPERPOWER PRAYERS FOR HEALTH AND FREEDOM SERIES

BOOK 1

MARIA T. TONELLO

My Pomegranate

Published by
My Pomegranate Inspiration Books
My Pomegranate LLC
United States of America
www.mypomegranate.me

For worldwide distribution printed in the
United States of America.
Cover and logo design by Tiffany Schramm

Library of Congress Cataloging-in-Publication Data has been applied for:

ISBN: 979-8-9915613-0-3 (Paperback)

ISBN: 979-8-9915613-1-0 (E-book)

ISBN: 979-8-9915613-2-7 (Hardcover)

TESTIMONIALS

"I think your prayer protocols (Leviathan, Python and Jezebel) are right on target not only for the USA but for the world. May God continue to be with you, guiding you, and filling you with abundant blessings. I thank you from the bottom of my heart for your dedication and leadership." S.B.

"We were praying against the mammon spirit in the courts of heaven. All of my life I've noticed overdrafts always ending up with a few dollars, getting cheated out of inheritances, but after going to the courts with you all and praying against the (mammon) spirit, my cable bill went from $222 a month down to $49.69. I see and hear our Father working in my life." J.R.

"I wanted to write and share how blessed I am by the recent turnaround in the Strike Force protocols. I am so grateful for your dedication to pray; to instruct the remnant how to unity (sic) and pray purposefully and scripturally. Through my weekly prayers, under your loving guidance, I have found myself set free from strongholds and demonic bastions that have set themselves upon against (sic) me. Through your prayer protocols I have seen myself walking in total freedom in Christ Jesus. Thank you for your time and countless hours spent on designing these prayer protocols. Never stop!! God bless the work of your hands. " S.D.

"I love your protocols. They have helped me cleanse so many aspects of my life - and to operate in the authority of Jesus." J.B.

"I know the python spirit had me bound since 1972. Something has been lifted off my chest and lungs. I am not kidding. I have had such an increase of joy as well as a revival to my breath. I also have such a new found freedom. The curse is gone. This has been a huge revival and yes, the healing of a woman's soul. Total miracle. Such huge joy and I am so glad to be able to share it with you. Healing and deliverance." P.M.

"Thank you so much for these powerful well thought out and Holy Spirit Full prayers! We do them in our Ekklesia groups regularly. God bless you in the New Year!" D. O.

ACKNOWLEDGMENTS

Thank you Jesus Christ Yeshua! You ARE the Son of the Living God and my life is a testimony that You are real and You do heal. Thank you Holy Spirit for being my writing partner. It has been a true co-creative process and I thank you for the honor of creating these works with you.

Thank you Heavenly Father, for your unwavering love, patience and guiding hand on my life, even when I did not believe it was there. Thank you for entrusting me with these teachings and revelations, to be able to help and serve your children on their journey home to You.

Thank you Michael Ortega for encouraging and supporting me in what God has been calling me to do. You taught me about the Heart of the Father by demonstrating it. Knowing the Heart of the Father has been a game-changer to live in His Divine Will and see others through His eyes and heart.

Much love and gratitude to our faithful Intercessors. When God was giving us a new wine and new wineskin, you courageously persevered and we all went to new, amazing heights together with the Holy Spirit, *Unity in the Spirit*. God love you!

Thank you to my father Francesco and my mother Rosalie for raising me in the Faith.

TABLE OF CONTENTS

FOREWORD

"You must continually be clothed
with the full armor of God
to enable you to stand
against the strategies of the devil:
because the wrestling for us is
not with blood and flesh,
but with the rulers,
with the powers,
with the world rulers of this darkness,
with the spiritual forces of wickedness
in the heavenlies."

Ephesians 6:11-12
ONM

PREFACE

"Your eyes have seen my unformed substance;
And in your book were all written
The days that were appointed for me,
When as yet there was not one of them
[even taking shape]."
Psalm 139:16

HOW TO GET THE MOST FROM THIS BOOK

This book is designed to take you progressively on a very personal journey to remove what has:

- Clouded over your indwelling spirit
- Blocked or denied your authentic self
- Kept you from fulfilling your God destiny
- Denied your true identity and life in Christ Jesus, who incarnated as our role model *made in God's image*
- Blocked you from being healed and reconciled to God through the Passion gift of Jesus Christ

We all have character flaws, weaknesses and bad habits that are not God's design for us. They are part of the kingdom of darkness through which hidden, demonic powers work and have their power over us.

We are peeling back layers and layers of programs, conditioning, traumas and yes, demonization. That may sound scary but the truth is that we have all been affected by the demonic realm, aka the kingdom of darkness, because we live in a fallen world.

Jesus Christ declared that the adversary aka satan is *"the ruler of this world."* He is a formidable enemy and has a hierarchy of demons that operate under him in his realm. It is an unseen realm. We have not been educated about this realm. For many of us, myself included, we have intentionally avoided knowing about this realm. It can seem a bit scary, negative and even intimidating.

Fear not — this book has been designed in collaboration with the Holy Spirit, to be as easy as possible to understand and quickly apply. I will provide a list of recommended books if you would like to learn more deeply about some of the strategies we will use. They are all excellent.[1]

This book is for people who do not have the time or inclination to read a stack of books. All the teachings and prayer protocols in this book are backed by the Holy Scriptures and are proven by hundreds of prayer warriors from all walks of life.

I recommend you do each protocol at least three times. New things can come up each time you do them. It can be more powerful the third time than the first! Even months or more later, you may feel called to repeat some protocols. Consider it part of spiritual hygiene.

Most importantly, you are never alone on your journey for health and freedom. God your Father, Jesus Christ your brother, and your friend the Holy Spirit, are always here for you!

"You have enclosed me behind and before,
and placed your hand upon me."
Psalm 139:5

IN THIS BOOK YOU WILL LEARN HOW TO:

- Identify demonic powers.
- Take authority over them in your life.
- Remove the unseen hand of demonic powers and influences.
- Identify self-limiting and self-sabotaging elements in your own character and personality that are traits of and food for these demonic powers.
- Learn protocols for overcoming these elements.
- Replace flaws and weaknesses with virtues and strengths which are an inoculation against demonic powers.
- Open to transformational growth.

TO RECAP:

- Read and speak OUT LOUD all of the prayer protocols in order.
- Do each prayer protocol at least three times.
- Repeat any of them as much as you want, even weeks or months after first doing them.
- Consider the protocols as part of your spiritual hygiene.
- Customize the protocols to fit your specific needs. They are templates.

EVERYTHING JESUS DID ACTIVATED OUR OWN ABILITY TO DO THE SAME WHEN WE ARE TRULY SAVED.

Please note:

This book is not for people who are demonically possessed. That requires an exorcist professional. However, exorcists say that most requests they receive can be resolved without a professional exorcist. This book is for people who are experiencing a degree of oppression (most of humanity) and are willing to do their part in breaking free and staying free. Please see the disclaimer on the Copyright page.

This book is ecumenical in nature. That is, it is inclusive of different Christian denominations. As such, different bible translations are used, as well as other citations, in order to offer a greater richness.

However, because the New American Standard Bible is open source, allowing for a higher number of citations, it is the most prevalent translation used. The Amplified Bible (AMP) typically contains content in parentheses. There are other translations cited on the Copyright page and referenced in the end notes.

When the exact scripture is provided, it is in both italics and quotations. When it has been customized to first person to use as a declaration, it is still in italics but without the quotations.

Lastly, we do not dignify the demons by capitalizing their names.

———

PART ONE

LAYING THE GROUNDWORK

CHAPTER 1

LET'S BEGIN!

WELCOME! And congratulations! On taking this step towards deliverance from bondage!

PURIFICATION IS THE KEY

Our emancipation comes through purification — purifying our mind, heart and soul of things that have bound us in suffering and limitations, sorrows and wounds. This involves releasing wounds, habits, beliefs and wrongs committed by yourself or others in your bloodline that are causing pain and negative repercussions in your life.

You can apply these prayer protocols to any situation or dimension of your life. The only proviso is that you must get permission for applying them to anyone other than yourself and your underage children. Free will must be honored.

We will be using spiritual power tools that have been proven highly effective in resolving stubborn and long-term issues.

There are easy-to-follow steps designed to get you quickly up and running to solutions, healing and breakthroughs.

We will be applying principles from the Courts of Heaven and Divine Restraining Orders throughout this book. The prayer protocols are unique with proven results. You can treat them as templates and customize them as you see fit. Don't worry, we will go over all the key principles and you will be given everything you need to fly on new wings!

What is a Demonic Power and How Did It Get in My Life?

A demonic power as spoken of in Ephesians 6:12 as "*against powers*", is a very powerful force from the demonic realm that has dominion over a specific set of traits, area of life and/or a region in a country. They have a strong hold and influence over people's lives, their relationships and their personalties without them even realizing it.

They are often referred to as "strongholds." They can control and operate through individuals, families, organizations, governments and geographic regions. Several are mentioned in detail in the Bible. You will learn how to recognize them. All that we present in this book has its basis in the Sacred Scriptures (Bible).

If you grew up in a particular environment — your family or ethnic culture for example, where one of these powers is active, you have most likely become acclimated to certain demonic powers and even normalized their very existence, influences and traits. You've normalized the way life is experienced with that demonic power affecting and infecting your life and your relationships. It is time for you to be free!

Demonic Powers Can Affect Our:

- Character
- Relationships
- Personality traits
- Beliefs, choices, actions, fate and destiny
- Filters of how we see, interpret and respond to life

It is impossible to live in this world and not have ever been exposed to and affected by these forces. This is because they are everywhere and embedded in our culture. People's behavior, thoughts, words and deeds actually feed them. They grow and strengthen through the negative speech and actions of individuals or groups of people. This is because people make the qualities of these demonic powers part of their own persona and become very comfortable and attached to them. Once a person is truly dedicated and committed to being delivered from them, healing and freedom will follow.

WE MAKE QUALITIES OF DEMONIC POWERS
PART OF OUR OWN PERSONA.

THIS IS HOW THEY HAVE ACCESS TO AFFECT OUR LIFE.

. . .

But no worries.... you are here! That means you ARE committed to being free and being your true authentic self as God designed and destined you to be.

Why Do I Need So Many Different Prayers for Healing and Deliverance?

This is a common (and reasonable!) question. If we need healing for a physical health issue for example, why should we address bloodline curses and territorial spirits? If I need help in my finances, why should I care about regional strongholds? Short answer: because your problems could be stemming from one or more sources or causes. We just don't always know where the problems are coming from or why they are so persistent.

Also our bondage is unfortunately, multi-dimensional. That is, there can be mental bondage through wrong beliefs and mental filters, emotional bondage that damages relationship happiness, and spiritual bondage that has been keeping you in a very small version of yourself and thus limiting or blocking your ability to fulfill your God destiny.

KNOWLEDGE OF DEMONIC POWERS IS EMPOWERING

Awareness of the existence of demonic powers is crucial and also empowering. Awareness of and understanding who they are, what they do and how they operate will build your confidence to overcome them. One reason they are so powerful and pervasive is because they are stealth. Most people don't know they exist. They don't know that these powers are lurking under the surface, behind trees, around the corner. Another reason they are so powerful is because people are afraid of them.

Learning how to recognize them operating in your life or situation is a huge step to taking greater charge over your life. Knowledge is power! Learning to recognize the signs and symptoms of demonic powers enables you to overcome your fear of them.

Demonic powers are so powerful and effective because most people don't know they even exist. People don't realize they are being controlled or affected by them. These demonic powers count on people never knowing who they are.

Your power tool is remembering who you are in Christ Jesus Yeshua; and that you have been *"given all authority to tread on snakes and scorpions, and over all the power of the enemy. Nothing will harm you."* Luke 10:19

> *"I will give you the keys of the kingdom of heaven,*
> *and whatever you bind on earth*
> *shall be bound in heaven,*
> *and whatever you loose on earth*
> *shall be loosed in heaven."*
> Matthew 16:19

OVERCOMING DEMONIC POWERS BRINGS FREEDOM

Remember, all non-divine (not from God) powers, forces and spirits have one thing in common: to make you forget your divine nature and identity made in God's image, to separate you from your divine nature, and to block your God purpose and destiny from being fulfilled. This is the very definition of bondage. This is why we are doing this kind of deliverance: to free you from their grip and help you reset to your God destiny path.

We are waking up to all the ways we have been programmed into bondage and are now breaking the shackles to be free as God designed and destined us to be. Demonic beings absolutely hate our divinity. They hate that we have what they will never have: the Divine Creator within us and the ability to truly create beautiful things including life itself. Now is your time to remember who you are and clear your life of all the bramble that has limited you!

JESUS IS THE WAY TO HEALTH AND FREEDOM

The proof is in the pudding![1] There is no other world figure, spiritual leader or healer that has over 2000 years of testimonials across all races and 100's of nationalities, ethnicities and cultures. None. Only Jesus Christ Yeshua. The name above all other names is the name by which countless miracles have occurred.[2]

100s of millions of people across the earth have been healed and delivered in the name of Jesus Christ.[3] There are so many documented miracles of His healing and deliverance. Drug addicts have been instantly healed of their addictions. There have been miracle healings and recovery from injuries. There have been miracles of relationship restoration, protection and favor in battle, hardened criminals reformed and transformed, breakthroughs and overcoming seemingly lost causes. Saints dedicated to His Gospel of Love have incorruptible bodies decades and centuries after their death.[4]

Ask God to reveal His Truth to You and He will do so. The Way is not complicated. The Kingdom of Heaven is for those who enter as children.

> Ask God to reveal His Truth to You
> and He will.

HEALING OUR HEART & SOUL BRINGS TRUE FREEDOM

Jesus' ministry is a ministry of healing and deliverance. It is a ministry of reconciliation; that is, reconciling and restoring us to a relationship with God the Father, and to our divine identity and purpose.

This reconciliation is fundamentally a healing of the heart and soul. We were created from pure love and are reconciled to return to that love. Jesus came as the Incarnation of pure love and as the Incarnation of God's Divine Mercy.

Jesus came to create the Way back to union with God the Father, back to pure love. He came to set us free from the ravages of this fallen world, which is riddled with demonic powers. He came to heal our wounds, to *"bind up the broken-hearted"* and *"set the captives free."*[5]

"For God did not send His Son into the world
so that He would condemn the world,
but so that the world would be saved through Him."
John 3:17

YOUR FAITH WILL HEAL YOU

The miracles Jesus performed were contingent on the faith of the individual wanting the healing or deliverance. He refused to minister in His own hometown because the people there lacked faith. They knew Him as the son of Joseph, as a simple boy growing up to be a carpenter like His father. What would He know about healing? How could He be special? So their lack of faith deprived them of incredible blessings.

Jesus healed people who were outcasts from society, people who were outside of His religious sect, people who were pagans or considered heathens. This is Divine Mercy Incarnate. It matters not your history, your background, what you have done or failed to do in your life. Divine Mercy offers you deliverance from demonic powers that have been running your life.

"For God so loved the world, that He gave His sonly Son,
so that every one who believes in Him would not die
but would have eternal life."
John 3:16

The Most High God is a deeply loving and merciful God. He is the God of Compassion. His Son Jesus is the incarnation of Divine Mercy. Have faith. Know that you are worthy of this profound gift. There are no special qualifications.

Here is your ticket to emancipation:

"If you confess with your mouth that Jesus is Lord
and believe in your heart
that God raised him from the dead,
you will be saved.
"For with the heart one believes and is justified,
and with the mouth one confesses and is saved."
Romans 10:9-10

CHAPTER 2
WHAT ARE DEMONIC POWERS?

"The wrestling for us is not
with blood and flesh,
but with the rulers,
with the powers,
with the world rulers of this darkness,
with the spiritual forces of wickedness
in the heavenlies."
Ephesians 6:12

IN THIS BOOK, <u>Deliverance from Demonic Powers That Run Our Lives</u>, we will learn about these "darkness" and "wickedness" elements. What do they govern? How do they affect us personally? Knowledge is power. We live our lives predominantly if not exclusively, by our five physical senses. We have not been trained or educated in things that are not perceived by our physical senses.

These demonic powers are a part of the unseen realm which requires more subtle senses to discern. Fortunately, we can learn about them and apply weapons to dispel them without requiring highly honed subtle senses.

What we are talking about from the unseen realm are aspects of the kingdom of darkness, part of satan's kingdom. Jesus called satan *"the ruler (prince) of this world."* Does a ruler act alone? Hardly. A ruler only rules if there is someone or something to rule over.

This Ephesians 6:12 verse provides an overview of what satan rules over. These four categories represent a hierarchy in satan's kingdom. Each of these categories has a level or span of influence and dominion, just as we have hierarchies in our world.

> *"Victory over the 'prince of this world' was won once for all at the Hour when Jesus freely gave himself up to death to give us His life.*
> *This is the judgement of this world, and the prince of this world is 'cast out.'"*[1]

A private in the army has basically no authority, but with progressive ranks, he gains greater authority and a bigger ruling or leadership domain. A general commands a large operation over a whole region. We will see how this looks in the kingdom of darkness and how these affect our personal life.

Most importantly, we will learn how to be free of their control over us. Fortunately for us, Jesus shed His Blood as a sin payment on our behalf. THAT is our freedom ticket.

Take Back Your Power. Receive Your Freedom.

This book is designed to train you up and equip you to take back your power and dominion from these unseen forces of darkness, to take back your identity and destiny as a child of the Most High God, and as a brother or sister of Jesus Christ Yeshua.

You will be provided knowledge and tools to:

- Cultivate your spiritual discernment
- Identify the causes of problems and challenges in your life
- Apply God's Word as powerful weapons of warfare
- Transmute weakness and wounds to strengths and victories

What do these demonic powers do? How do they control us?

"(Demonic) powers influence the thoughts and feelings of human beings. They can influence people to kill, steal, and indulge in all manner of destructive deeds. (Demonic) powers can influence us to gossip, backbite, slander people, bear grudges, cause people to have a lackadaisical attitude to the work of God." Derek Prince

. . .

In short, demonic powers can cause people to be less than what God created them to be. They can cause people to be petty, indulge in character flaws, have addictions, even cause them to commit crimes. Demonic powers can cause people to go utterly rogue and to misapply their abilities and gifts.

Someone may have a musical gift, a gift to sing and make music. If that person is under demonic influence, those gifts can get warped to create demonic music, and vulgar and violent lyrics; rather than uplifting, life-affirming, healing music. Satan loves to twist things to a perverted version of its original. Demonic powers seek to have dominion over people's lives, to re-direct them to a dark, distorted version of God's original design.

DEMONIC POWERS SEEK TO HAVE DOMINION OVER OUR LIVES, TO MISDIRECT US TO A DISTORTED VERSION OF GOD'S ORIGINAL DESIGN.

Power is About Domain & Dominion.

"Be still and know that I AM GOD."
Psalm 46:10

So much in this fallen world is about power and power plays. Why would anyone or anything want to have control and power over us? To take what is ours. To take out the king or queen on our chessboard. Satan and his minions have been stealing from humanity for millennia. We have been reduced to crumbs off the table of life that God intended for us. No more.

————

But God....

But God created us in His image and gave US dominion over the earth. That is our birthright. That is our fundamental case in restoring the real estate that demonic powers have stolen from our lives.

"Then God said,
*'**Let Us** (Father, Son, Holy Spirit)*
***make man in Our image**,*
according to Our likeness
[not physical, but a spiritual personality and moral likeness];
and let them have complete authority
over the fish of the sea,
the birds of the air, the cattle,
and over the entire earth,
and over everything
that creeps and crawls on the earth.'"
Genesis 1:26 AMP

*"**But God** has seen my hardship and the toil of my hands."* Genesis 31:42

*"**But God** did not permit him to harm me."* Genesis 31:7

. . .

"***But God*** *will be with you.*" Genesis 48:21

———

Let Truth Free You and Embolden You.

One of the biggest reasons people don't face demons to conquer them is because they are afraid of them. I want to encourage you to face these punks and vanquish them. YOU are made in God's image. Not them. YOU have been given authority over the entire earth. Not them. YOU have a Book in Heaven written for your life. Not them.

Because of the gift of free will, we must choose to overcome the wickedness in this world. We must choose to fight for our inheritance. God is on our side. Jesus gave His life to forge a way back for us.

"Before I formed you in the womb I knew you."
Jeremiah 1:5

God knew us before we were in our mother's womb. God created us in spirit and then gave us life in the physical. We are spirit from His Spirit. There is no more powerful spirit than the Spirit of God.

There is no demonic power or spirit that has more authority than you do, delivered through Christ Jesus. Under the protection of El Shaddai, God as our Shelter and Protector, we are hidden in His strength, according to Psalm 91.

THERE IS NO DEMONIC POWER THAT HAS MORE AUTHORITY THAN YOU, DELIVERED IN CHRIST JESUS.

Now let's learn about how to strengthen our spirit and restore it as the operating system of our lives.

THE SPIRITUAL GOAL IS TO RESTORE OUR INDWELLING SPIRIT AS OUR CORE OPERATING SYSTEM.

"He who the Son sets free is truly free."
John 8:36

———

CHAPTER 3
WAITING ON THE LORD

"I wait for the Lord, my soul does wait,
and in His word do I hope."
Psalm 1 30:5

THE DEEPEST EXPERIENCES of God can come in the silence. The most amazing answers and insights come in the silence. Silence comes through stillness. Be still and hear from God. God's Holy Spirit speaks to us in the silence and stillness. Our spirit syncs up with God's Spirit to bring us back on line, in oneness with our Divine Creator, His thoughts, His Heart, His Will for our life.

This is *"waiting on the Lord"*. It is taking time to be still and wait in silence to hear from God. There are many benefits to waiting on the Lord, waiting to hear from God's Heart. God's Heart reveals His greatest desires and plans for us, possibilities that our mind does not conceive.

. . .

When we wait on the Lord, we still our mind and all the limitations that it carries. We stop cycling through thoughts and worries, trying to come up with solutions from the confines of our mind and intellect. We give our nervous system a rest. True healing can come from this rest and stillness.

> "The Lord is good to those who wait for Him,
> to the person who seeks Him."
> Lamentations 3:25

The Soul Waits in Silence.
Sit or rest in silence. No distractions. No interruptions. Give Him your undivided silence.

> "My soul, wait in silence for God only,
> for my hope is from Him."
> Psalm 62:5

HOW TO WAIT ON THE LORD

There are two fundamental ways to *Wait on the Lord.*

The first way to Wait on the Lord is through a specific time and space set aside to sit or lie in quietness and stillness. No phones. No distractions or interruptions. Give God ten dedicated minutes a day. Gradually increase that time when you can. Empty your head of thoughts that run through worries, ideas, solutions or whatever. Yield to the Spirit, the

Holy Spirit. Yield to the stillness. Do your best to do this from your heart.

If you are a visual person, envision Jesus in front of you, with His heart radiating love into you and into your heart. Yield to His love.

The key to waiting on the Lord is to be silent and receive. No mental or physical activity or output.

> *"Be still and know that I AM God."*
> Psalm 46:10

The second way to Wait on the Lord is to surrender an issue to God and wait for Him to bring you the right answer or solution in His timing. If there is an urgency to receiving a solution to your problem, then carve out a bigger chunk of time to go away to a quiet place and spend time alone with God until you receive your answer.

Many issues are not on our timeline however; they are on God's timeline. So waiting on the Lord requires surrendering your own desire for the timing of something; as well as your own agendas and desires around the answer.

SUMMARY OF HOW TO WAIT ON THE LORD

- There are two fundamental ways to *Wait on the Lord*: through dedicated time and space or being patient over time to receive an answer or guidance on an issue.
- Give dedicated time each day, at least 10 minutes to start.
- 3 S's : surrender, stillness and solitude.
- Allow God to come to you; do not go seeking to hear with your mind. No efforting or striving!
- Be patient.
- Have faith. He WILL answer you in His timing and way.

WHAT WE RECEIVE BY WAITING ON THE LORD

Help!

> *"Our soul waits for the Lord;*
> *He is our help and our shield."*
> Psalm 33:20

God's help comes through waiting. Our soul waits in stillness to hear from Him. The stillness clears the static that is on the line when our mind is overactive. Trust the stillness.

Hope & Encouragement.

> *"Wait for the Lord;*
> *be strong and let your heart take courage;*

yes, wait for the Lord."
Psalm 27:14

Faith is a part of waiting on the Lord. It enables our heart to take courage. We are saying, "I know the Lord will come through for me. I know I will receive the answers or guidance I am seeking." Faith brings the fruits of hope and encouragement, when we experience the fruits of waiting on the Lord.

Insights & Answers to Prayers.

"I waited patiently for the Lord;
and He inclined to me and heard my cry."
Psalm 40:1

Patience is a part of waiting. Sometimes the answer we are looking for does not come right away. Do not be discouraged if it doesn't come in your timing. God brings new insights and revelations in the stillness.

"But as for me, I will watch expectantly for the Lord;
I will wait for the God of my salvation.
My God will hear me."
Micah 7:7

Hearing from God is not always on our timing or schedule. Rest in faith and patience.

"Now at the end of ten days
the word of the Lord came to Jeremiah."
Jeremiah 42:7

This passage refers to a time when a remnant of the Israelites came to the prophet Jeremiah and asked him to pray to God and receive guidance on what they should do. Jeremiah had to patiently wait on the Lord ten days before receiving an answer.

Ironically and unfortunately, the people did not heed the instructions from God and died just as it was predicted they would for not following His instructions. They used God's prophet to get the answer they wanted to hear. When it wasn't to their liking, they did what they wanted anyway, to their demise.

Unexpected Gifts.

"Lead me in your truth and teach me, for
You are the God of my salvation;
for You I wait all the day."
Psalm 25:5 (King David)

Why was King David such a *"man after God's heart"*? Because He sought God out to teach him. He had a humble heart. Waiting on the Lord with humility and love brings gifts. It brings truth and revelation. King David was a warrior. God directed him in how to deal with His enemies and receive victories over them. God guided David where to go to be protected from His enemies. God did all of this for David because he sought God with a sincere and humble heart.

GOD GAVE DAVID SUPERNATURAL STRATEGIES AND PROVISION BECAUSE DAVID KNEW HOW TO WAIT ON THE LORD.

David had a genuine relationship with God. David was a foreshadow, a partial form, of how his descendant Jesus Christ would walk the earth in a deep relationship with His Father.

Restoration.

"But they that wait upon the Lord will gain new strength. They
will mount up with wings like eagles.
They will run and not get tired.
They will walk and not become weary."
Isaiah 40:31

Waiting on the Lord brings refreshment, rejuvenation and restoration. Just resting the nervous system for ten or so minutes can really make a difference. It can bring a strength and ability to persevere. Waiting on the Lord can restore hope as well as the body. It can restore dreams and relationships. God can heal in the stillness.

GOD HEALS IN THE STILLNESS.

Taking Back Domain.

> *"Wait for the Lord and keep His way,*
> *and He will exalt you to inherit the land."*
> Psalm 37:34

Waiting on the Lord can bring advancements and gains that our own cleverness and actions cannot. Waiting on the Lord allows God and His supernatural ways to enter into our situations and life. It forces and requires us to step out of our own working of a problem.

In that humble surrender, we create space for God's solutions to enter in. This empowers us to take back domain, areas of our life that demonic powers have been running rampant.

GOD WANTS TO HELP YOU

> *"Therefore the Lord longs to be gracious to you,*
> *and therefore He waits on high to have compassion on you.*
> *For the Lord is a God of justice;*
> *how blessed are all those who long for Him."*
> Isaiah 30:18

There is so much juice in this verse! Let's unpack it.

"God longs to be gracious to you."
God wants to help you. He wants to give to you. We pray to God to receive from Him. How often do we allow God to be gracious to us? What would that look like for you? Opening

your heart? Consciously being in a place of receiving from God?

WHAT WOULD IT LOOK LIKE TO ALLOW GOD TO BE GRACIOUS TO YOU?

"*He waits on high to have compassion for you.*"

He has compassion for you and cares about you. He cares about your life and what you are going through. How many of us actually allow ourselves to receive compassion? Maybe that feels corny or weak or embarrassing, but compassion is a noble grace.

God feels our pain and cares about our suffering and hardships. Sometimes just knowing that someone cares about what we are going through can spark a healing. It is a salve. We cannot receive when we are on the go. Waiting on the Lord brings blessings, peace and healing to us.

"*The Lord is a God of Justice.*"

Now THAT is important to remember when you make your petitions to Him. God is on our side! He is the Just Judge. He wants to make right where we've been wronged. He wants to balance the scales and bring resolution, reparations and restoration through justice.

"*How blessed are those who long for Him.*"

There is an element of longing that is a part of waiting on the Lord. We long to hear from Him. We long for a closer and deeper connection. We long to feel His love and presence. We long to be comforted by Him. This is a kind of intimacy that is not easy for many of us. We are not accustomed to it. Many of us are not used to this kind of close connection with another human being, much less God.

If we are in a rush and someone really wants to speak with us, we're not usually very good listeners. But if we remove the distractions and multi-tasking, choose to be still and truly present, we can hear more deeply what they are wanting us to hear and understand. How often do we give God this kind of undivided attention?

WAITING ON THE LORD IS CHOOSING TO HAVE A GENUINE AND DEEPER RELATIONSHIP WITH HIM.

The great thing is that we don't have to know *how* to have a deeper relationship, we just have to be *willing* and create the space to be in that stillness. The Holy Spirit will truly *"lead us into all Truth"* in that stillness.

WHY WAITING ON THE LORD IS ESSENTIAL FOR DELIVERANCE

Waiting on the Lord Brings Revelations.

Waiting on the Lord is essential for our freedom because it is the place in which we receive revelations from God about what is contributing to our bondage. We receive revelations about what we need to repent of. Repentance is a super key to deliverance, health and freedom. To get to the deepest juice of repentance requires waiting on the Lord to have Him reveal what needs to be cleansed out of us.

WAITING ON THE LORD REVEALS KEYS TO REPENTANCE.

This is why it is so essential to wait on the Lord God in order to hear from Him. He will bring to our awareness things for which we need to repent. I can attest to having big breakthroughs after repenting for things in my own past and in my family lineage that I only discovered by waiting on the Lord in stillness.

Listen. Wait. Allow Him to bring the answers with your heart quiet and open. This brings purification, releasing what has been bottled up inside.

. . .

Waiting on the Lord Cleanses and Heals.

God will reveal things that are hidden or have been stuffed deep within us. Things that require an apology, grudges that need to be released, hurts that need healing. Just saying them out loud to God in private can be very healing. Deliverance is not just about being free of demons. We all need to be delivered from pain, traumas, offenses, betrayals, unforgiveness, failures and disappointments. We humans carry a lot of pain and suffering in our hearts, souls and bodies.

Waiting on the Lord is a good daily practice. Treat yourself to quiet stillness and allow God's healing love to fill you. Love heals all wounds.

Waiting on the Lord Brings Purification and Humility.

When we commit to truly being free — free from our past, from traumas and resentments, free from our own flaws and bad habits, God responds with incredible support. We've only to ask for it.

Purifying our character, our heart, mind and body is liberating. We ask God to reveal what in our own nature and past needs purification; to reveal our sins and mistakes; where we have wronged someone or dishonored ourself; what iniquity in our bloodline is affecting us today. Waiting on the Lord for these answers is humbling to be sure; but in that humility is a liberation.

"If we say that we have no sin,
we are deceiving ourselves
and the truth is not in us.
If we confess our sins,
He is faithful and righteous,
so that He will forgive us our sins
and cleanse us from all unrighteousness."
1 John 1:8-9

This is a beautiful passage of consolation. We are all flawed. It's the human condition. Yet we have a pathway to freedom and wholeness.

"He will forgive us our sins and cleanse us from all unrighteousness." What a precious gift! Once more, Apostle Paul reveals that in our sincere repentance, grace abounds. Grace may enter in.

"As St. Paul affirms, *'Where sin increased, grace abounded all the more.'*[1] But to do its work grace must uncover sin so as to convert our hearts and bestow on us 'righteousness to eternal life through Jesus Christ our Lord.' Like a physician who probes the wound before treating it, God, by His Word and by His Spirit, casts a living light on sin."[2]

WAITING ON THE LORD IS PREPARATION FOR GOING TO THE COURTS OF HEAVEN

In the next chapter we will learn about going to the Courts of Heaven as a means of being delivered from demonic powers. One of the key steps to this is repentance. It's important to take time for self-examination and to repent for things related to our problems or petitions.

For the most effective outcomes, take quiet time with God before going to the Courts of Heaven; it's always best not to assume anything. We may believe we understand the problem at hand sufficiently, but waiting on the Lord will frequently reveal factors, causes and events you were not aware of.

When we wait on the Lord in a still and quiet sitting, we can receive deeper insights. These are insights about the true nature and cause of the problem, previously unknown areas of repentance, things or people that we need to forgive. Healing can begin even before going to the Courts of Heaven.

Waiting on the Lord is the foundation of SuperPower Prayers.

CHAPTER 4

THE COURTS OF HEAVEN

WHAT ARE THE COURTS OF HEAVEN?

THE COURTS of Heaven are where we can go in the spirit to bring our petitions before God. It is where we can address head on the cases that satan has been holding against us, on account of our own actions and those of our bloodlines. It is an opportunity to examine our conscience, repent on behalf of ourselves and our bloodlines and seek forgiveness and justice. We are truly blessed to live in a time when this power tool has been given to the Bride of Christ.

This Courts of Heaven prayer protocol will walk you through nine key steps to receiving relief from recurring problems in your life. These steps are outlined in detail in Chapter 7.

Through a process of examination of your own conscience, asking the Holy Spirit to reveal to you past behavior and wrongs committed by yourself and your bloodlines, causes of these recurring problems can be revealed and addressed at their source.

A MEANS TO REMOVE CASES AND CURSES AGAINST US

The Courts of Heaven are a means for removing persistent yet often unknown cases and curses against us. These can be due to our own actions or inactions and/or those of our bloodlines. They are the legal access that satan has into our lives.

Revelations 12:10 talks about the adversary, "accuser", aka satan, going before God day and night accusing the brethren of the faith. This implies that there are legal cases against us that satan is using to give him and his demon minions legal access to us, to torment us, to rob us, to deprive us of our God destiny.

*"He who accuses them and keeps bringing charges
[of sinful behavior] against them
before our God day and night."*
Revelations 12:10

Recurring problems can also arise from curses placed on a bloodline. Curses are not the same as iniquities, though they may be related to them. Until broken, they can go on for many generations and run across a family tree, e.g. siblings, cousins, aunts and uncles. Sometimes curses are the direct consequence of iniquities, sometimes not.

. . .

For example, out of anger and hurt a great-grandmother put a curse on ensuing generations. It's an iniquity to place a curse but the curse is a specific action that can be removed with proper spiritual actions and petitions. On the other hand, iniquities may also require some kind of penance, reparations, to 'pay off' the debt incurred by them. That does <u>not</u> clear the iniquities on that great-grandmother's soul. She is responsible for her own actions and choices.

Deliverance comes by removing the legal cases satan has been holding against us through repentance, petitions and if necessary, some form of penance.

DELIVERANCE COMES BY REMOVING THE LEGAL CASES SATAN HAS BEEN HOLDING AGAINST US.

Iniquities and curses are the legal access that satan and his minions have into your life. Through God's mercy and His mercy gift of Jesus Christ, we have a way out of these prisons and traps.

TRANSGRESSIONS, SINS & INIQUITIES ARE THE LEGAL ACCESS THAT SATAN AND HIS MINIONS HAVE TO OUR LIFE.

. . .

To Summarize:

The Courts of Heaven can be used for legal cases which stem from:

- Curses, rituals, witchcraft, sorcery, occult
- Oaths, contracts, covenants, vows, agreements
- Bloodline strongholds and family iniquities passed down and affecting your life
- Iniquities, negative traits and inclinations in us
- The effects of sins, which include a weakening of our character, more engrained habits, flaws or traits

Please see the endnotes[1] for a detailed explanation of the differences between sin[2], iniquity[3] and transgressions[4].

Renunciation in the Courts of Heaven is a ritual to have God bear witness to our choice to recognize and renounce the effects of sin. This in and of itself can be considered a kind of penance. There is a value, yet different purpose to, the Sacrament of Reconciliation. Please see end notes.[5]

A GATEWAY TO MERCY AND GRACE

The Courts of Heaven are a gateway to receiving God's mercy and grace, and relief from our oppressors when we *"come to good terms with our accuser."*

. . .

Jesus taught this in a parable.

> *"Come to good terms with your accuser quickly,*
> *while you are with him on the way to court,*
> *so that your accuser will not hand you over to the judge,*
> *and the judge to the officer,*
> *and you will not be thrown into prison."*
> Matthew 5:25

The Courts of Heaven protocol provides a structure whereby we can identify and seek relief from our accuser. It is also an opportunity for self-examination, taking personal responsibility for our own and our bloodlines' actions, and building spiritual muscle and maturity.

ARE THE COURTS OF HEAVEN IN THE BIBLE?

Yes! Here Are Three Examples ...

1. Daniel 7:9-10 tells us:

> *"I kept looking until thrones were placed*
> *[for the assessors with the Judge],*
> *and the Ancient of Days [God, the eternal Father]*
> *took His seat,*
> *Whose garment was white as snow*
> *and the hair of His head like pure wool.*
> *His throne was like the fiery flame;*
> *its wheels were burning fire.*
> *A stream of fire came forth from before Him;*

a thousand thousands ministered to Him and ten thousand times
ten thousand rose up and stood before Him;
the Judge was seated [the court was in session]
and the books were opened."

This is one of the most potent and detailed passages in the Sacred Scriptures speaking of God's Court in Heaven. We will apply it in our prayer protocols.

2. In Isaiah Chapter 43, God encourages His people to make their case to Him and meet Him in court:

> *"Meet Me in court, let's argue our case together;*
> *state your cause, so that you may be proved right."*
> Isaiah 43:26

God is inviting us to argue our case with Him!

3. In Isaiah 41:21 the LORD God says:

> *"Present your case, set forth your arguments."*

On Petitioning God.
King David frequently went before God to plead his case when he needed help and when he knew he messed up. Petitioning before God is not some new invention.

·   ·   ·

In Psalm 17, King David petitions God to rule in his favor. Note the words "plea" and vindication" contained in this passage. Both words are legal terms.[6]. Psalm 17 begins with:

> "Hear me, Lord, my plea is just; listen to my cry.
> Hear my prayer— it does not rise from deceitful lips.
> Let my vindication come from You;
> may your eyes see what is right."
> Psalm 17:1-2

David perseveres, appealing to God's love for him:

> "I call on you, my God, for You will answer me;
> turn your ear to me and hear my prayer.
> Show me the wonders of your great love,
> You who save by your right hand those
> who take refuge in You from their foes."
> Psalm 17:6-7

David then asks for God's justice and judgment:

> "Rise up, Lord, confront them, bring them down;
> with your sword rescue me from the wicked.
> By your hand save me from such people, Lord,
> from those of this world whose reward is in this life."
> Psalm 17:13-14

Lest you think King David didn't do anything so serious as to request God's mercy and grace, think again. He committed some pretty terrible sins. We will look at how he appealed to God as we move through the steps of the Courts of Heaven.

. . .

Alchemizing Power.

This protocol can transform character flaws into holiness, suffering into joy, weakness into strength; through the alchemy of humility, self-examination and profession of mistakes. You will see how cathartic and healing it can be. There are all kinds of ghosts, so to speak, that lurk in the cellars of family lineages and within our own psyche. Recognizing them, owning up to them and releasing them to God is a powerful medicine.

GOING TO THE COURTS OF HEAVEN CAN ALCHEMIZE SUFFERING INTO JOY, FLAWS INTO VIRTUES.

For Healing Our Heart.

Jesus gave a sobering talk on harboring grudges and resentments towards others. He is exhorting us to keep our own heart clean; free from toxic emotions. Again, He uses court terminology.

"You have heard that the ancients were told,
'You shall not murder,' and 'Whoever commits murder
shall be answerable to the court.'
But I say to you that
everyone who is angry with his brother
shall be answerable to the court;
and whoever says to his brother,

'You good-for-nothing,'
shall be answerable to the supreme court;
and whoever says, 'You fool,'
shall be guilty enough to go into the fiery hell."
Matthew 5:21-22

Why is Jesus teaching us to empty ourselves of anger, cruelty, unforgiveness and resentments? He first references external laws on murder, etc., but then pivots to speaking about our interior life, **what is going on internally that is a form of spiritual violence and damage**.

He is concerned about our interior condition, the condition of our heart and soul. Emptying ourselves of anger, offense and grudges is key to experiencing true health and freedom.

TRUE HEALTH AND FREEDOM COME FROM EMPTYING OF ANGER AND UNFORGIVENESS.

On Settling Cases.

We've shared this passage earlier, but are highlighting it again to cover another lesson from it. What Jesus is instructing here is to *"settle matters quickly"*; do not haggle.

*"Settle matters quickly with **your adversary***
who is taking you to court.
Do it while you are still together on the way,

or your adversary may
hand you over to the judge,
and the judge may
hand you over to the officer,
and you may be thrown into prison."
Matthew 5:25

One the nine steps in the Courts of Heaven protocol is pleading guilty. We do this to disarm the adversary and because someone IS guilty or we wouldn't be getting harassed, we wouldn't be in bondage. We follow up with presenting the atoning Blood of Jesus.

Why would Jesus have given a teaching on the adversary taking us to court if this spiritual dynamic did not exist?

GOD AS MERCIFUL JUST JUDGE

God the Father is a God of Justice. His name as Adonai expresses Him as LORD, Sovereign over all of creation, the LORD of lords.[7] Psalm 103:19 proclaims: *"The Lord has established His throne in the heavens, and His sovereignty rules over all."*

The Prophet Isaiah was taken up in a vision and witnessed God as Adonai:

"I saw the Lord[8] sitting on a throne,
lofty and exalted,
with the train of His robe
filling the temple."
Isaiah 6:1

Learn from David.

King David understood and recognized the multi-dimensionality and multi-functionality of God the Father, LORD of lords. While many people fear God in His function of Just Judge, David viewed Him as merciful and loving in this role; and approached God accordingly with reverence and love. How might this knowledge influence your heart in how you choose to approach God?

Because David understood this merciful facet of God, he did not hesitate to go to Him with his sins and faults. This is the core of the admonition: *"You have not because you ask not."* [9]

"How blessed is he whose wrongdoing is forgiven,
whose sin is covered!
How blessed is a person whose guilt
the Lord does not take into account,
and in whose spirit there is no deceit!
Psalm 31:1-2

This passage tells us that God wants us to be free from our past through the grace of forgiveness.

. . .

Additionally, Psalm 103 beautifully describes the facets of God as a Merciful Judge and Father. Read Psalm 103 in its entirety. It contains comfort and assurance of God's loving mercy.

"Bless the Lord, my soul,
and do not forget any of His benefits;
Who pardons all your guilt,
Who heals all your diseases;
Who redeems your life from the pit."
Psalm 103:2-4

God as Merciful Judge shall pardon our guilt and redeem our life. How profound. He delivers us from oppression.

"The Lord performs righteous deeds (vindication)
and judgments for all who are oppressed."
Psalm 103:6

The Holy Scriptures tell us that we can come to Him to seek justice. Justice is sought in a court of law.

"Woe to those who enact evil statutes
and to those who constantly record unjust decisions,
so as to deprive the needy of justice
and rob the poor of My people of their rights,
so that widows may be their spoil
and that they may plunder the orphans."
Isaiah 10:1-2

God does not like good and innocent people to be mistreated!

Psalm 82 describes God as Adonai holding court in His own domain, *"His own assembly"*.

> *"God takes His stand in His own assembly;*
> *He judges in the midst of the rulers.*
> *How long will you judge unjustly and show*
> *partiality to the wicked? Selah.*
> *Vindicate the weak and fatherless;*
> *Do justice to the afflicted and destitute.*
> *Rescue the weak and needy;*
> *Deliver them out of the hand of the wicked."*
> Psalm 82:1-4

This passage encourages us to seek justice, to ask for deliverance from *"the hand of the wicked."* <u>This is the very purpose of this book.</u>

WHY DO I NEED TO DEFEND MYSELF?

> *"For the accuser of our brethren (satan)*
> *has been thrown down,*
> *he who accuses them*
> *before our God day and night."*
> Revelations 12:10

Satan accuses us before God day and night. That's a lot of accusing! What if we are praying for someone to stop badmouthing us at work and in the meantime, satan is reminding God of all the times we did the same thing! He's telling God, hey she has no right to be asking others to stop badmouthing her when she's guilty of it herself! Or it could be the "*sins of the father (or mother).... three generations back.*"

If there is an open case against us by the adversary aka 'the accuser', then we need to have the case overturned. We can have accusations and cases overturned by true repentance and presenting the Blood of Jesus as our atonement.

Going to the Courts of Heaven to atone for and clear these cases is also providing grace to your own children and bloodlines.

How Do I Know If God Will Allow Me Into the Courts of Heaven?

This is a common question. I personally felt very intimidated by the whole Courts of Heaven business. How do I know what I'm doing? What if I do it wrong? Will I get kicked out of the courtroom?

The short answer is, you have permission because of the shed Blood of Jesus Christ Messiah. His sacrifice gave us the opening and authority to attain victory over the forces of evil. His death and resurrection made His enemies His footstool. Satan has already been judged. What's more, the Blood of Jesus Christ breaks every curse.

> " *I, even I, am He Who blots out*
> *and cancels your transgressions,*
> *for My own sake, and I will not remember your sins.*
> *Put Me in remembrance [remind Me of your merits];*
> **let us plead and argue together**.
> **Set forth your case,**
> **that you may be justified** (*proved right*)."
> Isaiah 43:25-26 AMP

This is probably the most powerful and compelling verse in the entire Word of God regarding the Courts of Heaven. Use it in pleading your cases before God!

Did you notice the last verse? "***Set forth your case, that you may be justified.***" God is literally inviting you to plead your case, so that He may bring justice to you.

What Else is God Telling Us in Isaiah 43?

God is saying "*plead and argue with Me*"; let's have it out and discuss this. He is saying that if we rightly make our case before Him, He will blot out our sins. He will CANCEL our transgressions. When something is cancelled, the record of it is wiped out. God says, bring me your merits, make your case, bring your case before me, so that you may be justified (be made worthy, redeemed, absolved).

God is INVITING you to bring your cases before Him.

Present your petitions. He wants you to be FREED from your adversaries. <u>God wants you to be free</u>.

GOD WANTS YOU TO BE FREED FROM YOUR ADVERSARIES, FLAWS AND WEAKNESSES.

God is also saying "Remind me of your virtues and the case that you have." For one thing, before we were born God wrote a book in Heaven about our destiny here on earth. This is a purpose that God had for us before we were even born. "*And in Your book were written all the days that were ordained for me, when as yet there was not one of them.*" Psalm 139:16

I always remind God that if I am not set free and these cases against me are not dismissed, that it will seriously impair or could even prevent my being able to fulfill my God destiny.

> "*If God is for us, who can be against us?*"
> Romans 8:31

This means if we have the greatest Power on our side, who can win against us? If that weren't enough, Romans 8:32 ensures us:

> "*He in fact did not spare His own Son*
> *but gave Him over on our behalf —*

how then will He not freely give us all things with Him?"

So now are you convinced that God wants you to be free from demons, accusations and hardships? He also wants you to be free from habits, vices and flaws that bind you.

God wants a relationship with you. He wants you to be happy and have a healed and loving heart. He wants you to receive all the love that He has for you. He wants you to receive all the blessings and good that He has for you. He wants you to be holy as He is holy. He wants you to love as He loves. He wants you to be who He created you to be.

He wants to free you, as Romans 8:33 affirms:

> *"Who will bring any charge*
> *against those whom God has chosen?*
> *It is God who justifies."*

How Do I know If God Will Grant My Petitions?

God made you in His image. He has written a book in Heaven about you, about your purpose and destiny on earth. He WANTS you to fulfill your book! He wants you to be free of anything that is hindering your ability to fulfill your destiny!

*"Your eyes saw my undeveloped form and
in your book are written all my destined days,
when as yet there was not one of them."*
Psalm 139:16

All that God wants and has for you is in His Word. Find yourself in the pages of the Sacred Scriptures, the Old Testament and the New Testament Gospel. As God's son or daughter, ALL that He has promised for His people is available to you.

*"When He had disarmed the rulers and authorities
[those supernatural forces of evil operating against us],
He made a public example of them
[exhibiting them as captives in His triumphal procession],
having triumphed over them through the cross."*
Colossians 2:15 AMP

WHICH COURT OF HEAVEN SHOULD I GO TO?

We are going to keep things very simple in these books. There is a Throne (Court) of Grace often called the Throne of Mercy and Grace. We will go to this Court of Mercy and Grace for most of our petitions.

Hebrews 4:16 speaks of it: *"Let us then approach **God's throne of grace** with confidence, so that we may receive mercy and find grace to help us in our time of need."*

The author of Hebrews instructs us to go to God's throne of

grace with confidence! This tells us we should be confident that our petitions will be received and fulfilled by the Just Judge.

Genuine repentance, that is, course-correcting from vices, character flaws and bad habits, opens the door to God's Grace. The Courts of Heaven are a means and place to express our repentance and have God formally bear witness to our self-examination and self-responsibility.

The Courts of Heaven protocol is a powerful way to purify our heart and soul, and make way for genuine healing. Purification strengthens and matures our character. Purification becomes our inoculation against demonic oppression.

PURIFICATION BECOMES OUR INOCULATION AGAINST DEMONIC OPPRESSION.

Now let's look at the five keys to purification through the Courts of Heaven.

———

5 KEYS TO PURIFICATION
THROUGH THE COURTS OF HEAVEN

DELIVERANCE from demonic powers comes through purification — purification from all the sources and causes of their presence and effects in our lives. This is the purpose of this book.

PURIFICATION LEADS TO INOCULATION

One of the most important principles in this book is that purification of our bloodline, character and life leads to inoculation against demonic powers . The greatest empowerment is not in getting liberated; it is in staying liberated. It is *walking through life inoculated against demonic attacks and influences.* This is a key to lasting spiritual freedom.

That doesn't mean no one will ever again attempt to attack you through witchcraft or the use of demonic powers. It does mean that you can develop into a spiritual powerhouse, whereby these attacks will bounce right off of you and fall to the ground as dead seed.

. . .

Spiritual viruses so to speak, demonic powers, may be floating around all the time and everywhere, but your spiritual immune system will become <u>inoculated against the effects</u> of these "viruses". You will walk as the realization of Psalm 91.

> *"You will not be afraid of the terror by night,*
> *or of the arrow that flies by day;*
> *of the plague that stalks in darkness,*
> *or of the destruction that devastates at noon.*
> *A thousand may fall at your side*
> *and ten thousand at your right hand,*
> *but it shall not approach you.*
> *You will only look on with your eyes*
> *and see the retaliation against the wicked."*
> Psalm 91:5-8

Speaking from personal experience, this is possible. This author sat through a 2 1/2 hour "meeting" where someone lobbed demonic familiar spirits passed off as the Holy Spirit. If someone is nasty, cold, unkind, lacking compassion, they are NOT operating in the Holy Spirit.

Being baptized in the Holy Spirit transforms and cleanses the heart. Demonic attacks never feel like puppies and butterflies. You will know the difference. Another great benefit to spiritual purification is greater discernment.

PURIFICATION BRINGS DISCERNMENT

Because I had been doing these protocols for three years, the intended effects of this ambush meeting did not come to fruition. Oh, I was very ticked off to be sure, but not damaged from the attacks; *"not afraid of the arrow that flies by day."* Big difference. A fruit of purification is greater discernment.

One reason your discernment improves is because there is now a notable difference between your inner cleansed house and outer elements. These elements include the temperament and behavior of others. You will start to discern the jezebel spirit or the leviathan spirit traits in a person. As your spiritual, emotional and mental well-being improve, you will more easily discern dysfunctional behavior and traits in others. They are no longer normalized for you.

Learning the traits and qualities of the core demonic spirits we cover in this book will heighten your discernment in recognizing them in your environment. Discernment is power. Now let's look at the five keys to purification that will empower your health and freedom.

THE 5 KEYS TO PURIFICATION

The five keys to purification for deliverance from demonic powers are:

1. Examination of our own conscience
2. Repentance
3. Reparations or penance

4. Forgiveness

5. Perseverance

We can be liberated from mental, emotional, spiritual and other bondage by correcting our own bad habits and character flaws, taking responsibility for our wrong actions and choices, making amends, breaking off bloodline curses and strongholds and persevering until we see victory.

By purification of our character, heart, mind and life, we are removing entry points and food for demonic powers. We are closing up the breaches in our lives.[1] We are removing legal cases that the adversary has against us.

PURIFICATION REMOVES ENTRY POINTS AND FOOD FOR DEMONIC POWERS.

---

1. EXAMINATION OF CONSCIENCE.

Examination of our own conscience, self-examination, is the power tool of holy people. It is essential for routing out causes to recurring problems in our lives. It is the foundation for a thorough repentance to remove any and all cases held against us by the adversary. It is the pathway to humility and the means to cultivating noble virtues.

. . .

King David is a great example of someone who was aware of his faults and also asked God to search him out to purify him of his faults and mistakes.

"Search me, God, and know my heart;
Put me to the test and know my anxious thoughts;
And see if there is any hurtful way in me,
And lead me in the everlasting way."
Psalm 139:23-24

The key to transformational repentance is to examine your conscience and ask for the Holy Spirit to bring you revelation of what in your life and past needs to be rectified. It is an internal, very personal experience. You can follow this same process for revelation of generational sins. The Holy Spirit will reveal things to you if you ask and take the time and space to listen. Self-examination is the foundation for the next step, repentance. This is part of Step 1 in the Courts of Heaven protocol covered in Chapter 7.

2. REPENTANCE.

Repentance is a master key to healing and deliverance. It was the first instruction Jesus gave to the masses when He began His ministry, believed to be at the time of Yom Kippur, the Judaic feast of collective atonement. How spiritually poetic!

Repentance is a way for you to talk to God and feel safe in admitting your mistakes and flaws, to bring your pain and suffering before Him to be healed. It is a means to remove persistent legal cases against you to bring deliverance from demonic powers and influences.

Jesus brought the keys to the Kingdom of Heaven to earth and provided a roadmap for people to enter into it by repenting; literally meaning to turn around and have a transformation in our thinking, our way of life and our being. In the original Greek translation of the Gospel, the word for repent was 'metanoia' which means transformation, a change of thinking and being. It is not merely saying, oops sorry. It is much deeper and more powerful.

> *"From that time Jesus began to preach and say,*
> *'Repent [change your inner self,*
> *your old way of thinking,*
> *regret past sins,*
> *live your life in a way that proves repentance;*
> *seek God's purpose for your life],*
> *for the kingdom of heaven is at hand.'"*
> Matthew 4:17 AMP

Fruitful repentance requires a sincere examination of conscience, to reveal and take responsibility for wrong actions, character flaws and patterns. Jesus instructed on this:

> *"Why do you look at the speck*
> *of sawdust in your brother's eye*
> *and pay no attention*
> *to the plank in your own eye?*
> *How can you say to your brother,*

'Let me take the speck out of your eye,'
when all the time
there is a plank in your own eye?
You hypocrite,
first take the plank out of your own eye,
and then you will see clearly
to remove the speck from your brother's eye."
Matthew 7:3-5

In repenting, which is expressing sincere remorse for harmful or wrong actions towards God, others and ourself, we take full responsibility for what is in our life, the negative patterns and recurring problems. Thankfully, we are going before a merciful judge, a loving Father, who brings redemption and the forgiveness of sins through the sin payment of Christ Jesus.

"Interior repentance is a radical reorientation of our whole life, a return, a conversion to God with all our heart, an end of sin, a turning away from evil, with repugnance toward the evil actions we have committed. At the same time it entails the desire and resolution to change one's life, with hope in God's mercy and trust in the help of His grace."[2]

If repentance, a conversion of our heart, mind and soul, is the work of the grace of God, we can approach it feeling safe and loved. Now the act of repentance becomes a profound exchange of love between you and your Creator. How glorious!

. . .

REPENTANCE BECOMES A PROFOUND EXCHANGE OF
LOVE BETWEEN YOU AND GOD.

This is how the powerful exercise of repentance through examination of conscience is such a powerful means of purification. The heart is cleansed. The conscience is cleansed and relieved of heavy burdens. The heart changes its orientation from outer attachments and desires, to things of a deeper, richer value — a new or restored relationship with God and all the love that it offers; a new identity seeded in the heart of God.

"The human heart is heavy and hardened. God must give man a new heart. Conversion is first of all a work of the grace of God who makes our hearts return to him: 'Restore us to thyself, O LORD, that we may be restored!'[3] God gives us the strength to begin anew. It is in discovering the greatness of God's love that our heart is shaken by the horror and weight of sin and begins to fear offending God by sin and being separated form him. The human heart is converted by looking upon him whom our sins have pierced."[4,5]

THROUGH REPENTANCE, GOD GIVES US A NEW
HEART.

In summary, repenting for the mistakes we have made, owning up to our character flaws and weaknesses, repenting on behalf of our lineage, is a key to purification because it purifies our character, heart and soul. It purifies our bloodline. It strengthens our character by fortifying our integrity. It cleanses our conscience and is key to lifting the burden of guilt we may be carrying. Repentance is Step 3 in the Courts of Heaven protocol covered in Chapter 7.

3. REPARATIONS ~ PENANCE.

This step involves some form of making amends or providing reparations for wrong actions, for the effects of sins. It is a repairing of relationships. It is an act of love to compensate for, make amends for hurtful or damaging actions or words. It is also making amends for inactions, such as neglect. Reparations and penance purify our soul and heal relationships. Reparations of love involve some kind of external material action and agent.

Penance is of a spiritual and more internal nature, like prayer offerings, fasting and charitable giving. Penance is also called atonement, though both reparations and penance are forms of atoning for sins, making amends for damaging actions. These sins and damaging actions can be against others as well as our own self.

. . .

A thief must repay what they have stolen. Someone who lies must come clean and repair the damage done by the lies. Doing it grudgingly is not spiritually or morally elevating. It is not cleansing. It taints the action. We're called to do it with love, to do it *for* love. In this way, reparations and penance are cleansing for the heart and soul, helping them to mature and grow. This atonement is also purifying for relationships and bloodlines.

Sometimes the reparations cannot be made directly to the wronged person. In this case, there can be an action of penance, such as doing something selfless for someone else, giving time or money to a charity or church ("almsgiving"), or offering prayers to recompense for our mistakes or inactions.

"Fools mock at reparation,
but among the upright there is favor."
Proverbs 14:9

What the Bible Says About Reparations.

This scripture in Numbers gives a good summary of how to clear a debt of wrong or hurtful action:

"When a man or woman commits
any of the sins of mankind,
acting unfaithfully against the Lord,
and that person is guilty,
then he shall confess his sin
which he has committed,
and he shall make reparations

in full for his wrong and
add to it a fifth of it,
and give it to him whom he has wronged.
But if the person has no redeemer
to whom reparations
may be made for the wrong,
the reparations which is made
for the wrong
must go to the Lord for the priest."
Numbers 5:6-8

So this passage provides a guideline for reparations of love: giving a fifth more added to the wrong, if it is quantifiable. Making a charitable reparations, donating to the priest/church is recommended if the reparations cannot be made to the individual person. If it is not a money reparations, there are actions such as the examples just provided here.

Some people devote hours to prayer as their reparations or atonement. They pray for that person or their family, for example. You can also pay it forward by helping someone else out financially or through other good deeds.

What the Bible Says About Penance.

Penance is a spiritual action to atone for the sin. We can do penance for ourself and also for our lineage. We can even do penance for our country, for example. What's important is to **do it with love.**

. . .

Penance can be some kind of personal sacrifice, prayer, fasting or alms-giving (charity), or some combination thereof. Matthew Chapter 6 provides some simple guidelines for genuine penance: do your prayers and give in secret, not seeking attention from others. Pray sincerely and in private from your heart. Bragging or announcing your giving nullifies its spiritual value.

> *"Take care not to practice your righteousness*
> *in the sight of people, to be noticed by them;*
> *otherwise you have no reward*
> *with your Father who is in heaven.*
> *But when you give to the poor,*
> *do not let your left hand know*
> *what your right hand is doing,*
> *so that your charitable giving will be in secret;*
> *and your Father who sees what is done*
> *in secret will reward you."*
> Matthew 6:1 & 3-4

Penance is an Inner Conversion of the Heart.

Penance is a turning inward to God. It is an inner conversion of the heart, from rebelliousness to humility, from headstrong to obedient (doing God's will), from bitterness to forgiveness, from selfishness to considerate, from anger to peace, from resentment to love, from hate to compassion, from victimhood to self-responsibility.

This is the transformational value expressed in Joel Chapter 2.

"'Yet even now,' declares the Lord,
'Return to Me with all your heart,
and with fasting, weeping, and mourning;
and tear your heart and not merely your garments.'
Now return to the Lord your God,
for He is gracious and compassionate,
slow to anger, abounding in mercy
and relenting of catastrophe."
Joel 2:12-13

Penance & Reparations of Love Build Character.

A key insurance policy against demonic powers effecting or running our lives is strong, upright, moral character. Demonic powers feed off of weakness. They feed off of character flaws. This is because weak character and character flaws take us out of oneness with God's law.

Once we are lawless, so to speak, we are fair game for the demonic realm. We are now on their turf basically. They possess power and authority on their own turf. They are empowered by our immoral and unethical actions. They feed off of our vices and flaws.

DEMONIC POWERS FEED OFF OF OUR VICES AND FLAWS.

Conversely, admitting a mistake and course-correcting rebuilds weak character. Making amends or offering a penance with true repentance and humility builds moral character. It deepens spiritual maturity. It cleanses our soul. It can even heal our own heart. It can definitely heal relationships. Making reparations with love builds character. Penance cleanses our character of flaws and grows us to walk in the virtues of Christ.

Penance & Reparations of Love Pay Off Debts.

Making amends or some kind of penance pays off the debt that is incurred by damaging and unlawful (by God's law or man's law) actions. It brings justice to a situation. It helps to clear cases that are being held against us by satan. Reparations of love balance the books and give us a clean start.

Doing something with genuine love clear debts from our ledger. God is love. Genuine love with humility can alchemize hurtful situations, traumas and strife, and bring healing and restoration to relationships and lives.

As Peter the Apostle teaches: *"Above all, keep fervent in your love for one another, because love covers a multitude of sins."*[6]

ATONING WITH GENUINE LOVE ALCHEMIZES AND HEALS.

Penance and Reparations of Love Restore Us to Christ.

This is to say, when we offer sincere penance and reparations of love, we are restoring ourselves to our life in Christ and made-in-His-image. We are sacrificing and dying to self as Christ Jesus did. We are loving selflessly as Christ does. We are giving without expectation of a return, as Christ did. We are humbling ourselves as Christ modeled for us. We are offering up our own comforts and desires for the good of others as Christ modeled for us.

Penance and reparations of love are profound spiritual practices that purify us, sanctify us, transform us and yoke us to Christ Jesus — body, mind and soul. They are Step 5 in the Courts of Heaven protocol covered in Chapter 7.

4. FORGIVENESS.

Part of the roadmap to redemption, freedom and healing is forgiving others for what they have done to us. Forgiveness purifies us of bitterness, resentment, offense, anger, trauma, sorrow, victimhood, and vindictiveness. Through The Lord's Prayer, Jesus provides a beautiful prayer for forgiveness and explains why forgiveness is so vital for our own spiritual well-being.

"This, then, is how you should pray:
'Our Father in heaven,
hallowed be your name,
your kingdom come,
your will be done,
on earth as it is in heaven.

Give us today our daily bread.
And forgive us our debts,
as we also have forgiven our debtors.
And lead us not into temptation,
but deliver us from the evil one.'

For if you forgive other people when they sin against you,
your heavenly Father will also forgive you.
But if you do not forgive others their sins,
your Father will not forgive your sins."
Matthew 6:9-15

This last passage from the Gospel of Matthew, 6:14-16, instructs us that we have no legal right to ask for and expect forgiveness if we are holding a grudge and unforgiveness towards someone else.

Forgiveness is **not** absolution of a violation. It is not saying "it's ok" that someone violated or betrayed you. It is saying: "I release any and all unforgiveness." It is to release ourselves from the bondage of torment and toxic emotions. Leave justice in the hands of God.

Forgiveness is Purifying and Liberating.

Forgiveness purifies our heart, mind and soul. It frees us from gnawing and haunting memories and experiences. In this way, we are purifying our mind. Forgiveness releases bitterness from our heart, purifying our heart. Forgiveness breaks unhealthy remaining connections to those who have hurt or harmed us, thus purifying our soul.

Forgiveness makes a way for a new beginning by closing the door to our wounded past. Forgiveness is a gateway to emotional, mental and spiritual freedom. It is part of Step 3 in the Courts of Heaven protocol covered in Chapter 7; but is an on-going spiritual practice in our daily life.

5. PERSEVERANCE.

The fifth key to purification is perseverance. Perseverance is purifying because we are pushing through our fears, laziness, discouragement, biases, weakness, negativity; wrong, unhealthy or fixed views and beliefs; pessimism and disbelief; to persevere and not take no for an answer. Perseverance purifies our character and strengthens us from the inside out. It is the *"persistence in faith"* that Jesus exhorts us to possess.

Jesus Encourages Perseverance.

In Luke 18:1-8, Jesus Christ instructs His disciples to have persistence in going before the "Just Judge" to attain justice:

*"Now He was telling them a parable to show that at all times they ought to pray and **not become discouraged**, saying,*

"'In a certain city there was a judge who did not fear God and did not respect any person. Now there was a widow in that city, and she kept coming to him, saying, 'Give me justice against my

opponent.' For a while he was unwilling; but later he said to himself, 'Even though I do not fear God nor respect any person, yet because this widow is bothering me, I will give her justice; otherwise by continually coming she will wear me out.'

*"And the Lord said, 'Listen to what the unrighteous judge said; now, will God not bring about justice for His elect **who cry out to Him day and night**, and will He delay long for them? I tell you that He will bring about justice for them quickly. However, when the Son of Man comes, will He find **(persistence in) faith** on the earth?'"*

What Do We Learn From the Persistent Widow Parable?

- We must not give up, lose heart or lose faith. We must persevere until justice is served!
- With sincerity for our cause and persistence, God WILL avenge injustices against us.
- God IS a Just Judge for His sons and daughters. He is compassionate. He WILL defend, protect and avenge us.
- God wants us to receive justice! He wants us to be free!
- Persistence in faith, not giving up, is a spiritual virtue. It is rewarded.

A Personal Testimony

I can personally attest that the persistent widow approach

does work. I had a very stressful legal issue that went on for a year. I had gone to the Courts of Heaven. Truthfully tho, I had become battle weary. That's just what the enemy wants! Thankfully, I got my second wind. I went yet again (a third time) to the Courts of Heaven. I always pray and ask for guidance and revelation BEFORE I go into the Courts of Heaven.

I asked the Holy Spirit to reveal anything else in my bloodline that was causing this issue and/or the blockage to resolution. I did receive information about the actions of one of my grandfathers. Based on this, I added new repentance and requests. I was forceful. I was not a wimp or self-pitying. As I went through my petitions, I grew stronger and more resolved. I left the Courts of Heaven feeling stronger, renewed in my spirit. I was no longer battle weary.

Days later, I received a notice of my victory. It was far beyond what I had asked and hoped for. God had something much better than what I had requested. I believed that the less I asked for, the more likely I could win the case. I was wrong. My Just Judge had a much better outcome in mind. He truly did avenge me, as I was wronged more than I had realized.

A new judge was assigned to my case and he literally dropped the whole case. It was expunged as if it had never happened. I then received a check in the mail from this other party. It was 10 times what I had expected. God avenged the injustices against me. He could not and would not have done so if I had given up.

. . .

In my persistence, I grew stronger. I faced the bullies, these demonic powers, and my Just Judge came through for me. I pressed forward to remove the remaining legal case that was being held against me through my bloodline. I grew stronger from that experience and gained more inner peace as a result.

About a week later I was speaking with my cousin who is a great knowledge keeper of family history and he shared some stories about that grandfather. The stories confirmed what the Holy Spirit had told me with regards to my legal case. My grandfather had done some legally questionable activities and that 'case' was hanging over my head, as satan's legal right to harass me through the legal system.

In my third and last Courts of Heaven session for this issue, I repented specifically for the action of my deceased grandfather and presented the Blood of Jesus as atonement. This does <u>not</u> release my grandfather from what is on his soul, but it <u>released me from that inherited legal case</u> satan was using against me.

Perseverance Purifies Character.

That situation was truly a trial and tribulation. It was quite stressful and upsetting. However, if I hadn't persevered the way that I had, I would not have received that amazing outcome. Best of all, was the personal growth and spiritual maturation that I experienced on account of my perseverance. I hope this inspires you to alchemize your own trials and tribulations through perseverance!

PERSEVERANCE ALCHEMIZES TESTS AND TRIALS.

The following scripture from Romans perfectly sums up how we can apply perseverance to our difficulties to purify our character.

"We also celebrate in our tribulations,
knowing that tribulation brings about perseverance;
and perseverance, proven character;
and proven character, hope."
Romans 5:3-5

Perseverance purifies our mind and character. We often hold self-limiting and mistaken beliefs in our mind, which shape and come to define our character. When we persist, we are choosing to break through these self-imposed barriers and comfort zones.

Persistence purifies our mind and character of false beliefs about ourself, others and the world. It purifies us of insecurities, fears, hubris, stubbornness, sloth and spiritual laziness.

Now let's look at a Courts of Heaven secret weapon to overcoming persistent problems and receiving breakthroughs — the Divine Restraining Order.

CHAPTER 6
DIVINE RESTRAINING ORDERS

A DIVINE RESTRAINING Order is a kind of petition or request, that we can present to God in the Courts of Heaven. Just as its name conveys, it is a legal restraint granted from God's Courts against a person, party, entity, power, principality or stronghold. It is for a particular timeframe of God's choosing. It could be granted for the span of time the requestor is living in a geographical area for example.

There are other petitions we can request from God in the Courts of Heaven. Divine Restraining Orders are just one of them.

When Should a Divine Restraining Order Be Requested?

A Divine Restraining Order should be requested when there is a persistent problem or issue that has come from a very powerful or persistent source, either in the spiritual or physical realm.

. . .

In the spiritual realm, this would include principalities, strongholds or demons. This includes the specific demonic powers that we will cover in this book: leviathan, jezebel, mammon, python, baal and their cohorts and minions. These demonic powers can be operating through a specific person who is causing the harassment.

Strongholds can also include territorial or regional principalities that rule over and operate out of a particular region. A region could be a town, city, county, state or a region within a state. These principalities are associated with specific conditions or areas of life. They are mentioned in Daniel 10:20.

For example, there can be a regional spirit of poverty, crime, indebtedness or violence. An example is a large retreat property — very outwardly beautiful — that had a spirit of murder on it. There were several incidents that demonstrated this spirit of murder: three people killed on a retreat, the owner choosing premature death on account of a 'death wish', a resident undergoing environmental poisoning that almost took him out. A murder stronghold was ruling over this property regardless of who was the owner of it.

Another example of application for requesting a Divine Restraining Order is when a curse has been placed upon someone. A family member had a "harassing spirit" curse placed upon him. I went to the Courts of Heaven and requested a Divine Restraining Order against this demon punk. The result was remarkable. Immediately he attained relief and has not experienced that harassment since.

. . .

How Do I Know When or If I Should Request a Divine Restraining Order?

Circumstances which could warrant requesting a Divine Restraining Order include:

- Curses or demons sent out against you or a family member.
- Forces that are beyond our ability to personally control, such as a territorial spirit or a principality. This is because the people who live in that region continue to act in ways that feed that spirit. We cannot control the choices and actions of the population, but we can request our own relief and protection from territorial spirits.
- A problem or party that is so big or so powerful, you need help.
- Family issues — a deep ancestral curse like premature or violent death.
- Attacks from someone — behavioral or spiritual attacks from a troubled person.
- A territorial spirit — to protect yourself, your community or your neighborhood.
- A principality — that governs your country.

———

SCRIPTURES FOR REQUESTING DIVINE RESTRAINING ORDERS

God's Word contains everything we need to present a compelling case to Him in His Courts of Heaven. God's Word is His law, His promises to us, His justice. Therefore, we present Sacred Scriptures that are relevant to the case we are bringing before Him, just as an attorney presents settled law or cases to convince the judge to rule in his or her favor.

There is a spiritual power to God's Word. There is a credibility to God's Word. When we declare God's Word out loud, it strengthens our spirit and builds our confidence. We are presenting and declaring God's laws, His relationship with us, and His Covenant promises to us.

WHEN WE DECLARE GOD'S WORD OUT LOUD, IT STRENGTHENS OUR SPIRIT AND BUILDS OUR CONFIDENCE & FAITH.

Remember, a restraining order is to limit the actions of a demon or person, to put a boundary around you, to keep you safe, to protect you. God always wants His children to be safe and protected. The following are Scriptures that speak of God providing boundaries and protection. You can use any of these when you are petitioning God to issue a Divine Restraining Order on your behalf.

God Will Set Boundaries.

- Psalm 104:7-9 — "*At your rebuke they fled, at the sound of your thunder they hurried away. The mountains rose; the valleys sank down to the place which You established for them.* **You set a boundary that they may not pass over**, *so that they will not return to cover the earth."*

- Proverbs 15:25 — *"The Lord will tear down the house of the proud and arrogant (self-righteous), but* **He will establish and protect the boundaries** *[of the land] of the [godly] widow."*
- 1 Samuel 7:13 — *"So the Philistines were subdued and* **came no more into** *Israelite* **territory.** *And the hand of the Lord was against the Philistines all the days of Samuel."*
- Isaiah 17:13 — *"The nations rumble on like the rumbling of many waters, but He will rebuke them and* **they will flee far away, and be chased like chaff** *in the mountains before the wind, or like whirling dust before a gale."*

God Will Protect You.

- Psalm 17:7 — *"Wondrously show your [marvelous and amazing] lovingkindness, O Savior of those* **who take refuge at your right hand** *from those who rise up against them."*
- Psalm 141:8 — *"For my eyes are toward You, O God, the Lord; in You I take refuge;* **do not** *pour out my life nor* **leave me defenseless**.*"
- Psalm 143:9 — *"Rescue me, O Lord, from my enemies;* **I take refuge in You**.*"
- Luke 18:3 — *"There was a [desperate] widow in that city and she kept coming to him and saying,*

*'**Give me justice and legal protection** from
my adversary.'"*

- Luke 18:5 — "*Yet because this widow continues to
bother me, **I will give her justice and legal
protection**; otherwise by continually coming she
will wear me out.*"

WHEN TO PETITION FOR A DIVINE RESTRAINING ORDER

Based on the information in this chapter, reflect on current and
recurring problems or issues in your life and/or in your family.
They may be candidates for requesting a Divine Restraining
Order from God.

We can petition for Divine Restraining Orders in Step 7 of the
Courts of Heaven protocol. We cover this in the next Chapter,
"*9 Steps to Petitioning in the Courts of Heaven.*"

———

CHAPTER 7

9 STEPS TO PETITIONING
IN THE COURTS OF HEAVEN

NINE KEY STEPS outline a foundational protocol for going to the Courts of Heaven. While you're first learning the protocol to apply it to your personal cases, it may be helpful to have paper and pen handy to write down your customized content for these steps.

THE NINE STEPS

1. Preparation
2. Presentation of Purpose
3. Renounce and Repent
4. Plead Guilty
5. Reparations ~ Penance
6. Justification ~ Plead your Case
7. Petitions
8. Wait on the Lord's Response
9. Thanks and Praise

1. PREPARATION.

You may want to write out your answers to these points.

- Be clear about what you are requesting and why.
- What is the issue that is causing you to go to God?
- What are your petitions? (For example, to request a Divine Restraining Order, to be delivered from a stronghold, an addiction, a recurring problem.)
- What will happen or not happen if you do NOT get your petitions granted? This can also include what might happen to your children or other family members if you do not receive the relief you are seeking. You can remind God that you have a life purpose in Him that needs be fulfilled.
- Pray and ask the Holy Spirit to reveal what you need to repent of. It could be for yourself or it could be on behalf of your bloodline or both! He is the Spirit of Truth and reveals all truth. Use this Courts of Heaven experience to cultivate a relationship with Him. He is the Holy Advocate.
- This 'examination of conscience' is very key for receiving an effective outcome from your Courts of Heaven petitions. It is a powerful tool to purify, strengthen and transform our character. <u>Integrity and maturity are the foundation for living in happy union with God and others.</u>
- Ask the Holy Spirit to help you with this. Ask him to reveal anything in your bloodline that is contributing to your problem or issue and from whom in your bloodline it originated. Ask him to reveal character flaws and bad habits that are contributing to your problems. Ask him to reveal

past mistakes, sins or inactions that are contributing to or are the cause of your current issues.

- Identify what you need to personally repent for.
- Identify what in your family lineage to renounce.

Gather Scriptures To Make Your Case.

Identify and have with you Scriptures that back up why God should grant your petitions. Don't worry, we are providing several in this book. They are sufficient to get you started. The reason for using Sacred Scriptures is because they are God's law. To win in a court of law, a good lawyer presents "settled law" to make a strong case.

How to use Scriptures in presenting your case in the Courts of Heaven is actually very simple. You can begin by saying something like, "Dear God, just as You did for your people in (name the scripture book, chapter and verse), where You (recite the verse), so too am I asking for You to set a boundary around me so that so and so can no longer torment me."

When you present the ramifications (consequences) of *not* being granted your request, such as a Divine Restraining Order, you can reference one of the many Scriptures that speaks of God's promises. Don't worry, all the *SuperPower Prayers* in this book have Scriptures provided for you.

You don't need more than a few Scriptures. As you get more comfortable with this, you will branch out and find others to make your cases. It's not because God needs or requires you to be a Bible scholar. It is to strengthen your indwelling spirit, because His Word exists beyond time and space in its supernatural attributes and functions.

Learning and knowing God's Word brings comfort, inner strength, greater confidence, faith and peace. Understanding God through His Word strengthens faith, hope and love. These three virtues become the catalyst for personal transformation. We will cover them in deeper detail in Chapter 20.

PROCLAIMING GOD'S WORD HELPS YOU GROW IN FAITH, HOPE AND LOVE, THE THREE VIRTUES FOR TRANSFORMATION AND NOBLE CHARACTER.

As you discover how much God wants you to be free and supports your valid cases, your confidence and faith will grow. You will feel closer to God. Your heart will open more to God. You will be able to receive more of God's love for you. Love is healing. God's love will heal you.

GOD'S LOVE WILL HEAL YOU.

---

2. PRESENT YOUR PURPOSE.

- You enter God's Courtroom with Scriptural protocol (Daniel 7:10).
- You tell God why you have come before Him at this time; e.g., "To break off of my life the stronghold of having my work and efforts always sabotaged."
- You tell God what recourse you're looking for; e.g., "Issue a Divine Restraining Order against harassing and sabotaging spirits."

3. RENOUNCE AND REPENT.

We renounce things from our bloodline such as iniquities, character traits, oaths, contracts, covenants, agreements that may be the source and cause of curses and other problems in our life. We do this to remove legal access and cases against us on account of our ancestors.

Repentance is key to removing the repercussions of sins, iniquities and transgressions from our spiritual ledger. The word 'repent' has been poorly translated from its New Testament Greek source. As shared previously, the Greek word was 'metanoia'[1], literally a change of mind, a purification of soul and character which brings deep transformation; specifically a transformational change of heart and even a spiritual conversion. Jesus was exhorting people to have a spiritual conversion!

WHEN JESUS CALLS TO "REPENT!", HE IS CALLING
US TO A SPIRITUAL CONVERSION!

This is much more powerful than its current understanding as
a superficial action that is just words saying "I'm sorry", but not
actually changing behavior and habits.

True Repentance is the Desire for Transformation.
To genuinely repent means a declaration of committing to
course-correct from bad habits or unproductive thoughts, to
correct mistakes or mis-directions, to correct character flaws, to
identify and determine to put and end to repeating negative
patterns, and to atone for past sins. This requires thoughtful
self-examination to assess what is working well in our life and
what is not; and what are the possible sources or causes of
things that are repeatedly not working well for us.

Wrong or negative thinking, habits such as worry and
negativity, expectations of things going wrong are examples of
mental habits that can benefit from a metanoia, transformation.
Lying, yes even fibbing 'white lies', manipulating, deceitfulness
are character flaws that become engrained as habits. God sees
everything we are doing. We are only kidding ourselves if we
believe we're getting away with lying, cheating or stealing.
There is always a price to pay eventually.

. . .

True repentance also involves a sincere and intimate conversation with God, where you recognize and admit to Him where you are holding hurts, offenses or unforgiveness.

Repentance Requires Self-Examination.

Repentance also involves a deep and honest self-examination of any mistakes, bad habits, flaws and weaknesses. Sometimes we can't remember everything off the top of our head and it requires going to a place of quiet and stillness to wait and hear from God. Ask the Holy Spirit to come to you and reveal to you what to bring before God.

This is also an opportunity to identify patterns in our life: patterns in our behavior, relationships, responses or reactions to people and events. If there are patterns, we are at the center of them.

King David recognized the value of confessing his sins to God.

> "When I kept silent about my sin, my body wasted away.
> I acknowledged my sin to You,
> And I did not hide my guilt;
> I said, 'I will confess my wrongdoings to the Lord';
> And You forgave the guilt of my sin."
> Psalm 32:3 & 5

We can tend to withhold the worst from God because we do not trust that He will actually forgive us. See the faith of

David! David slept with another man's wife and then had that man killed on the battlefield. That's pretty heavy. If he can go to God to ask for forgiveness, we surely have this same pathway to freedom, freedom through repentance.

REPENTANCE BRINGS HEALING TO OUR HEART, SOUL AND OUR LIFE.

Repentance Involves Waiting on the Lord.

Set aside a quiet time and place to ask the Lord to reveal to you what it is you need to repent of. Make sure you allow quiet time to hear from God. Sit still and wait on the Lord. It may take a few minutes. It may reveal itself over a period of days or more. Be patient. He needs you to be quiet and still with no distractions.

There is a divine purpose and value to waiting on the Lord for deeper and full revelation on what needs repentance. God prepares our heart and soul in this process. He begins the metanoia, our transformation, in this process of waiting to receive deeper revelation on repentance. Allow it to be joyful and uplifting.

Trust that if you truly wait on the Lord, yield to His stillness within you, that you *will* hear from Him. Try to yield from your heart. You can yield to the stillness within you even when you are active in your daily life. It becomes its own spiritual practice. It will sync you up with the Holy Spirit and cultivate your ability to operate from your indwelling spirit.

WAITING ON THE LORD SYNCS YOU UP WITH THE HOLY SPIRIT.

When you are in a genuine place of surrendering and opening to God's revelations, He will infill you, download to you what requires repentance. Often it's something for which you had no idea existed or you had long since forgotten. Frequently, it is something that happened in your lineage but is being held against you by the accuser.

For example, if you've had a recurring problem with people stealing from you — not just money, but perhaps promotions, jobs, etc. — it could be from an iniquity in your bloodline; someone who engaged in theft. God's mercy can release you from that family iniquity. He WANTS to set you free!

Repentance for Our Family.

Your repentance may also include renouncing or repenting on behalf of your family, back at least four generations, who engaged in a certain behavior or subject at hand; or their inactions regarding that topic. I always like to cover my bases and say "and back to Adam and Eve." I know some say, "well the Bible says it's only three to four generations." That's true, but curses can go on for centuries, even millennia. We don't always know what is the actual originating cause of a problem — an iniquity or a curse. I'm covering my bases. The choice is yours of course.

So we can ask the Holy Spirit, what did someone in our family lineage do or not do that has caused this problem in our life? There are things that I did not know of that came to me in the stillness of waiting on God. Afterwards, I received confirmation of what I had received directly from the Holy Spirit in the stillness with God.

Please note, that renouncing or repenting on behalf of our bloodline does NOT free that person from their own sin burden. It can however, break that sin payment or curse off of our own life and future generations.

Be Sincere and Humble.

Sincerely ask God for forgiveness. If there is not sincere repentance, you have no credible case going before God. James 4:5 says: *"God opposes the proud but gives grace to the humble."* Ask God if there are any reparations or penance that He would like you to do for those iniquities. It could be fasting and prayer. It could be giving to a charity or doing some volunteer work for a good cause in your community.

Obviously, your repentance will have something to do with the topic or party in your specific petitions. For example, someone is incessantly badmouthing you in the workplace. You have gone to your boss. You have tried to make nice with them.

Nothing's working. Your repentance would include any time you or someone in your bloodline badmouthed others, engaged in gossip and spread falsehoods about others.

4. PLEAD GUILTY.

We always plead guilty to the charges the adversary is holding against us. We plead guilty because we are guilty. Someone in our bloodline is guilty. Remember Jesus teaches this element of spiritual law in Matthew 5:25: *"Come to good terms with your accuser quickly, while you are with him on the way to court."*

The title of this book contains the word *"Deliverance."* This is because deliverance is freedom; freedom from an accusation, freedom from a court case, freedom from oppression, freedom from bondage.

We have already learned that the accuser, aka satan, accuses us day and night before the Lord God. Pleading guilty diffuses the accusation. It is a part of removing the legal leverage that the accuser is holding against us.

Immediately after we plead guilty, we present the atoning Blood of Jesus to remove the case against us. The following passage from Colossians Chapter 2 is a most compelling argument for how and why the Blood of Jesus removes legal cases and debts against us. We are always using God's Word as the legal document of Covenant Law.

GOD'S WORD IS THE LEGAL DOCUMENT OF HIS
COVENANT LAW.

When we reconcile with God through the Five Keys to
Purification, we are on solid ground to argue our case applying
His Covenant Law.

> *"When you were dead in your sins*
> *and in the uncircumcision of your flesh*
> *(worldliness, manner of life),*
> *God made you alive together with Christ,*
> *having forgiven us all our sins,*
> ***having canceled out the certificate of debt***
> ***consisting of legal demands (decrees)***
> *against us and which were hostile to us.*
> ***And this certificate He has set aside***
> ***and completely removed by nailing it to the cross.***
> *When He had disarmed the rulers and authorities*
> *[those supernatural forces of evil operating against us],*
> *He made a public example of them*
> *[exhibiting them as captives in His triumphal procession],*
> *having triumphed over them through the cross."*
> Colossians 2:13-15

This passage is so powerful and compelling, that we will use it
quite a bit in the prayer protocols in this book — specifically,
the words in bold.

. . .

Remember, in Isaiah 41:21 the Lord God says: *"Present your case, set forth your arguments."* And from Isaiah 43:26: *"Meet Me in court, let's argue our case together; state your cause, so that you may be proved right."* Let these scriptures fill you with boldness and confidence to go before God's Throne of Mercy and Grace!

5. REPARATIONS ~ PENANCE.

In this step, we ask God to guide us to some form of penance, if necessary. Penance or atonement is also called reparations.[2] "Atone"[3] is associated with the word repentance and refers to actions taken to compensate, "make right", for sins, violations to others, wrong actions, inactions, behaviors that have been hurtful or damaging to others and/or ourselves.

Penance responds to the Third Law of Thermodynamics which says that for every action there is an equal and opposite reaction. Penance fulfills the spiritual law that we reap what we sow. Penance is God's mercy allowing us to make reparations for wrong actions or inactions.

PENANCE IS A MEANS OF SEEKING AND RECEIVING GOD'S MERCY.

The spiritual value to penance is that we are proffering to pay back rather than waiting for the reaping to come to us, as best we can. Three fundamental ways of penance are prayer, fasting and "alms-giving". The latter can include giving of money, time and energy to charity, as well as tithing. At its core, penance is personal sacrifice — sacrifice of desires, comforts, money, time and energy.

The Gospel provides an example of making reparations. A tax collector, one of the most dreaded and shunned persons in those times, seeks salvation from the Lord Jesus.

> *"But Zacchaeus stood up and said to the Lord,*
> *'Behold, Lord, half of my possessions*
> *I am giving to the poor,*
> *and if I have extorted anything from anyone,*
> *I am giving back four times as much.'*
> *And Jesus said to him,*
> *'Today salvation has come to this house,*
> *because he, too, is a son of Abraham.*
> *For the Son of Man has come*
> *to seek and to save that which was lost.'"*
> Luke 19:8-10

In fact, this notion of repaying four-fold is found in 2 Samuel 12:6: *"So he must make reparations for the lamb four times over, since he did this thing and had no compassion."*

The point of this step is that repentance and pleading guilty are important, but there may be situations where reparations or a form of penance is needed as well. Apologizing for stealing is a good step, but the thief also has to return the stolen goods.

. . .

Jesus came to bring a pathway back to God through redemption. This does not mean that we do not have to recompense if we steal. It means we are given a means for redemption, to make right, when we do steal. We are not thrown in jail without a key, so to speak. There may still be a debt to pay however.

JESUS CAME TO BRING A PATHWAY BACK TO GOD.
PENANCE IS FOOD FOR THE JOURNEY.

---

6. JUSTIFICATION. PLEAD YOUR CASE.

This is part of your compelling case for why God should grant you your petitions. You can petition for yourself and your underage children. You will need permission from others to include them in these protocols. This is what you will share with God:

- What will happen to you and/or your loved ones if you are not granted your petitions? What consequences?
- What good thing will *not* happen to you? What might you be deprived of?
- What might you lose? Your shelter? Your job? Your marriage? Your destiny fulfillment?
- What will be prevented or blocked if you do NOT get your petitions granted?
- What does God's Word, the Holy Scriptures, say about your topic or need? How does it back up

your requests or purpose for coming before His Court?

- Don't hesitate to be totally real with God; like, "I am at the end of my rope. I don't know where else to turn if You won't help me with this."
Vulnerability opens the soul to God's grace.

VULNERABILITY OPENS THE SOUL TO GOD'S GRACE.

---

7. PETITIONS.

This is when you share with God what you are asking for that will help you in your life. <u>It is your specific request to remove a hindering problem.</u>

Petitions can include resolution or removal of a problem or situation; cancelling curses; dissolving and nullifying ungodly oaths, contracts, covenants and agreements; issuing Divine Restraining Orders; being delivered from demonic powers that have been running your life.

If you are not sure of what to ask for, sit in quiet and ask the Holy Spirit to reveal to you what petitions you should seek. Don't overthink it though. It really should be clear to you based on persistent or recurring issues you have been experiencing.

. . .

You do not need to always know any or all of the causes of the problem; but be clear about <u>what you need relief from</u>. You may receive deeper revelation of a cause *after* you have gone to the Courts of Heaven. You can then go back to God's Courts for a deeper petition of that issue. Sometimes removal of problems is like peeling the layers of an onion. Have faith that <u>there is a deeper spiritual value and purpose to the process</u> itself; which is deeper transformation, healing and deliverance.

8. WAIT ON THE LORD'S RESPONSE.

- Sit in silence to hear from the Holy Spirit and out of respect for being before the Throne of God.
- You may hear that there is something else for which to repent. You can do so at this time. Repentance is not confined to one place or moment in this process.
- You may feel in your spirit that God is granting all of your petitions.

9. THANKS AND PRAISE.

- Thank God for receiving you into His throne room, for listening to your repentance and for hearing your petitions.
- Thank God for answering your petitions.
- Giving thanks and praise is letting God know you appreciate His listening to you.
- It builds our faith to believe that our petitions and prayers ***will*** be answered.
- Jesus Christ always gave thanks to God the Father *before* performing a miracle.

. . .

Now we will look at the profound gift we have been given for
our forgiveness and redemption, the Sacred Blood of Jesus. The
more deeply we understand this gift, the more we will value it,
and the more precious and holy it is to us.

The Sacred Blood of Jesus Christ is the redemption for our
sins. It is key to having cases against us dropped or receiving a
grace dispensation. The Blood of Jesus is not just a catch
phrase. It has been repeatedly discovered to possess supernatural qualities.

How might knowing this affect your faith in its redemptive
value and power?

———

CHAPTER 8

THE SUPERNATURAL BLOOD AND NAME OF JESUS

THE SUPERNATURAL BLOOD OF JESUS

A *SUPERPOWER* PRAYER for redemption and deliverance includes the application of the supernatural Blood of Jesus. The Blood of Jesus is a real and profound gift from God, and has been at the center of many incredible miracles verifying the Glory of God and the truth of Jesus Christ as the Son of God.

Jesus disarmed the demonic powers when He shed His blood and gave His life for humanity. His blood was the atoning sin payment for the sins of humanity.

When He gave His last breath, an earthquake shook the area. Apostle Matthew describes the scene.

"And when Jesus had cried out again in a loud voice,
He gave up His spirit.
At that moment the curtain of the temple
was torn in two from top to bottom.
The earth shook, the rocks split
and the tombs broke open."
Matthew 27:50-52

BLOOD ON THE MERCY SEAT

2000 years later, a Holy Spirit-led amateur archaeologist and devoutly humble Christian man named Ron Wyatt[1], was given the honor of discovering the Ark of the Covenant.[2] It was deep below the ground in a cave directly under the cross upon which Jesus was crucified.[3]

When the earthquake shook at Christ's last breath, it created a crack in the earth right below the cross. The Blood of Jesus poured off of His bloodied body, down into the crack and fell upon the lid of the Ark of the Covenant, known as the Mercy Seat.

In the times of the Levitical priesthood of God's Judaic people, the priests offered the blood of animals, a spotless lamb or goat, to atone for the people's sins. The most important feast day for this was the Feast of Passover in early spring. It required the offering of a spotless lamb for the atonement of family and collective sins.

.   .   .

The blood of these lambs was placed on the Mercy Seat of the Ark of the Covenant for the atonement. Jesus, as the spotless (sinless) Lamb of God, gave His blood as atonement for the sins of humanity. He did so on the Feast of Passover, *pesach* in Hebrew. Later, He would be called the *Paschal Lamb*.

Upon discovering the Ark, Ron recognized dried blood on the Mercy Seat. As a medical professional, Ron decided to take some of the dried blood to a lab in Israel and have it reconstituted and tested. He did not tell them anything about the blood or where he got it. They shared their findings about the blood:

- The blood is still alive.
- The blood is from a human being.
- The blood has only 24 total chromosomes; (normal human blood has 46 chromosomes).[4]
- The blood has 23 X chromosomes from the mother but only one Y chromosome, indicating it has a human mother (23 X chromosomes) and is the blood of a human male (one Y chromosome).
- The blood is from a human being who has a human mother but not a human father. (Ergo the missing 22 Y chromosomes.)

Jesus Christ has a human mother Mary; the Holy Spirit is His father.[5] His blood is still alive 2000 years later. No one before or since Ron Wyatt's discovery of the Ark of the Covenant has been allowed to find it again. Those who have attempted, have died crawling through the cave to find it. This is consistent with the Scriptures' accounts of unauthorized parties dying when coming into contact with the Ark of the Covenant. [6]

THE SUPERNATURAL BLOOD OF JESUS ENABLES US TO BE DELIVERED FROM DEMONIC POWERS AND SET FREE FROM THE CONSEQUENCES OF OUR MISTAKES AND TRANSGRESSIONS.

THE BLOOD IS ATONEMENT

IF you are truly repentant (turn away and course correct) from your mistakes, flaws and transgressions, and you present the Blood of Jesus as your atonement, then God will forgive your sins. More than 700 years before Jesus Christ sacrificed His life for humanity, Isaiah prophesied Jesus' profound act of sacrifice.

"But He was wounded for our transgressions,
He was crushed for our wickedness
[our sin, our injustice, our wrongdoing];
The punishment [required] for our well-being fell on Him,
And by His stripes (wounds) we are healed."
Isaiah 53:5 AMP

God is real. The Passion of Jesus Christ is real. There is no other spiritual figure by whose name millions of people have been healed, delivered of demons and experienced profound transformations. No one.

THERE IS NO OTHER SPIRITUAL FIGURE BY WHOSE
NAME MILLIONS OF PEOPLE HAVE BEEN HEALED AND
DELIVERED.

This gift is given freely to all of humanity. The supernatural, shed Blood of Jesus Christ gives you access to the Courts of Heaven to bring victories over demonic powers, your adversaries, hardships and oppression.

"For we do not wrestle against flesh and blood,
but against the rulers, against the authorities,
against the cosmic powers over this present darkness,
against the spiritual forces of evil in the heavenly places."
Ephesians 6:12

At the Last Supper, the night before His crucifixion, Jesus foretold of the power of His shed blood to free humanity from their internal bondage. He called it the Blood of the New Covenant.

"On the eve of His Passion, while still free, Jesus transformed this Last Supper with the apostles into the
memorial of His voluntary offering to the Father for the
salvation of men: *'This is my body which is given for
you.' 'This is my blood of the covenant, which is poured
out for many for the forgiveness of sins.'*"[7]

JESUS AS HIGH PRIEST EMPOWERS THE BLOOD

Jesus Establishes the New Covenant.

A priest performs covenant rituals and rites. When do we
see Jesus in this role? Jesus as the High Priest of the New
Covenant performs the sacrifice ritual at Passover, the Last
Supper, where He transmutes the Passover bread into His body
and the Passover wine into His blood. It was God's given law
that blood must be shed for the forgiveness of sins. Hebrews
9:22 confirms this:

*"And almost all things are cleansed with blood,
according to the Law[8],
and without the shedding of blood
there is no forgiveness."*
Hebrews 9:22

The Last Supper was not a farewell party. It was the institution
of a supernatural gift that Jesus Christ gave to humanity. It was
a sacrament that enabled His disciples to fulfill His command
in 1 Corinthians 11:25: *"In the same way, He took the cup of
wine after supper, saying, 'This cup is the new covenant*

between God and His people—an agreement confirmed with my blood. **Do this in remembrance of me as often as you drink it.'"**

Jesus is saying that when you partake of this sacrament of remembrance, His supernatural blood is this wine. He knew that He was about to transmute His blood into supernatural blood that would purchase eternal redemption for humanity.

As we will see later in this chapter, this supernatural blood has appeared in numerous remarkable ways in a variety of places throughout the world. It is on account of the supernatural nature of the Blood of Jesus that we can present it as our atonement for remission of sins; because it speaks on our behalf.

> *"And to Jesus, the mediator of a new covenant,*
> *and to the sprinkled blood,*
> *which speaks better than the blood of Abel."*
> Hebrews 12:24

WE PRESENT THE SUPERNATURAL BLOOD OF JESUS
AS ATONEMENT FOR REMISSION OF OUR SINS.

> *"But when Christ appeared as a high priest*
> *of the good things having come,*
> *He entered through the greater*
> *and more perfect tabernacle,*

not made by hands, that is, not of this creation;
and not through the blood of goats and calves,
but through His own blood,
He entered the holy place once for all time,
having obtained eternal redemption."
Hebrews 9:11-13

The Wine of the New Covenant is His Supernatural Blood.

In His first miracle, the wedding at Cana, Jesus transmuted purification water into fine wine. He was the groom that saved the best wine for last.[9] Now at the Last Supper, He is changing the wine of the old covenant into the wine of the New Covenant. The wine of the old covenant was of the earth (represented by the six clay pots that held the purification water that was transmuted into wine).

The wine of the New Covenant is of Heaven, Christ's blood. This miracle of the wine presages the transmutation of our own earthly bodies (clay) into heavenly bodies in eternal life.

Consider:

- The wine of the New Covenant is Jesus' Blood.
- It has proven to possess supernatural properties.
- ***What does this mean for your relationship with Him?***
- ***How can the High Priest of the New***

Covenant draw you closer to God through
His sacrifice?

"And when He had taken a cup and given thanks,
He gave it to them, saying, "Drink from it, all of you;
for this is My blood of the [new and better] covenant, which is
being poured out for many [as a substitute atonement]
for the forgiveness of sins."
Matthew 26:27 AMP

The Supernatural Blood of Jesus has appeared in many different places and circumstances across the ages. Thanks to modern technology, we are able to assess it.

MIRACLES IN THE EUCHARISTIC HOST

There have been several recorded cases of blood showing up on a Eucharistic host[10], often after it has been desecrated.[11] This can include it falling on the floor or being placed outside of a sanctified container. Incidences of blood showing up in consecrated hosts have occurred in different places around the world, from South America to India to Europe.[12]

That is to say, on several separate incidents the consecrated Eucharistic Host was placed in a sealed container; yet blood spontaneously showed up *in* the Host. See the previous end notes for some examples. There are numerous of these miracles recorded.

. . .

The blood type is always AB, similar to the one found in the famous Host of Lanciano and in the Holy Shroud of Turin.[13]. It is a rare blood type this is called a "universal recipient." Of course, the heart that is "hard soil" will not believe any amount if evidence. We only share what is a preponderance of findings.

There are 158 documented and verified Eucharistic miracles referenced in the end notes for this chapter. When there are one or maybe two occurrences of an anomaly, it can easily be tossed off as a coincidence or aberration in nature. When there are many occurrences with the same findings, any sound person of science would take notice.

The Blood of Jesus Yeshua ransomed people from every tribe, every race, every language, every ethnicity, every nation. How profound.

*"And by your blood you ransomed people for God
from every tribe and language and people and nation."*
Revelation 5:9

———

JESUS CHRIST CAME AS THE DIVINE TEMPLATE

Jesus Christ came as a human man made in God's image, operating in God's perfect will, expressing God's perfect love as the Son of Man. Jesus came as the template, a divine template, of who God created us to be in our own unique expression. He came to pay the price for our sins and mistakes by dying as a blood sacrifice.

His supernatural blood found on the solid gold mercy seat of the Ark of the Covenant tells us Jesus Yeshua is real. He is divine AND human. The blood analysis confirms this. Yet so do the millions upon millions of miracles and testimonials over the past 2000 years. His story is real. His sacrifice is real. His dying in our place to free us from the bondage of this world is real. Receive this gift!

The blood sacrifice of Jesus is like a coupon that must be redeemed in order for it to have any value. Redeem the coupon! Cash in the Blood. Claim the Blood of Jesus. Take it, grab hold of it as His gift to you, to set you free from the bondage of this world! His divine power is in His Blood. It is this divine power and sin offering gift that have overcome the demonic powers of this world.

"And everyone who calls on
the name of the Lord will be saved."
Joel 2:32 [14]

THE SUPERNATURAL NAME OF JESUS

"And she will give birth to a Son,
And you will call his name Y'shua[15]*;*
For He will save His people from their sins."
Matthew 1:21

There is Power in the Name of Jesus Christ Yeshua.

Throughout the Holy Scriptures, from the prophets of the Old Testament to the apostles and saints of the New Testament, we find a consistent theme and message: there is power in the name of Jesus Yeshua. His Hebraic name, *Y'shua* means 'salvation' or 'he who saves (or delivers).'

In the West, we know Him by the name Jesus, which derived from the Greek translation of Yeshua. He will answer to any language's version of His name. God knows what is in our heart.

> *"And there is salvation in no one else,*
> *for there is no other name under heaven*
> *given among men*
> *by which we must be saved."*
> Acts 4:12

The power of application of His name is not contingent on language or pronunciation. God knows the hearts of men and women (and children), whom they are invoking to make their supplications to God. The proof of this is 2000 years of miracles that have occurred by invoking the name of Jesus Christ Yeshua in hundreds of languages and pronunciation variations, and throughout many cultures, ethnicities, races and nations.

"But the one name that contains everything is the one that the Son of God received in His incarnation: Jesus. The divine name may not be spoken by human lips, but by assuming our humanity The Word of God[16] hands it over to us and we can invoke it: 'Jesus,' 'YHWH saves'. The name 'Jesus' contains all: God and man and the whole economy of creation and salvation. To pray 'Jesus' is to invoke him and to call him within us. His name is the only one that contains the presence it signifies. Jesus is the Risen One, and whoever invokes the name of Jesus is welcoming the Son of God who loved him and who gave himself up for him."[17]

There is a concept and expression of language in Sanskrit called *nama-rupa*, name-form. That is, the name produces the form, the form or sound expresses the name. The sound value is creational, creating the very word's meaning.

Jesus as The Word became flesh and His creational form and power is in His name, *Y'shua*, "He who saves", "He who brings salvation, freedom." There truly is power in the name of Jesus Yeshua.

The extraordinary phenomenon is that the supernatural power of the name of Jesus transcends all human differences. It is equal opportunity deliverance and salvation, mercy and forgiveness.

"If you declare with your mouth, 'Jesus is Lord,'
and believe in your heart that God
raised him from the dead,
you will be saved.
For it is with your heart that you believe
and are justified,
and it is with your mouth that you
profess your faith and are saved.
As Scripture says, 'Anyone who believes in him
will never be put to shame.'
For there is no difference between Jew and Gentile —
the same Lord is Lord of all
and richly blesses all who call on him, for,
'Everyone who calls on the name of the Lord
will be saved.'"
Romans 10:9-13

"There is no other way of Christian prayer than Christ. Whether our prayer is communal or personal, vocal or interior, it has access to the Father only if we pray 'in the name' of Jesus. The sacred humanity of Jesus is therefore the way by which the Holy Spirit teaches us to pray to God our Father."[18]

Jesus' Name Alchemized With Faith.
When Jesus performed healing miracles, He proclaimed:

"Your faith has healed you." Our faith is our conscious engagement with the gift of healing that is being transmitted.

FAITH IS THE APPLICATION OF OUR FREE WILL WITH
AN OPEN AND WILLING HEART, TO RECEIVE THE
BLESSINGS OFFERED TO US THROUGH JESUS CHRIST.

Saint Paul the Apostle described this alchemy of the name of Jesus with our personal faith.

"By faith in the name of Jesus,
this man whom you see and know was made strong.
It is Jesus' name and the faith that comes through him
that has completely healed him,
as you can all see."
Acts 3:16

YOUR EMANCIPATION TICKET: THE SALVATION PRAYER

The necessary key is to recognize and accept that Jesus came as the Son of Man to free us from our sins through His sin offering on our behalf. Luke 19:10 says: *"For the Son of man is come to seek and to save that which was lost."*

A coupon is only of value once it is actually redeemed. It is of no use sitting in the bottom of your purse or buried in your wallet.

. . .

Here is one version of the Salvation Prayer:

"Dear God, I know I have gone astray. I want to return to You now. I believe that Jesus is Lord, your only begotten Son who was crucified, died, buried and resurrected; who shed His blood as a sin payment on my behalf. I ask You Lord Jesus to come into my heart, come into my life. I release my past and all my pain to You now. I want to be in a true relationship with You. Help me to receive your healing love for me. I make You the Lord over my life. Amen."

———

CHAPTER 9
THE SUPERPOWER
PRAYER OF GRATITUDE

JESUS ALWAYS BEGAN His prayers to His Father by saying, *"Thank you Father..."* Before He performed incredible miracles and they even manifested, Jesus always thanked God the Father. Because His will was at one with the will of His Father, Jesus knew that whatever He petitioned from God, God would fulfill.

Before He performed the miracle of loaves, turning five loaves of bread and two fish into enough to feed over 5,000 people, He gave thanks and praise to His Heavenly Father.

Depending on the Bible translation, Matthew 14:18 says that Jesus gave thanks or He praised God: *"Taking the five loaves and the two fish and looking up to heaven, **He gave thanks (praised God**) and broke the loaves."*

Before Jesus Christ raised Lazarus from the dead: *"Jesus said to her, 'Did I not say to you that if you believe [in Me], you will see the glory of God [the expression of His excellence]?' So they took away the stone. And Jesus raised His eyes [toward heaven] and said, 'Father, I thank You that You have heard Me. I know that You always hear Me and listen to Me; but I have said this because of the people standing around, so that they may believe that You have sent Me.'"* John 11:40-42 AMP

KEEP THANKING GOD THAT HE HAS ANSWERED YOUR
PRAYERS EVEN BEFORE THEY HAVE BEEN ANSWERED.

ADORATION

There is another level of connecting heart to heart with God. That is adoration. Adoration is a silent outpouring of love from your heart to the heart of God the Father or to the heart of Jesus. It is a meditative practice that you can enjoy anytime and anywhere.[1]

The power of adoration is inexpressible. I have found it to be a medicine that calms and soothes, that strengthens my bond to God and Jesus, that anchors me more deeply in the stillness of God, the ocean of mercy and grace.

"Adoration is the first attitude of man acknowledging that he is a creature before His Creator. It exalts the greatness of the Lord who made us and the almighty power of the Savior who sets us free from evil. Adoration is homage of the spirit to the 'King of Glory,' respectful silence in the presence of the 'ever greater'

God. Adoration of the thrice-holy and sovereign God of love blends with humility and gives assurance to our supplications."[2]

"Gives assurance to our supplications." What does this mean? Supplications are our prayer petitions. Why would adoration give assurance, a peaceful faith, in the fulfillment of our petitions? It's because by pouring out loving adoration from our own heart, we are connecting more intimately with God and Jesus. A deeper bond develops. Our hearts begin to merge into one.

Adoration creates a spiritual pathway between your heart and the heart of Jesus, your heart and the heart of God the Father. In this act of adoration, you can't help but be in humility, because there is no ego involved. This humility blended with adoration brings peace and faith of a good outcome.

ADORATION CREATES A SPIRITUAL PATHWAY & BOND BETWEEN YOU AND JESUS.

The act of adoration also "gives assurance to our supplications" because now we are synced up with the will of God which is an emanation from the heart of God. When we are synced up with the heart and therefore the will of God, we see and understand from His perspective. We see with His eyes of love.

Understanding and seeing from Divine Love enables us to accept and naturally live God's Will.

GOD'S WILL IS AN EMANATION FROM HIS HEART.

Our supplications and petitions are either aligned with God's Will or they aren't. If they are, the practice of adoration brings us peace that our petitions will be fulfilled in God's way and timing. If our petitions do not align with God's heart, then our desires will naturally adjust to His. These are the profound gifts of adoration, which is a higher octave of thanks and praise.

ADORATION NATURALLY ADJUSTS OUR WILL TO GOD'S HEART.

READY FOR YOUR BREAKTHROUGHS?

When obstacles, hardships and adversities are put on our path, they can strengthen us, but they can also hinder us from fulfilling our God destiny if they keep repeating. If a type of hardship keeps recurring, it is usually for one of two reasons: it is not from God or we have not learned the lessons that situation is presenting us.

The beauty of the Courts of Heaven protocol is that it requires self-examination, which fosters self-awareness. These two virtues can bring us revelation of what is causing a recurrence of a particular problem or issue in our life. Armed with this revelation, we can go to the Courts of Heaven to repent and obtain a remedy.

God wants us to grow and learn from our mistakes, but if we are stuck, then there is some underlying cause to the problem. We should not be continually hindered from fulfilling our purpose on earth.

GOD WANTS YOU TO FULFILL THE DESTINY HE CREATED YOU FOR!

NOW IT'S TIME FOR SUPERPOWER PRAYERS!

I've shared these words of encouragement with you to impress upon you how important you are to God. How much you are loved and cared for. No matter what the trials and tribulations, God wants to bring you healing, peace and freedom.

Let this encouragement drive you to persevere. It can take several times to be free of a problem. That does not mean God doesn't care or the prayers don't work for you. We are in a fallen world and there are many forces working against us as brothers and sisters of Jesus Christ. The dark side hates the light. We are here to grow and become strong, to be free and live in joy, peace and love.

The fiercest warriors of God were hindered in the fulfillment of their God destiny.

The prophet Daniel got held up for 21 days by the adversary: *"But the prince of the kingdom of Persia was standing in my way for twenty-one days; then behold, Michael, one of the chief princes, came to help me, for I had been left there with the kings of Persia."*[3]

St. Paul the Apostle wrote his disciples: *"For we wanted to come to you—indeed I, Paul, tried again and again—but Satan obstructed us."*[4]

So press on until you get your breakthroughs! Many people have experienced the transformative power of these prayer protocols; but like anything of true value, it takes commitment and perseverance. Follow and do these *SuperPower Prayers* out loud with conviction. Don't back down. If you don't get your breakthrough right away, keep doing them with sincere dedication, genuine repentance, and you *will* be victorious.

We are learning that God's Word is not just words in a book or religious dogma. God's Word is a supernatural hand over your life, ready and waiting for you to call upon it. God's Word is a living guide and roadmap to health and freedom, peace, joy and love. God's Word is His love letter to you.

God's Word is His love letter to you.

Now let's go to the Courts of Heaven for deliverance from demonic powers that have been running our lives.....

"His divine power has given us everything we need
for life and godliness,
through the knowledge of Him who called us
by His own glory and virtue."
2 Peter 1:3

———

PART TWO

DELIVERANCE FROM 5 KEY PRINCIPALITIES & HEALING SOUL WOUNDS

CHAPTER 10
DELIVERANCE FROM
THE LEVIATHAN SPIRIT

———

"Can you draw out leviathan with a fishhook?
Or press down his tongue with a cord?
Can you put a rope of rushes into his nose or pierce his jaw
through with a hook?
Will he make many supplications to you
[begging to be spared]?
Or will he speak soft words to you
[to coax you to treat him kindly]?
Will he make a covenant or an arrangement with you?
Will you take him for your servant forever?"
Job 41:1-4

———

WHAT IS THE LEVIATHAN SPIRIT

THE LEVIATHAN SPIRIT is described in detail in Chapter 41 of the Book of Job. This unseen beast is very pervasive and yet so covert. He is the kingpin of pride. Pridefulness is a trait that few humans escape. It can hide itself behind spiritual or religious righteousness, moral superiority, arrogance, self-importance, righteous indignation and virtuous ambition. It frequently operates in church communities to divide and conquer. It is rampant in our culture at large.

God hates pride. It is the greatest cause of human downfall. It is the most difficult force to be fully free of, delivered from, because pride by its nature enjoys being right, being superior, lording over others. It is rewarded in our culture. This is a hard drug to give up. It is one of the biggest roadblocks to fulfilling our God destiny.

Jesus called His disciples to be humble. He demonstrated this by washing their feet at the Last Supper. It's impossible to be humble and proud at the same time. Just before He began to wash their feet, an argument had broken out amongst His disciples. They were debating which of them was superior — pride!

> *"Now a dispute also arose among them*
> *as to which of them was regarded to be the greatest."*
> Luke 22:24

In the culture of those times, the students would have washed the feet of their rabbi, not the other way around. This was unheard of. After Jesus had washed all of their feet, He encouraged them to do the same for one another. It is hard to be pridefully competitive when you are washing someone's filthy feet.

Jesus continued: *"I gave you an example so that you would also do just as I did. Most assuredly I say to you, a servant is not greater than his master and one sent is not greater than the one who sent him. If you know these things, blessed are you if you would do them."* John 13:15-17

Pride separates. Pride divides. Pride keeps us from having a pure and deep relationship with God, as well as others. Pride keeps us from knowing and living God's perfect will for our life. Separation from God is a barrier to our destiny fulfillment. It is not possible to truly and completely fulfill our God destiny with pridefulness.

People lose their anointing on account of pride; one of the wages of our celebrity culture. It is not possible to truly love others when pride is present. <u>Pride is a barrier to true intimacy</u>.

> *"Pride goes before destruction,*
> *and a haughty spirit before a fall."*
> Proverbs 16:18

In doing deliverance work, this kingpin must be addressed first before all other spirits and strongholds. Pride is considered one of the 'capital sins' because it is the basis for so many others.

Apostle John the Beloved refers to it as *"the boastful pride of life."*[1].

"Envy often comes from pride. The baptized person should train himself to live in humility."[2]

In our modern culture, we are marinating in this leviathan spirit. It saturates every area of our lives. It is in the media, entertainment and social media cultures. Pridefulness is a trait that is encouraged, lauded and awarded. We are expected to boast on our social media profiles, boast on our resumes, boast on dates. It eventually bites its own tail however. Let's take a look at the underbelly of this leviathan beast.

So long as we allow Leviathan traits in our personality and life, it has legal access to work its devious agendas in and through us.

THE LEVIATHAN SPIRIT CAN BE DESCRIBED BY 5 D'S

1. **D**eceptive
2. **D**ivisive
3. **D**evious
4. **D**ragon-like
5. **D**isplays in our character

. . .

1. DECEPTIVE.

The leviathan spirit twists and turns. It is slippery with words, perceptions and meanings to intentionally deceive, mislead and create confusion and deception.

How the leviathan spirit deceives:

- Twists words (deception, psy ops, deceptive media).
- Turns (pits) people against one another.
- Counterfeits the true light and fire of God.
- Takes advantage of our own self-doubts to sow seeds of doubt about others, in others.

Self-examine:

- What can you think of in yourself, your environment and the culture that expresses these traits?
- What things, people, habits, relationships in your life create or contribute to deception and confusion?
- Is this habit or trait in your family culture?
- Do you have some of these habits? If so, how do they show up? Is there a pattern to when/how/where/with whom they show up?
- Have you been the recipient of this kind of deception?

- Is it a pattern in your life that indicates a blindspot or flaw?

"His sneezes flash forth light,
And his eyes are like the eye of dawn.
From his mouth go burning torches;
Sparks of fire leap forth.
From his nostrils smoke goes out
As from a boiling pot and burning reeds.
His breath sets coals aglow,
And a flame goes forth from his mouth."
Job 41:18-21

Burning torches coming out of his mouth? That sounds like verbal weapons such as slander, gossip and rumor mongering. A critical spirit can work as a cohort to the leviathan spirit. Unfortunately, this is very pervasive in certain religious denomination cultures.

IF WE HAVE ANY OF THESE HABITS OR TRAITS, WE ARE ALLOWING THE LEVIATHAN SPIRIT LEGAL ACCESS INTO OUR LIFE TO WREAK HAVOC.

---

2. DIVISIVE.

The leviathan spirit is often called the "spirit of separation". It likes to divide in order to conquer. Do you see this happening anywhere in our culture today? Is it happening anywhere in your life — within your family, your workplace, your church?

Divisiveness can accompany and support pridefulness. There can be a false sense of superiority that comes from creating factions, pitting one party against another or having a critical spirit.

Job 41:8 says: *"Lay your hand on him; remember the battle with him; you will not do such an ill-advised thing again!"*

How the leviathan spirit divides:

- Drives wedges between God and His people.
- Creates divisiveness amongst loved ones, amongst people working together, in a group, in the Body of Christ.
- Shows up as triangulating (subversively involving a third party in an issue), back-biting, bad-mouthing, accusing, fault-finding, a trouble-maker.
- Works with the cohorts of a critical spirit, a judgmental spirit and/or a mocking spirit.
- Works with other principalities such as jezebel and python.

Self-examine:

- How do these dynamics currently show up in your life?
- Are you the recipient of someone who creates divisiveness?
- Do you create divisiveness? Is it a dynamic in your own family system? Did you learn it from someone?
- Do you possess traits or habits that feed divisiveness?
- Is this a recurring theme in your life?

3. DEVIOUS.

The leviathan spirit likes to stir up negativity, agitate emotions, create disharmony and disturbances. If you are afflicted by the leviathan spirit (most people are to some degree), it could show up as either or both sides of the equation: contentiousness and picking fights, or victimization.

When the leviathan spirit is activated in your life, it's possible to be both the giver and/or the receiver of these dynamics. It's also possible that you are being attacked by someone operating in this spirit, though you yourself are not operating in it.

An example is growing up with a parent who operates in the leviathan spirit, so you attract others who do so. The opportunity is to <u>learn how to respond in a healthy manner</u> and learn not to engage in relationships with leviathan types.

. . .

The leviathan spirit is sneaky, covert and deceptive, so contentiousness can be disguised. Someone with fundamentally good intentions can still have character traits of acting contentious and belligerent. It can also be expressed as passive-aggressive behavior patterns. Someone may present as having noble intentions or agenda, yet be acting covertly with a hidden agenda.

Self-examination and self-awareness are the keys to dispelling these unhealthy habits; as well as observing if you are repeatedly a recipient of someone operating in the leviathan spirit. Good people can be targeted, and are called to be attentive and discerning in order to neutralize leviathan attacks. If you grew up in a leviathan spirit environment, you may have normalized its traits in others.

How the leviathan spirit is devious:

- Creates or perpetuates victimhood; victimizes others, as well as a pattern of playing the victim or being perceived as a victim.
- Creates dissent, disharmony and conflict.
- Plots and schemes for disharmonious outcomes.
- Hides this deviousness behind 'good intentions' or victimhood as the justification.
- Feigns regret or apologies but is insincere.

Self-examine:

- Do any of these dynamics show up as recurring themes in your life?
- Are you frequently the recipient of someone with these traits?
- Are these dynamics in your family system?
- Is the leviathan spirit your blind spot? E.g., trusting someone with hidden agendas and then getting blindsided.
- Are you guilty of any of these behaviors or traits yourself?

4. DRAGON-LIKE.

The leviathan spirit is a marine - serpentine spirit. It is displayed in cultures across the world as a dragon or a big serpent-like creature living in the sea. It is so fierce, only God can defeat it. We *can* get delivered of it however!

> *"Can you fill its hide with harpoons*
> *or its head with fishing spears?"*
> Job 41:7

What to remember about the dragon-like leviathan:

- He is a formidable foe as Job 41:12-16 describes him.
- We cannot bind him. We call on God to confine him.

. . .

5. DISPLAYS in Our Character.

The leviathan spirit has a menu of traits. If there are a number of these displayed in a personality, not necessarily every single one, then most likely the leviathan spirit is manifesting.

How the leviathan spirit displays in our character:

- Ego, pridefulness, bragging, conceited, haughty, superiority, arrogance, jealousy, competitive, stiff-necked, stubborn, defensive, narcissistic, manipulative. *"He is monarch over all the sons of pride."* Job 41:34
- Insufficient or no self-examination & self-awareness; which feeds into insufficient or no self-responsibility.
- Uses religion, dogma, power-authority as a weapon to justify these traits and create divisiveness or dissension.[3]
- Stubborn, resists deliverance. *"Who can penetrate his outer armor?"* Job 41:13

Self-examine:

- Can you identify any of these leviathan traits in yourself?
- Do you see any of these as common traits in your

family culture? Were they prevalent in either of
your parents?

- Have any of these traits caused you to lose or be
denied important things in your life?

- Do people with this profile repeatedly show up in
your life? If so, what is the pattern of
when/how/where they show up? For example, is it
when you are gaining momentum?

- Could it be that narcissists repeatedly show up in
your life to reflect a self-centeredness within you?
Or perhaps you've normalized narcissism on
account of a narcissistic parent, for example.

WHY WE NEED TO BE DELIVERED FROM THE LEVIATHAN SPIRIT

- The leviathan spirit keeps us in bondage.

- It keeps us cycling through very unhealthy patterns
and experiences in our life.

- It keeps us in a lower version of ourself that is not
how God created us to be.

- It keeps us in dysfunction that we normalize; we
come to accept its hold on our life and our own
psyche. This is profound bondage.

- It is very damaging and hurtful to others. We are
accountable to God for all those we have hurt.

- It can be the vehicle through which your good works and momentum are sabotaged.

- Fortifying against it will help to nullify future attacks from the leviathan spirit.

THE WICKEDNESS OF LEVIATHAN

- The leviathan spirit sabotages our Covenant relationship with God and therefore denies us our Covenant promises and blessings.

- It sabotages key relationships and opportunities that are a part of fulfilling our destiny and bringing us a joyful life.

- When manifesting through someone directed at us, the leviathan spirit seeks to weaken us, throw us off our game, demoralize us and puncture our confidence.

- It keeps us from, or can limit us from, being filled with the Holy Spirit, receiving the gifts of the Holy Spirit, and having our deepest relationship with God, Jesus Christ and our loved ones.

- It counterfeits the light and fire of God, so you might get a flavor of God without going for the whole banquet. People often stop at the flavor which is leviathan's goal! He seeks to deny us the fullness of who we are, made in God's image.

- The leviathan spirit fosters spiritual and personal stagnation. The leviathan traits of arrogance ("I know best"), close-heartedness, stubbornness and being stiff-necked stop the flow, love and will of God from operating in our life.

- It prevents us from moving *with* God, truly knowing God and being one with Him.

THE LEVIATHAN SPIRIT PREVENTS US FROM MOVING WITH GOD AND HIS DESIGN FOR OUR LIFE.

The leviathan spirit is deeply woven into our culture, so it is virtually impossible to escape its grip. Therefore, there is no condemnation in needing to be delivered of it! We can't remove the leviathan spirit from earth, but we can get *delivered from its grip* personally.

Now let's go to the Courts of Heaven to receive God's help in becoming emancipated from the leviathan spirit!

COURTS OF HEAVEN PROTOCOL TO BE DELIVERED FROM THE LEVIATHAN SPIRIT

1. Preparation.

Before you go into the Courts of Heaven, take the time to identify your petitions and purposes, what remedies you are seeking, what in your life and character require repentance and what in your family lineage requires renunciation. Ask the Holy Spirit to reveal to you these things before you go in to the Courts of Heaven. Often times, when you are in the Courts of Heaven, the Holy Spirit will bring other things to mind for which to repent.

You may receive information about specific family members who have already passed on. This can include activities they engaged in such as crimes, rituals, oaths, covenants, contracts and curses. You renounce, repudiate, and disavow the sins, transgressions and iniquities of your ancestors <u>to remove any legal cases against yourself.</u>

We repent and plead guilty for all personal sins, transgressions and iniquities, present the Blood of Jesus as our atonement, and then ask God to pass judgements on our behalf. The adversary operates through legality, which is why we go to God's Court-room to remove any legal cases the enemy is using against us or our family.

Remember to speak the entire protocol OUT LOUD!

. . .

2. Presentation of Purpose.

LORD God, Just Judge, I come before your Court of Mercy and Grace and ask that the courts be seated and the books be opened, according to Daniel 7:10. I ask for the Lord Jesus Christ and the Holy Spirit[4] to be my Holy Advocates to represent me in your Court. I give them full power to speak on my behalf. I put on robes of righteousness[5] and loose the Blood of Jesus Christ over myself so that satan and his minions have no access to me.

As I stand before your Court, I thank you Jesus Christ for everything you've done for me, that when You died on the Cross, You gave your blood to redeem me, to deliver me from curses and demonic powers. That sacrifice is speaking for me right now. Thank you for your sin payment on my behalf.

LORD God Adonai[6], I come before your Court to seek relief from the leviathan spirit; to renounce, repent of and shed leviathan traits in myself; to receive your forgiveness, grace and help to be free of all leviathan influences and oppression over my life once and for all.

Heavenly Father, when I say that "I repent", I am declaring that I am releasing, giving up, turning away from all ungodly habits, traits and impulses, and committing to their opposite – from arrogance to humility, from divisive and critical to conciliatory and peace-making, from insensitive to kind and thoughtful, from prideful to selflessness. When I say that "I repent", I am committing to being the kind of man/woman that You designed and destined me to be, my truth in Christ Jesus.

. . .

I ask LORD God that You release your Notification Angels, Enforcement Angels and Hosts of Heaven to all those humans and non-humans who will be affected by your Court decisions, to duly inform them of and immediately enforce all of your judgements in my case today.[7]

3. Renounce & Repent.

Dear Heavenly Father, I come in the name of Jesus Christ to repent of all my sins, iniquities and transgressions, and to renounce, repudiate, and disavow all the sins of my ancestors back to Adam and Eve, having to do with opening doors to satan, lucifer, the leviathan spirit and all of leviathan's cohorts and minions including the traits, flaws and spirits of jezebel, criticism, judgmentalness, religion, haughtiness, stiff-necked, willfulness, pridefulness, stubbornness, hard-heartedness, aggression, cruelty, superiority, jealousy, envy, competitiveness, gossip, slander, divisiveness, trouble-making, sabotage, victim-hood, momentum-breaking and stealing, false prophecy and false gifts of the spirit.

I hereby renounce, denounce, divorce and break all soul ties, oaths, contracts, covenants, agreements with all of these spirits now. I commit to not re-opening the door to them. I reject and renounce the normalization of these spirits and traits which have been passed down through my bloodlines.

I understand that *repent* means to turn away from, to change and transform my mind and way of living. It is a commitment to cease and turn away from activities and habits that are detrimental to my spirit which was made in your image. It is a commitment to nurture your indwelling spirit and to *"Guard, through the Holy Spirit who dwells in me, the treasure which has been entrusted to me,"* according to 2 Timothy 1:14.

I repent for all the times and ways the leviathan spirit and any of its cohorts and minions have been used and allowed to control, manipulate or damage myself, other human beings, and my relationship with You, the Holy Spirit and Jesus Christ. I renounce all leviathan seeds and fruits from all of my bloodlines back to Adam and Eve.

I forgive all those who contributed to my beliefs, behaviors and traits connected to leviathan and these other spirits. I ask You to forgive my family and ancestors LORD God.

Heavenly Father, I renounce, sever, divorce and cut forevermore all ties with leviathan and leviathan-related spirits, including all ungodly relationships, sources, systems, organizations, agendas and parties, and every leviathan seed implanted in me, my belief systems and body. Let every leviathan seed in me die now. In Jesus name!

I repent of all of my own sins and character flaws that have given the leviathan spirit a place or a foothold in my life. I repent of and renounce the leviathan spirit and all of its attributes, habits, traits, cohorts and minions including:

- Pride, conceit and arrogance
- Stubbornness and rebelliousness
- Haughtiness, vanity and jealousy
- Irritation, impatience and intolerance
- Spiritual pride and jealousy, focusing more on myself and my own spiritual gifts than on You Abba Father
- Stealing the glory for myself that only belongs to You LORD God and Jesus Christ
- Wanting to be honored, rewarded and acknowledged by others rather than serving You and your perfect will
- Being unteachable and having a know-it-all mentality
- Intellectualism and rationalization
- Thinking more of myself than I should
- Fearfulness in talking about You and sharing You with others
- Ministering in your name without a holy fear and reverence for who You truly are
- Allowing others with the leviathan spirit to sow seeds of doubt, divisiveness and negativity about other people
- Judging, finding fault and being quarrelsome
- Using and abusing others for my own benefit
- Seeking my own benefit in situations etc. (List what the Holy Spirit has shown you personally about yourself and your ways.)
- Seeking power, position, status, control, authority
- Distrust in God, self-reliance and a self-serving agenda
- Atheism, antichrist spirit and rebellion against God

- Indulging in a critical spirit; others are always wrong
- Self-deception, confusion and twisting of the truth
- Not giving God the glory that only He deserves
- Spiritual blindness and deafness, in denial, inability to see and realize when I'm lost and in need of salvation and deliverance
- Anger, irritability, impatience, intolerance and resentment
- Contentious in relationships, sowing divisiveness and separation with others
- Argumentative, quarrelsome, wanting to prove I'm right, needing to have the last word
- Not taking responsibility for my own faults and mistakes but rather blaming others
- Self-righteousness – blaming God and everybody else for what goes wrong
- Putting my own intellect and ability to reason above God and God's Will
- Being controlling and possessive (submitting to and even yoking to the jezebel spirit, and people who possess it)
- A cutting and critical tongue, gossiping about people and a habit of judging others
- Creating an environment for others to slander and not stopping it
- Rejecting dependence upon and total submission to God
- False humility and false peace that is not from God
- Believing in masculine superiority and masculine dominance in an ungodly way that subjugates or demeans others

. . .

Dear LORD God, I ask for your forgiveness for all of these behaviors, habits and traits, and commit to an earnest undertaking to permanently turn away from them.

I renounce, denounce and divorce all ungodly oaths, contracts, covenants, agreements, curses, rituals, witchcraft, sorcery, occult practices having to do with the leviathan spirit and its programs committed by my bloodlines; and all related demonic strongholds and iniquities passed down and affecting my life.

I renounce and repent of all traits, habits, character flaws and inclinations that I have inherited, indulged in and expressed on account of these ancestral iniquities and having to do with the leviathan spirit and programs. I recognize that they are wrong, hurtful to myself, others and You Heavenly Father. Please forgive me.

LORD God, I also forgive my ancestors and particularly _____ (name those that the Lord has revealed to you) including those that are already deceased and whom I have not even known, who passed on the spirit of leviathan and its accompanying spirits, habits, traits and character flaws.

4. Plead Guilty.

Father God, for everything I have repented of and renounced here, I plead guilty to remove all the cases that satan and his demonic powers have been holding against me. I present the Blood of the Lamb of God, Jesus Christ Yeshua, as atonement. I present the Voice of the Blood of Jesus[8] which speaks "Tetelestai"[9], "paid in full" to clear these transgressions from my record and my bloodline.

Father God, I ask for redemption from the curse, by the Blood of Jesus and ask You to break all curses of leviathan and all other related demonic spirits, systems and agendas over me and my bloodline. Let the Blood of Jesus break all of these curses now!

For indeed your Word in Colossians 2:13-15 confirms that charges against us are cancelled with the atoning Blood of your Son: "*He forgave us all our sins, having canceled the charge of our legal indebtedness, which stood against us and condemned us; He has taken it away, nailing it to the cross. And having disarmed the powers and authorities, He made a public spectacle of them, triumphing over them by the cross.*"

Thank You LORD God, for this mercy gift of compassion and grace.

Cleanse, Clear & Release.

LORD God, I now ask that You take me back in the spirit to the point of conception in my mother's womb. I ask that any bloodline curse of leviathan be cancelled over me at the point of conception in my mother's womb by the power of the Blood of Jesus, and that I am set free now!

· · ·

I cut all unholy soul ties between me and anyone who has been a slave to leviathan in the spirit. Let the spiritual seed of leviathan die in me (and my children).

Dear Heavenly Father, let the spiritual cord coming through the bloodlines that bound me to this stronghold of leviathan be severed now by the Sword of the Spirit of Truth.

LORD God, order the spirit of leviathan and all its cohort spirits to leave my soul, my body and my life now! In the name of Jesus!

Dear Jesus, I now ask You to teach me humbleness and meekness whilst also being able to take up my full spiritual authority in You. Teach me the difference between pride and spiritual authority. Teach me *your* ways. Please make me less in my own ego so that your Spirit in me can become more, and become my actual operating system.

Jesus in me must increase, but I must decrease, according to John 3:30. Help me LORD God, to trust your indwelling spirit, to discern truth from lies, to never again be swayed by or manipulated by the leviathan spirit operating through others or in the atmosphere.

Help me LORD God, to discern when it is operating in someone else and to neutralize all attacks against me by remaining in the love of Christ dwelling in my heart and soul.

. . .

LORD God, pour your healing balm of Gilead into all of my places of stored habits, traits, filters, beliefs, memories, imprints and traumas having to do with leviathan and its cohorts. Clear them out now. Purify and cleanse my body, brain, mind, heart and soul, my conscience, my subconscious and unconscious mind, my memory bank and everywhere in me where leviathan and its cohorts have been imprinted and operating.

Pour your healing balm of Gilead into all the places where hooks, cords and connections to the leviathan spirit and its cohorts have existed within me to regenerate and rejuvenate them now. Restore me to "factory settings", your design for me.

1 John 4:4 tells me that I am from God and *"Greater is He who is in me than he who is in the world."* LORD God, I recognize, honor and accept that your potential for holiness in Christ Jesus dwells in me, that I am born of your seed of divinity, created in your image, and that You are healing, blessing and restoring me, my body, mind, heart, soul and life. Thank you for transforming me through your anointing, your grace and your love.

~ Pause in Silence to Receive God's Healing ~

5. Reparations ~ Penance.
Dear Heavenly Father, please guide me to right reparations

and/or penance for all the violations I have committed regarding the leviathan spirit and its accompanying character traits, habits, personality flaws and behaviors; as well as any reparations on behalf of my family lineage.

Speak to me through your Holy Spirit. Convict me in mind and heart of right restitution to make through my actions, relationships, charity, teaching, sharing, giving, sacrifices, prayers and fasting.

6. Justification ~ Plead Your Case.

LORD God, Righteous Judge, I am presenting my legal case to You based upon your legal document, your Word, which contains your laws, statutes and covenants. Please receive your Word as the key to my freedom from the bondage of the leviathan spirit and its cohorts. Father God, your Word declares the following:

I Have a Pre-Ordained God Destiny.

Psalm 139:5 says: *"You have enclosed me behind and before, and You have placed your hand upon me."*

Psalm 139:16 shares: *"Your eyes have seen my unformed substance; and in your book were all written the days that were appointed for me, when as yet there was not one of them [even taking shape]."*

. . .

Father God, I want to fulfill my book of life, my God destiny. Your Word declares that this is my potential and infers that anything that stands in the way of that is in violation of your will and your laws. Remaining under the yoke and oppression of the leviathan spirit will hinder and even prevent the fulfillment of my purpose and destiny in You.

You Have Called Me to be One with You.

Your Word in John 17:22-23 says: *"And the glory which You gave Me I have given them, that they may be one just as We are one: I in them, and You in Me; that they may be made perfect in one, and that the world may know that You have sent Me, and have loved them as You have loved Me."*

Heavenly Father, the leviathan spirit seeks to separate me from You and deny me this oneness. Stand for me against its attacks and grips. Free me once and for all from the leviathan spirit! I want to be one with You and your Son Jesus Christ.

I commit to listening to *your* voice over lying voices. Give me the discernment to always recognize your voice from whispering lies, your Spirit from demonic spirits. I commit to not allowing false spirits to separate me from You and Jesus. I submit my will to your will.

My Sins Have Been Nailed to the Cross.

Your Word in Colossians 2:13-14 promises me: *"When you were dead in your sins and in the uncircumcision of your flesh (worldliness, manner of life), God made you alive together with Christ, having [freely] forgiven us all our sins, having canceled out the certificate of debt consisting of legal demands [which were in force] against us and which were hostile to us. And this certificate He has set aside and completely removed by nailing it to the cross."*

Father God, your Word clearly states that there can be no more accusing voice against me, so long as I turn from my bad habits (repent) and commit to living dead to sin, continually self-examining and course-correcting when needed. Therefore, shut down the voice of the adversary coming against me through the leviathan spirit and its cohorts. Give me a fresh start and new life in Christ Jesus!

You Will Disarm the Enemy & Punish Leviathan.

Your Word in Ephesians 1:22-23 assures me: *"And He put all things under His feet, and gave Him to be head over all things to the church, which is His body, the fullness of Him who fills all in all."* So Jesus Christ has put leviathan under His feet, so that I, this captive, would be set free!

Your Word in Colossians 2:15 further declares: *"When He had disarmed the rulers and authorities [those supernatural forces of evil operating against us], He made a public example of them [exhibiting them as captives in His triumphal procession], having triumphed over them through the cross."*

This Word makes it abundantly clear that the shed Blood of

Jesus can disarm leviathan from wreaking havoc in my life and family.

Your Word in Isaiah 27:1-3 promises: *"In that day the Lord will punish leviathan the fleeing serpent with his fierce and great and mighty sword, even leviathan the twisted serpent; and he will kill the dragon who lives in the sea. In that day, a vineyard of wine, sing in praise of it! I, the LORD, am its Keeper; I water it every moment. So that no one will harm it, I guard it night and day."*

LORD God Just Judge, I ask you to punish leviathan, the fleeing serpent, for all the trouble he has made in my life and family lineage.

Father God, according to Psalm 74:11-14, I ask You: *"Don't hold back! Unleash your might and give it, leviathan, a final blow. You have always been, and always will be, my King. You are the mighty conqueror, working wonders all over the world. It was you who split the sea in two by your glorious strength. Smash the power of Tannin, the sea monster. Crush the might of leviathan, the great dragon, take it as crumbs and feed it to the sharks."*

LORD God, it is evident in your Word that You created me to be yours. If this leviathan spirit, its cohorts and minions are allowed to continue to control, steal or compromise any part of me or my life, I will not be able to fulfill my God destiny, as they always seek to destroy the call on my life and damage my relationship with You.

If I am not granted these requests from your Court, I will not be able to fulfill your plans for me. It is also clear from your Word that only You can harness and eliminate leviathan. So if You do not grant my petitions, leviathan, his cohorts and minions will be allowed to continue wreaking havoc in my life. Have mercy on me LORD God. Have mercy on my family.

7. Petitions.

Therefore LORD God Just Judge, the judgements that I am requesting from your Court of Mercy and Grace are:

- Grant all of my petitions in the case I have presented to You here.
- Grant me a divorce decree from and a Divine Restraining Order against leviathan and all leviathan cohorts, minions, entities and agendas from operating in my life, so that I will no longer be tormented by anything having to do with leviathan, so long as I do not do anything in the future to feed that beast, including reverting to leviathan traits.
- Grant me a Divine Restraining Order against leviathan and all his cohorts and minions purposing to create disunity, disharmony and strife in my life, marriage, family, vocation and other relationships.
- Neutralize the leviathan spirit in my life, take away the breath of leviathan, that it may die and return to dust, according to your Word in Psalm 104:29.
- Crush the head of leviathan and give him as food

for the creatures of the wilderness according to
Psalm 74:14.

- Punish leviathan, the fleeing serpent, with your
  fierce and great and mighty sword. Kill the dragon
  who lives in the sea, according to your Word in
  Isaiah 27:1.
- Extinguish all the holds that satan, lucifer,
  leviathan and all of their cohorts and minions have
  had on my destiny, family, marriage, relationships,
  finances, joy, success and well-being.
- Replace every lie in my belief system with your
  Truth that shall set me free. Fill me to overflowing
  with the true Holy Spirit and gifts of the Holy
  Spirit.
- Release all supports and resources, both spiritual
  and material, for me to fulfill my God destiny.
- Restore to me seven-fold everything leviathan, his
  minions and cohorts have stolen from me that has
  not been on account of my own actions and
  choices, according to your promises in Proverbs
  6:31: *"But when the thief is found, he must repay
  seven times what he stole; he must give all the
  property of his house."*
- Yoke me fully, eternally and exclusively to YOU,
  your heart, your perfect will, Father God.

8. Wait on the Lord's Response.

This is a pause, allowing for stillness and silence to respect
God's response to our petitions. This is cultivating an awareness and sensitivity to our relationship with God, just as we
would communicate with someone sitting right in front of us.

. . .

9. Thanks and Gratitude.

[Dedicate time to thank God after all of your petitions. You may want to play or sing praise music, dance; however you express thanks.]

- Thank you LORD God for granting my petitions!
- Thank you for your Justice, Mercy and Love!
- Thank you Father God and Jesus Christ, for healing, restoring and redeeming me!
- Thank you LORD God for delivering me from leviathan!
- To You alone be all the glory in Heaven and upon the earth forever and ever! AMEN!!!

"This is what the Sovereign Lord says:
'None of my words will be delayed any longer.
Whatever I say will be fulfilled,
declares the Sovereign LORD."
Ezekiel 12:28

———

CHAPTER 11

DELIVERANCE FROM THE JEZEBEL SPIRIT

"But I have this charge against you,
that you tolerate the woman Jezebel,
who calls herself a prophetess [claiming to be inspired],
and she teaches and misleads My bond-servants so that they
commit immorality and eat food sacrificed to idols.
Revelations 2:20

WHAT IS THE JEZEBEL SPIRIT

IN THE ABOVE passage from Chapter 2 of the Book of Revelations, Jesus is speaking of the *jezebel spirit*. The actual woman named Jezebel lived hundreds of years prior to this revelation given to John the Beloved by the Lord Jesus Christ. Jezebel was the wicked queen consort of Ahab, King of Israel.[1] Clearly, Jesus was not referring to the actual Queen Jezebel but *the spirit* which embodied Jezebel's character traits, and so named the spirit *"the woman Jezebel."*

Jezebel was infamous for her wicked and wily ways. She worshiped baal, a pagan god who fed off of the sacrifice of children. She had filled the court with hundreds of her baal-worshiping false prophets. She was deep into witchcraft and had a bloodthirsty ambition for power and domination. She was a nasty woman. King Ahab basically let her dominate him and so was a weak, spineless man.

WHAT TO KNOW ABOUT THE JEZEBEL SPIRIT

All of these traits may not manifest in one person, but there will be a preponderance of these tendencies. Though it is given a woman's name, it is *not* exclusive to women! Men, women and children can all be controlled by the jezebel spirit. She frequently works in tandem with the leviathan spirit.

- Narcissistic, lying, deceitful, manipulative controlling, uses people, uses information to create deceit and divisiveness
- Refuses to admit guilt or wrong, never wrong, insincere apologies; based on pride and insecurity
- Takes credit for everything
- Covertly and overtly controlling in many forms
- Uses people to accomplish its agenda
- Provokes others to anger and upset as a form of manipulation and control
- Uses information as a weapon
- Withholds & sequesters information to yield control of a situation or agenda
- Uses information as a form of manipulation (e.g. who gets access and who doesn't)
- Talks in confusion, obfuscates the topic or purpose as a means of hiding agendas
- Operates in hidden agendas; volunteers excessively to have their hand in everything, deceitful motives

- Habitual liar; uses charm to hide lies and motives
- Ignores and isolates people who disagree with their agenda
- Never or rarely gives credit or expresses gratitude
- Critical nature, puts down others to build up themself
- One-upsmanship, upstages others, threatened by others taking the limelight, credit or plaudits
- Talks excessively, dominates conversations as a form of narcissism/self-centeredness
- Spiritualizes everything to avoid taking responsibility, very "religious", but low self-awareness & self-responsibility
- Insubordinate, anti-authority, rebellious, trouble-maker
- Pushy, domineering, authoritative
- Works with familiar spirits acting as clairvoyant; operating from the mental realm passing off as from the Holy Spirit (common in churches)
- Uses element of surprise to catch others off guard
- Sows discord, contentious, belittles others, divisive
- Commands attention, must be center of attention, not a team player
- Vindictive and vengeful, never forgets a wrong, will seek to destroy another's reputation
- Projects their own traits on others, twists & manipulates others' genuine experiences to frame others
- Unsupportive, not supportive of others work, projects, etc. if they are not under jezebel's control
- Know-it-all, blind ambition, lone operator, their way or the highway
- Manipulation thru generosity and gift-giving

- Often dwells in the church but doesn't like authority unless IT is in the position of authority
- May hide; seemingly a person is delivered of this jezebel spirit, then suddenly without warning a situation will arise and the spirit is wreaking havoc again

WHY WE NEED TO BE DELIVERED FROM THE JEZEBEL SPIRIT

- Creates strife, stress, dramas and chaos as a recurring dynamic.

- Ego-centric, superiority, domination, arrogance, rigid belief systems including religious denomination judgementalness and superiority.

- Prohibits us from growing into spiritual and personal maturity, realizing our calling and *"doing the greater works"* that Jesus Christ prophesied.

- Distracts us and takes us out of attunement with God's Will, by keeping us looping in our own ego, desires and agendas.

- Destroys relationships and allows the enemy to steal and co-opt God's plans and purposes for our lives, relationships and vocations.

- Seeks legal entry and ground through victimhood, anger, righteous indignation, misapplied/faux 'righteousness'.

- Hinders us from being the fullness of Christ Jesus that we are called to be: righteous, holy and "loving one another as He has loved us."

- We remain a target for the jezebel spirit and lack keen discernment of it.

Reading through these lists of jezebel traits and agendas, it is very evident that the jezebel spirit is a dominating force in our culture and throughout the world at this time. This spirit is a lying, deceiving, seducing spirit. It is a powerful force behind the disinformation wars we find ourselves in.

There are women and men who currently dominate the world stage and news who clearly embody this jezebel spirit. It causes rifts in families and ruptures in marriages. It wreaks havoc in the workplace and in church communities. It is very common for a woman with the jezebel spirit to gain great power and authority in churches. It is time to take charge over it and dispel it from our lives!

We can't control other people choosing to be under the spell and control of jezebel, but we can control our own character and choices. <u>We can develop discernment about what is going on around us and with whom we are interacting</u>. We can make healthy decisions about relationships and circumstances in our lives.

There are leviathan-jezebel situations that we may have to walk away from for our own well-being. Knowledge is power. Going through this protocol and learning about the behaviors of these demons is empowering.

WE CAN CONTROL OUR OWN CHARACTER AND CHOICES. WE CAN DEVELOP DISCERNMENT ABOUT WHAT IS GOING ON AROUND US.

As you learn about the jezebel spirit's features and behaviors, you will cultivate the ability to discern it in action. Discernment is power. As your awareness and discernment grow, you will be able to take more charge over your environment and your life.

NO LONGER WILL YOU BE A VICTIM OF YOUR ENVIRONMENT.

You now have tools at your disposal that will assist you in being delivered from the demonic powers of the jezebel spirit. You will develop the strength and courage to walk away from unhealthy people and environments. You will also be able to neutralize jezebel demonic attacks.

KEY TO REMEMBER:

Character traits are your choice.

Personality and character traits are a free-will choice. If you choose to hold these traits, you are 'feeding the beast.' It is easy to fall back into habits even after doing these protocols. That is why it is important to repeat them from time to time. Old habits can sometimes die hard.

Attacks may still come.

The jezebel spirit is very, very pervasive in our society and therefore in the personalities of many people. Therefore, it is not unlikely you will find yourself getting attacked by this spirit even after you have done these protocols.

It wants to pull you into its lair by upsetting and hurting you, especially if you are coming into your godly power and in a momentum of destiny. Doing this protocol will build up your shield so that attacks will not be fruitful for the perpetrator.

Release offenses.

If you hold onto offenses, you are pulled back into its power over you.

Release unforgiveness.

Cut cords with the persons involved and soak yourself in the purifying Word of God. Shake the dust off your feet and move on!

COURTS OF HEAVEN PROTOCOL TO BE DELIVERED FROM THE JEZEBEL SPIRIT

1. Preparation.

Before you go into the Courts of Heaven, take the time to identify your petitions and purposes, what remedies you are seeking, what in your life and character require repentance and what in your family lineage requires renunciation. Ask the Holy Spirit to reveal to you these things before you go in to the Courts of Heaven. Often times, when you are in the Courts of Heaven, the Holy Spirit will bring other things to mind for which to repent.

You may receive information about specific family members who have already passed on. This can include activities they engaged in such as crimes, rituals, oaths, covenants, contracts and curses. You renounce, repudiate, and disavow the sins, transgressions and iniquities of your ancestors <u>to remove any legal cases against yourself.</u>

We repent and plead guilty for all personal sins, transgressions and iniquities, present the Blood of Jesus as our atonement, and then ask God to pass judgements on our behalf. The adversary operates through legality, which is why we go to God's Courtroom to remove any legal cases the enemy is using against us or our family.

Remember to speak the entire protocol OUT LOUD!

. . .

2. Presentation of Purpose.

LORD God, Just Judge, I come before your Court of Mercy and Grace and ask that the courts be seated and the books be opened, according to Daniel 7:10. I ask for the Holy Spirit and the Lord Jesus Christ to be my Holy Advocates to represent me in your Court. I put on robes of righteousness and I loose the Blood of Jesus Christ over myself so that satan and his minions have no access to me.

As I stand before your Court, I thank you Jesus, for everything you have done for me, that when you died on the Cross, you gave your blood to redeem me, to deliver me from curses and demonic powers. Thank you for your sin payment on my behalf.

LORD God Adonai, I come before your Court to seek relief from the jezebel spirit; to renounce, repent of and shed jezebel traits in myself; to receive your forgiveness, grace and help to be free of all jezebel influence and oppression over my life once and for all.

I ask LORD God that You release your Notification Angels, your Enforcement Angels and Hosts of Heaven to all those humans and non-humans who will be affected by your Court decisions to duly inform them of and immediately enforce all of your decisions in my case today.

3. Renounce & Repent.

Father God, I come in the name of Jesus Christ to repent

of all my sins, iniquities and transgressions, and renounce, repudiate, and disavow all the sins, transgressions and iniquities of my ancestors back to Adam and Eve, having to do with opening doors to satan, the jezebel spirit, and all of their cohorts and minions including spirits of occult, witchcraft, temple priestess, false religion, idolatry, wizardry, sorcery, seduction, incubus, succubus, manipulation, nahash, ahab, leviathan and python.

I understand that *repent* means to turn away from, to change and transform my mind and way of living, to transmute flaws into virtues. It is a commitment to course correct, to cease and turn away from activities and habits that are detrimental to my spirit which was made in your image. I commit to becoming a new creation in Christ Jesus.

I repent of:

- Engaging in and indulging in criticizing, back-biting, condemning and putting other people down
- Living in self-centeredness and not taking responsibility for my own actions and behaviors
- Destroying, opposing and slandering people, including your true prophets, prophecies and teachings
- Destroying, opposing and slandering your ordained leaders and anointed ones
- Satisfying the ego at the expense of your Will and others' considerations
- Opposing the work of the Holy Spirit, obstructing the flow of your Spirit

- Idolatry, including idolizing knowledge, my own views & beliefs, people, traditions, celebrities, money, social status and trends
- Engaging in witchcraft, sorcery, occult, curses, emotional manipulation, controlling behavior, rebellion
- Walking after the desires of the flesh including over-indulgence in food, drink, sex, work, t.v., entertainment
- Evoking the ahab spirit in others; leading others to wrong action
- Allowing the ahab spirit to manifest through me; being wrongly passive and permissive
- Abuse of power, authority and leadership
- Distorting other peoples' words and actions to make myself look good
- Distorting your words, even by speaking in your name that which You have not really spoken (sharing false prophetic words downloaded from the astral realm and familiar spirits)
- Lying, underhandedness, putting blame and suspicion on others
- Dominating, intimidating and manipulating
- Disobeying your Word, not asking, listening and obeying *your* Will
- Discouraging others from following and obeying You
- Rebellion and stubbornness in all forms in my life; my way rather than *your* way
- Pride, arrogance and argumentativeness
- Falsely accusing others, discouraging them and causing hurt and bitterness in them
- Criticizing, lying and cutting down others

- Being led astray by allowing drive and desire for material wealth and ambitions to overshadow You
- Ignoring promptings and warnings from the Holy Spirit
- Sexual immorality in all its forms; manipulation and sorcery through sex
- Transferring this spirit to my children and descendants
- Attempting to intimidate others with fear, manipulation and threats
- Following tradition and social trends instead of revelation
- Enforcing legalism (a religious spirit) instead of the Holy Spirit
- Bringing others into bondage (spouse, friends, employees, and children)
- Controlling others through a religious pretense and works, secretiveness, long and empty prayers, 'unique' experiences and super-spirituality (second heaven/astral experiences)
- Angry outbursts and the hurt and confusion created as a result
- Stepping on and using people to get what I want

I renounce, denounce and divorce all ungodly oaths, contracts, covenants, agreements, curses, rituals, witchcraft, sorcery, occult practices, activities, vocations, avocations, beliefs, hexes, vexes, voodoo having to do with the jezebel spirit and its programs committed by my bloodlines; and all related demonic strongholds and iniquities passed down and affecting my life. I renounce all jezebel seeds and fruits from all of my bloodlines back to Adam and Eve. Burn them all to ashes now in the name of Jesus.

I renounce and repent of all traits, habits, character flaws and inclinations that I have inherited, indulged in and expressed on account of these ancestral iniquities and having to do with the jezebel spirit and its programs. I recognize that they are wrong, hurtful to myself, others and You Heavenly Father. Please forgive me.

Father God, I renounce, repent of, divorce and break all oaths, contracts, covenants, agreements, altars, portals and temples that I and my bloodlines have created, participated in, been at all yoked to, having to do with the jezebel spirit and all of its cohorts and minions; including any jezebel temple built inside of me, any throne, crown, robes, regalia, scepter, jewels, ring and anything else belonging to jezebel not mentioned here.

LORD God, destroy with your Holy Fire anything in me having to do with jezebel walls, furnishings, dungeons, trap doors, hidden staircases, and every other internal structure having to do with the jezebel spirit and all its cohorts and minions. Burn them all to ashes now in the name of Jesus Christ.

Heavenly Father, I repent for all the times and ways I have allowed, enabled, indulged in, proliferated and tolerated the spirit of jezebel, all its cohorts and minions, and every seed implanted in me, my belief systems and body. I come to You, humbling myself before You because I desire *your* standard of righteousness and holiness.

LORD God, on behalf of myself and all of my l bloodlines back to Adam and Eve, I renounce, reject, forbid and divorce all cohorts and minions of jezebel including the demonic spirits and curses of: a bed of anguish and suffering, humiliation, rejection, downheartedness, utmost judgement, death and premature death, slavery, senility, cancer, sexual perversion, schizophrenia, divorce, bad marriages, adultery, female domination, male domination, incest, blasphemy, loss of children, loss of marriage partner, desertion, betrayal, infidelity, promiscuity, disasters and evil, loneliness and desolation, witchcraft, persecution, all offspring of satan and his demons, and any satan seed implanted in me.

I repent for all the times and ways I have allowed the jezebel spirit and all other demonic spirits including seducing, beguiling, divination, domination, controlling, manipulating and apollyon to damage other human beings, my own soul and my relationship with You. I forgive all those who contributed to my beliefs and behaviors connected to jezebel and these other demonic spirits, habits and traits.

I renounce, divorce and cut all ties with ungodly relationships, now and forever more. I renounce, sever, divorce, and close all doors permanently to all ungodly sources, parties and persons, including soul ties with former spouses, lovers and others that have been connected to me in the spirit. I return all soul parts to them now.

. . .

4. Plead Guilty.

Father God, for everything I have repented and renounced here, I plead guilty to remove all the cases that satan and his demonic powers have held against me. I present the Blood of the Lamb of God, Jesus Christ Yeshua as atonement. I present the Voice of the Blood of Jesus which speaks "paid in full" to clear these transgressions from my record and my future bloodline.

Father God, I ask for redemption from the curse, by the Blood of Jesus, and ask You to break all oppression from and curses of jezebel, ahab and all other demonic spirits, systems and agendas over me and my family line! Let the Blood of Jesus break all these curses now!

Father God, please forgive me for every way I have opened myself up to this jezebel spirit and its cohorts and minions. I ask for your forgiveness on behalf of myself and my entire bloodline. I stand before You today on the grounds of your mercy and the perfect work of Jesus Christ on the Cross, the reconciliation that He has worked for me.

Cleanse these hands of mine from all of these sins, even those sins I haven't realized yet. Please cleanse my heart also, Father God, in the precious name of Jesus Christ.

Cleanse, Clear & Release.

LORD God, pour your healing balm of Gilead into all of my places of stored habits, traits, filters, beliefs, memories, imprints and traumas having to do with the jezebel spirit, its cohorts and minions. Clear them out now. Purify and cleanse my body, brain, mind, heart and soul, my conscience, my subconscious and unconscious mind, my memory bank and everywhere in me where jezebel and its cohorts have been imprinted and operating.

Pour your healing balm of Gilead into all the places where hooks, cords and connections to the jezebel spirit and its cohorts have existed within me to regenerate and rejuvenate them now. Restore me to "factory settings", your design for me.

Let all stolen or scattered parts or fragments of my soul be fully healed with the Blood of Jesus and returned to me now.

Father God, cleanse me now. Cleanse my body, my life and my bloodline with your holy healing love, oil and fire. Heal me with the sacred Blood of Jesus from all arrogance, pridefulness, egoism, stubbornness, rebelliousness, willfulness, insecurities, jealousy, competitiveness, envy, anger, irritation, resentment, as a result of the jezebel spirit and all of its cohorts and minions. Heal me from all the sources and causes of these character flaws.

I receive by faith your healing because, *I am from God and have overcome demonic powers, and greater is He, Jesus, who is in me than he who is in the world*, according to 1 John 4:4.

. . .

LORD God, I recognize, honor and accept that your potential for holiness in Christ Jesus dwells in me, that I am born of your seed of divinity, created in your image, and that You are healing, restoring and blessing all of me. Thank you for transforming me through your healing grace and love.

~ Pause in Silence to Receive God's Healing ~

5. Reparations ~ Penance.

Dear Heavenly Father, please guide me to right reparations and/or penance for all the violations I have committed regarding the jezebel spirit and its accompanying character traits, habits, personality flaws and behaviors; including any oaths, contracts and covenants on behalf of my family lineage.

Speak to me through your Holy Spirit. Convict me in mind and heart of right restitution to make through my actions, relationships, charity, teaching, sharing, giving, sacrifices, prayers and fasting.

6. Justification ~ Plead Your Case.

God, Righteous Judge, I am presenting my legal case to You based upon your legal document, your Word. Father God, your Word declares the following:

. . .

You Promise Me Deliverance.

- Psalm 108:12 says: *"Give us help against the adversary, for deliverance by man is in vain [a worthless hope]."*

- Ephesians 1:7-8 declares: *"In Him we have redemption [that is, our deliverance and salvation] through His blood, [which paid the penalty for our sin and resulted in] the forgiveness and complete pardon of our sin, in accordance with the riches of His grace which He lavished on us."*

- Revelations 12:10-11 proclaims: *"Now the salvation, and the power, and the kingdom (dominion, reign) of our God, and the authority of His Christ have come; for the accuser of our [believing] brothers and sisters has been thrown down... and they overcame and conquered him because of the blood of the Lamb and because of the word of their testimony."*

- Father God, the jezebel spirit wants to deceive me into believing that I need its traits to make me strong, protected and keep people from taking advantage of me. I reject these lies! Your Holy Spirit in me is my strength, protection and victory!

- Father God, send your healing and glory angels to strengthen me. Fill me to overflowing with your healing love and joy.

Humility Is Rewarded & Required.

- Your Word in Proverbs 22:4 says: *"The reward of humility [that is, having a realistic view of one's importance] and the [reverent, worshipful] fear of the Lord is riches, honor, and life."*
- In 1 Peter 5:5 You instructed: *"Clothe yourselves with humility toward one another, for God is opposed to the proud [the disdainful, the presumptuous, and He defeats them], but He gives grace to the humble."*
- Heavenly Father, I commit to clothing myself everyday with humility, the antidote to the jezebel spirit that seeks to control through egoism, vanity, competitiveness and pridefulness. I commit to not bragging about myself or flattering others.
- Heavenly Father, I commit to submitting my will to yours, seeking your heart every day, listening to what YOU want and need, and devoting myself to fulfilling your heart.

I Seek Humility and Righteousness.

- Your Word in Zephaniah 2:3 says: *"Seek the Lord [search diligently for Him and regard Him as the foremost necessity of your life], all you humble of the land who have practiced His ordinances and have kept His commandments; seek righteousness, seek humility [regard them as vital]. Perhaps you will be hidden [and pardoned and rescued] in the day of the Lord's anger."*

- Father God, jezebel wants me to believe that I am always subservient to and victim to its agendas. It seeks to keep me *out* of humility and righteousness. I reject jezebel's agendas! I choose humility and righteousness as my walk and truth. I submit my character to You. Cleanse me with your lovingkindness and forgiveness. Transform me with your love.

You Created Me for Holiness.

- 2 Corinthians 7:1 says: *"Therefore, since we have these [great and wonderful] promises, beloved, let us cleanse ourselves from everything that contaminates body and spirit, completing holiness [living a consecrated life—a life set apart for God's purpose] in the fear of God."*
- Ephesians 4:24 says: *"Put on the new self [the regenerated and renewed nature], created in God's image, in the righteousness and holiness of the truth [living in a way that expresses to God your gratitude for your salvation]."*
- Father God, I choose holiness in Christ Jesus. Fill me with your Glory and Love so that jezebel has no place in me.
- Father God, with these Sacred Scriptures, I am cleansed of everything that has contaminated me. I put on my new and true self of righteousness and holiness. I commit to remembering each day that I am made in your image. I am new and renewed

every day. What a glorious miracle and gift! Thank
you Dear God!

I AM Pre-Destined as Yours.

- Your Word in Psalm 139:16 says: *"Your eyes have
  seen my unformed substance; and in your book were
  all written the days that were appointed for me,
  when as yet there was not one of them [even taking
  shape]."*
- Father God, I now realize that I am pre-destined as
  yours. I accept this truth from your Word. I belong
  to You and not demonic powers and the counterfeit
  light.
- Father God, silence the jezebel spirit that speaks
  against this and whispers in my ears false
  prophecies. I reject these and choose your Truth
  for my life! Silence the jezebel spirit once and
  for all!

Your Plans to Prosper Me.

- Your Word in Jeremiah 29:11 promises: *"For I
  know the plans I have for you, plans to prosper you,
  to give you hope and a future."*
- Father God, the jezebel spirit has co-opted, blocked
  and even destroyed my covenant blessings,
  supports and relationships, even my hope and
  morale. I say enough! No more! I contend for the

plans You have for me to prosper, to have hope and a good future in You.

Heavenly Father, it is indisputably clear throughout your Word which is your record of law, that You have created a way of deliverance and redemption from the curses and controls of the jezebel spirit and all of her cohorts and minions. Your Word provides the tools of deliverance and the weapons of warfare to be fully and finally free from oppression. Halleluia!

I call on the redemptive Blood of your Son, the Lord Jesus Christ. It is clear that if I am not granted these requests from your Court, I will not be able to fulfill your plans for me.

7. Petitions.

Heal the Battlefield in My Heart.

Heavenly Father, You designed my heart in your image. It was created to love in purity. Therefore, heal the battlefield in my heart and all the causes thereof. Heal me from the ravages of jezebel; who has deceived me into relying on her instead of You.

Dear Heavenly Father, it is said that Mary, the mother Jesus, loved so perfectly, she never counted the cost, the cost to her personally. She modeled and activated for women the divine blueprint for loving perfectly to counter the jezebel spirit. As

Jesus exhorted to His disciples in Matthew 5:48: *"Be ye perfect as your Heavenly Father is perfect."* Jesus spoke this as part of His instruction to love those who persecute us.

True love is unselfish. It does not count the cost. It does not have ulterior motives. It is not manipulative and deceitful. The jezebel spirit is counterfeit love and a counterfeit womanhood. I reject and renounce this deceit. Heal my heart Lord God. [For women: Heal my womanhood Lord God.]

Remove the battlefield that has been erected between man and woman by satan in the Garden. Heal the rift between us. Heal within me the primordial wound and rift that occurred between man and woman. Heal this in your Holy Church, your one flock under your one shepherd (John 10:16), our Lord Jesus Christ Yeshua.

Bring Healing & Discernment to Men.
[For men, this can be prayed from first-person.]

Proverbs 31:11-12 says: *"The heart of her husband trusts in her, and he will have no lack of gain. She comforts, encourages, and does him only good and not evil all the days of her life."*

Dear Heavenly Father, bring healing discernment to your men, that they shall see through the jezebel spirit, that they will go beyond just outer appearances and having their ego flattered by jezebel; that they will resist jezebel seduction and manipulation to discern and appreciate that a real woman does not seek to flatter and stroke the ego, but to be a 'help meet' as God designed; to help a man meet God.

A godly woman does not exploit a man's fears, insecurities, needs, vulnerabilities, vanities and ambitions. She builds him up in the most holy of Faith. She loves and supports him without personal agendas and motives, with purity of heart.

Dear Heavenly Father, remove the scales and veils off the eyes of your sons, to reveal the jezebel spirit controlling them and infecting their lives. Bring men the spiritual strength, discernment and maturity to resist the manipulations and deceit of jezebel.

Convict your sons to cast jezebel out and to turn to You, to replace her with YOU, within their own hearts and lives. Place in them the yearning and will to place their trust back in You; that they don't need an external force building them up, protecting them, fighting their battles for them. YOU are what they need to be made strong from the inside out. Let them see and know this, and return to You.

Heavenly Father, convict your sons to be delivered of the ahab spirit, the spirit of weakness that feeds and supports the jezebel spirit. Bring them supportive role models that are strong men in Christ Jesus.

.   .   .

Replace Jezebel with Your Virtuous Woman.

Your Word in Proverbs 31:10 says: *"An excellent woman [one who is spiritual, capable, intelligent, and virtuous], who is he who can find her? Her value is more precious than jewels and her worth is far above rubies or pearls."*

Lord God, it is not enough to remove the evil from our society. It must be replaced with your holiness and righteousness. Please replace this jezebel harlot with your virtuous women; that the world shall be healed by true women of God, who are virtuous, kind, loving, humble, holy and pure.

Heal the horrors of desecrated womanhood. Heal the soul of women and the soul of womanhood in me, in my family, in the Body of Christ and in my country.

Let the Virtuous Woman Heal the Family.

Proverbs 31:12 says: *"She comforts, encourages, and does him (the husband) only good and not evil all the days of her life."*

Dear Heavenly Father, raise up your virtuous women, wives and mothers to model and encourage other women and girls in how to be the healing presence of unconditional love for their families and loved ones; to teach and demonstrate nurturing and tender love; to embrace femininity as a strength and virtue.

Teach women the virtues of gentleness and tenderness; that they are not forms of weakness but rather true inner strength on a foundation of compassion, kindness and unconditional love.

Let the Virtuous Woman Heal the Business World.

According to Proverbs 31:16: *"She considers a field before she buys or accepts it [expanding her business prudently]; with her profits she plants fruitful vines in her vineyard."*

Dear Heavenly Father, replace the jezebel harlot with this model of the virtuous woman: prudent, responsible, trustworthy and honorable in all business dealings and throughout the mountain of business.

Bring forth the virtuous women to heal the business world, to bring healing to beleaguered workers, to restore compassion, honoring, fairness and kindness to the business culture.

My Additional Petitions.

Additional petitions that I am requesting from your Court are:

- Grant all of my petitions in the case I have presented to You here.
- Grant me a divorce decree from and a Divine Restraining Order against jezebel and all jezebel cohorts, minions, entities and agendas from operating in my life and that of my bloodline, so that I will no longer be tormented by anything from jezebel, and shall be fully and permanently

delivered from all of her traits, traps and programs; provided I do not re-activate her in my life through my own actions and choices.

- Grant me a Divine Restraining Order against jezebel and all of her cohorts and minions purposing to create disunity, disharmony and strife in my life and in any of my relationships.

- Replace every unrighteous habit and trait in my personality with your holiness, that I am *"in holiness [being set apart] and righteousness [being upright] before You all of my days,"* according to Luke 1:75.

- Loose the holds that satan, lucifer, jezebel and their cohorts and minions have had on my life, my destiny and my provisions.

- Release all supports and resources, both spiritual and material, for me to fulfill my God destiny.

- Direct these supports to be forthcoming so that my work and life may go on unhampered and I may fulfill my true life purpose, as well as all collaborative work and destiny with others that You have so appointed for me.

- Restore to me seven-fold everything jezebel, its minions and cohorts have stolen from me that has not been on account of my own actions and choices, according to your promises in Proverbs 6:31, which says that when the thief is caught, he must repay seven-fold all that he has stolen.

- Yoke me fully, eternally and exclusively to YOU Heavenly Father, and your destiny and purposes for me.

8. Wait on the Lord's Response.

This is a pause, allowing for stillness and silence to respect God's response to our petitions. This is cultivating an awareness and sensitivity to our relationship with God, just as we would communicate with someone sitting right in front of us.

9. Thanks and Gratitude.

[Dedicate time to thank God after all of your petitions. You may want to play or sing praise music, dance; however you express thanks.]

- Thank you LORD God for granting my petitions!
- Thank you for your mercy, compassion and love!
- Thank you for healing, restoring and redeeming me!
- Thank you for delivering me from jezebel demonic powers!
- To You alone be all the glory in Heaven and upon the earth forever and ever! AMEN!!!

CHAPTER 12

DELIVERANCE FROM THE MAMMON SPIRIT

"No one is able to serve two masters:
for he will hate the one
and will love the other,
or he will be devoted to one
and he will despise the other.
You are not able to serve God and mammon."
Matthew 6:24

WHAT IS THE MAMMON SPIRIT

MAMMON IS a pervasive spirit or force that is associated with a corrupted system, supply and pursuit of money; as well as the addiction to money as greed and materialism. It is a driving force in this carnal world that impairs our relationship with God. It works with other spirits and forces to control people and keep them in mental, material and spiritual bondage. It is the *"love of money at the root of all kinds of evil."*[1]

"For the love of money [that is, the greedy desire for it
and the willingness to gain it unethically]
is a root of all sorts of evil,
and some by longing for it
have wandered away from the faith
and pierced themselves
[through and through]
with many sorrows."
1 Timothy 6:10

IT'S ABOUT WHERE OUR VALUES LIE

What is Most Cherished.

The previous verse is talking about placing a priority on money, even obsessing over money and the pursuit of money. What precedes and follows that passage bring deeper understanding to it. Apostle Paul lays the groundwork: *"But godliness with contentment is great gain."*[2] Paul is exhorting us to place a greater value on inner virtues of godliness and inner contentment regardless of what are external conditions. This is in fact, a master key to true freedom — inner contentment regardless of outer circumstances.

TRUE FREEDOM IS INNER CONTENTMENT REGARDLESS OF OUTER CIRCUMSTANCES.

Paul continues: *"But you, man of God, flee from all this, and pursue righteousness, godliness, faith, love, endurance and gentleness. Fight the good fight of the faith. Take hold of the eternal life to which you were called when you made your good confession in the presence of many witnesses."*[3]

Of course, this does not imply fleeing from responsibly providing for yourself and your family. It does however, provide the scaffolding for creating a life built on a foundation of godly values, virtues and priorities. The opposite is implicitly trusting in and becoming a part of a corrupt system and/or organization to provide you with sustenance and security. Have you ever witnessed someone attached to this mammon money system and anyone in fear of being disconnected from it? <u>This is true bondage</u>.

God can and will always make a way for provision when we trust Him above all manmade creations and live out our gifts the way He calls us to do so. *"With God, ALL things are possible."*[4] This verse invites us to unlimited faith and helps us to examine wherein we place our faith.

Where We Place Our Faith.

The word mammon derives from a Hebrew word *Emonah* or *Emunah*. In the spoken language of the times, Aramaic, *mamon* meant wealth. The Hebrew word *mamone* actually means believer, faithful, devoted, steadfast, what is trusted in.[5]

Many places throughout the Sacred Scriptures Jesus and other teachers used word plays; that is, words that sound similar yet have different or even opposite meanings. These more nuanced elements of Jesus' teachings become lost in translation to the less subtle English language.

In His teachings from Matthew 6:24, *"You are not able to serve God and mammon,"* Jesus is using the word *mammon* to refer to those material things in which we put our trust and faith, rather than trusting in God. Jesus warns: *"No one is able to serve two masters."*

The "two masters" are the master of materialism and the Master God, Creator of Heaven and earth, Master Provider. The master of personal will and the Master Divine Will of God. The master of control and manipulation and the Master of Infinite Love and Infinite Supply.

Jesus' teaching on mammon as money or wealth, is a teaching on where we place our faith, to whom or what do we yoke ourselves. Do you choose to be driven by the system of wealth of this world or God's plan and treasures for your life?

Choose This Day.

Fundamentally, the choice is about in whom or what we put our faith and trust. American currency has the motto "In God We Trust" imprinted on it. Imagine if we actually returned to that practice in our financial system and currency — both of which are utterly mercurial and at the mercy of mammon overlords.

. . .

Jesus elaborated: *"You are not able to serve God and mammon."* This is because they are opposing elements. One is God-made, one is man-made. As Joshua the mighty and obedient warrior of God said: *"Choose this day who you will serve. As for me and my house, we will serve the Lord Most High."* Joshua was speaking to the Israelites who had begun to worship pagan gods yet again. He reminded them that over and over the One True God had come to their rescue and provided for them, against all odds and reason.

Joshua and Yeshua are two forms of the same Hebrew name which means salvation or deliverer. Salvation is "the preservation or deliverance from destruction, difficulty, or evil."[6] So we see the warrior Joshua as a foreshadow of the Salvation Messiah Jesus Yeshua; both warning the people about which master to choose over their lives. Trust and faith are two sides of the currency of man when he chooses to be yoked to God.

TRUST AND FAITH ARE THE CURRENCY FOR TRUE FREEDOM.

GOD HAS NOT ABANDONED US

One of the core reasons why people do not place their true trust and faith in God is because they feel abandoned, left to their own devices, left to fend for themselves in this wild and crazy world.

. . .

What if you knew you weren't in fact, abandoned? What if you believed that God wants to look out for you, to protect you and guide you on your path of life? What if dependence on God could bring you greater freedom, peace and joy than relying on your own devices or cleverness?

"With creation, God does not abandon His creatures to themselves. He not only gives them being and existence, but also, and at every moment, upholds and sustains them in being, enables them to act and brings them to their final end. Recognizing this utter dependence with respect to the Creator is a source of wisdom and freedom, of joy and confidence."[7]

Reading this passage, how does it make you feel? Do you feel any peace, any relief? Are you open to considering the gentle practice of surrendering, giving over your worries and burdens to God? If you hold on to the steering wheel with both hands tightly gripped to it, He cannot enter in to help drive the car or steer it in a better direction. Are you willing to share the wheel with God?

Allow yourself to make it a practice that you gradually grow in — little by little every day giving this moment or that moment over to God; giving over to Him this worry or that issue or burden. Believe it or not, our brilliant human minds cannot think of all the amazing possibilities by which a problem can get solved or a need satisfied.

ALLOW FOR THE WONDER OF GOD'S WORKINGS IN
YOUR LIFE!

Allow for the wonder of God's workings in your life! <u>This is
divine love in action</u>. Surrender brings freedom and a deeper
experience of God's love for you into your heart and life. "Utter
dependence on your Creator" is <u>not</u> weakness. It is profound
liberation and a gateway to deeper love and healing. It is
allowing true love in.

"The desire for God is written in the human heart,
because man is created by God and for God; and God
never ceases to draw man to himself. Only in God will
he find the truth and happiness he never stops searching
for."[8]

This beautiful passage tells us that "God never ceases to draw
man to himself." We've but only to allow this drawing to God.
It is the true nature and impulse of our being. Choose to be a
mamone, believer, who puts your trust in God. This is literally
putting yourself in God's current, His currency, as He draws
you back to Himself.

WE CAN CHOOSE GOD'S CURRENCY WHICH IS
ANCHORED IN HIS HEART, ETERNALLY STABLE &
RELIABLE.

Imagine being a leaf, a branch or a boat floating with and in
God's current of life and provision. We are still working and
being of service in the world. The difference is a deep inner
peace and joy, knowing that God has our back. We have yoked
to God in His current, His currency, which is eternally stable
and reliable unlikes the world's.

YOKING TO THE SOURCE OF FREEDOM BRINGS TRUE FREEDOM

Marry Up!

Salvation — that is, true and abiding freedom in and
beyond time and space, comes from serving and yoking to the
source of freedom, the Author of freedom. This is not a religious notion. This is practical and logical. God is the source of
all true freedom because He *is* freedom itself. God is infinite.
He is infinite freedom. He IS infinite love, infinite freedom and
infinite grace.

YOKE TO INFINITE FREEDOM AND GRACE TO BE IN
TRUE FREEDOM.

Why not marry up and yoke to this unlimited source of love, freedom and grace? Why not yoke to the One who loves you absolutely unconditionally through thick and thin? Why not bond yourself to the One who created you and wrote the divine blueprint for your purpose and destiny?

Since He created you with specific gifts, wouldn't He know best what life work you are called to do, the best way to express your gifts? Wouldn't He want the absolute best for you? Wouldn't He have a vested interest in making sure that His own sons and daughters were provided for, protected, guided and supported to live their best godly life?

Submission Brings Freedom.

In our culture, we have a very negative connotation of the word 'submission.' It's associated with a kind of bondage or subjugation. But let's look at it in spiritual terms from a spiritual perspective. You are "a spiritual creature," made from God the Spirit, as spirit in form; designed and destined to know and love God, and return to Him a fuller, more perfected expression of spirit in form.

SUBMISSION MEANS TO YOKE, RE-CONNECT WITH YOUR CREATOR, THE AUTHOR AND SOURCE OF LOVE.

In this regard, "submission" means to yoke, re-connect with your Creator, out of the exercise of your free will. God so loved us, He gave us free will to choose whether or not we want a relationship with Him, whether or not we will choose to return to the source of Love as a greater version of love than when we were born into this world. *"Be ye perfect as your Father in Heaven is perfect"*, exhorts Jesus, encouraging us to grow in our capacity to love others.[9]

"God created man in His image and established him in His friendship. A spiritual creature, man can live this friendship only in free submission to God..... The 'tree of the knowledge of good and evil' symbolically evokes the insurmountable limits that man, being a creature, must freely recognize and respect with trust. Man is dependent on his Creator and subject to the laws of creation and to the moral norms that govern the use of freedom."[10]

So "renouncing and divorcing mammon" is a statement that you are choosing the One True God to yoke to, to follow and trust as the source for your sustenance in this world; rather than the money supply programs of this world that frankly, are rigged against most of us.

This is not to imply that we sit and naval gaze and wait for God to take care of us. It is an internal choice and way of walking in life that is <u>choosing not to be psychologically gripped and controlled by mammon-money systems and programs</u>. It is a practice of submission, heart to Heart, spirit to Spirit, to the source of all good supply.

WE ARE CHOOSING TO NOT BE CONTROLLED BY MONEY PROGRAMS & SYSTEMS.

THE DECEPTIVE VIEWS OF MAMMON

There are prevalent emotions of fear, worry and anxiety that attach to many people regarding the mammon system. We come to believe that our security and freedom will come through engagement with and reliance on the things of mammon and mammon systems. Nothing that controls or grips us provides true and lasting freedom. Anxiety and worry are causes of physical and emotional unwellness.

In fact, millions of people have lost their pension funds to unscrupulous corporate raiders. Employees "played by all the rules," yet still were robbed of their savings and retirement hopes and dreams. So much for relying on the mammon system. Who creates and owns it, creates the rules and can change the rules at any time without you ever knowing about it. God's rules are unchanging and eternal. Which system sounds safer?

NOTHING THAT CONTROLS OR GRIPS US PROVIDES TRUE AND LASTING FREEDOM.

MAMMON IS BY NATURE LIMITED

By its very nature, mammon is limited. It is limited to the minds and imaginations of men. Some people view mammon as an actual spirit. It certainly has a demonic affect on many people. It is definitely a mental and societal program and is embedded in financial and economic systems of the world. These systems have overlords that decide what money and currency is worth, who gets to have most of it, and where, when and to whom the flow of wealth and abundance gets directed and aggregated.

Whatever term one chooses to ascribe to mammon, it is surely a force that grips masses of people. That in and of itself qualifies mammon as a form of bondage. Jesus clearly stated: *"You are not able to serve both God and mammon."* <u>Not able</u>. They are two different systems. They are two separate universes. By its nature, mammon is of this world and therefore restrictive. God is infinite. *"With God, all things are possible."*

God can create out of nothing. Mammon must create out of what already exists. God has ways of bringing us support and sustenance that can come completely out of the blue. Mammon follows predictable, linear means of providing money.

God's ways provide more possibilities than the ways of mammon. The only reason it is harder to trust in and only serve God is because we have been habituated to serving mammon. Our ego-mind is wired to seek linear, logical, limited, worldly solutions and sources. Now we will learn how to break old habits and create new ones, to establish true freedom.

NOW WE WILL LEARN HOW TO BREAK OLD, SELF-LIMITING HABITS AND CREATE NEW ONES, TO ESTABLISH TRUE FREEDOM.

WHAT TO KNOW ABOUT THE MAMMON SPIRIT

- Mammon is the god of this world, the god of wealth *competing with God* for attention and worship.
- Mammon is the most prevalent idol on earth. It promises security, importance, influence, prestige, chics, renown, happiness, success, independence, power, even immortality.
- Money is needed and necessary, but ***it is the controlling grip of the spirit and programs of mammon*** that compromises us, our morality, our ethics, and our ability to live fully aligned with God's Will and heart for our life.
- It is a slave system designed to capture our divinity and snuff out or seriously compromise our God destiny.
- Jesus warns against it in Luke 16:15: *"God knows your hearts [your thoughts, your desires, your secrets]; for that which is highly esteemed among men is detestable in the sight of God."*
- Mammon has cohorts, including: the spirits of pride, greed, avarice, debt, poverty, covetousness, to name a few.

WHY WE NEED TO BE DELIVERED FROM MAMMON

Why we need to be delivered from the mammon spirit is because it is a major cause of overall bondage. Money, finances and material issues are at the root of most stress, conflict and problems. It is the #1 cause of marital strife. The value that people place on money and material things is a core area of compatibility or conflict between two people. It drives people's ethics and morals, as well as key life decisions including choice of spouse and career. It is a top driver to committing crimes.

Other reasons include:

- Relying on sources of money over the power of God is allowing the spirit of mammon to control and dominate our life.
- It has had a deep psychological grip on humanity for millennia.
- Psychological and emotional grips block or compromise our ability to live out our God gifts.
- Mammon keeps us contracted and small.
- Mammon keeps us from operating from our spirit, our divine nature.
- Mammon is a bondage force that supports bondage programs.

OTHER THINGS TO CONSIDER ABOUT MAMMON

- Mammon operates through systems such as the stock market and our social security numbers.

There are many mammon systems to divorce & be delivered from.[11]

- Being a part of mammon systems is a form of bondage.

- These systems are often unknown and/or unseen to us. Nevertheless, we are in bondage to them.

- Deliverance and renouncing are the means to breaking free from this bondage.

- Luke 16:13 warns: *"You cannot serve both God and mammon [that is, your earthly possessions or anything else you trust in and rely on instead of God]."*

- The top 1% of Americans have 16 times more wealth than the bottom 50% combined. Billionaires grew their wealth by over 27% in just four months *during* the covid shutdowns. They know who they are serving and how to work within that mammon system and spirit. This disparity in wealth suggests a system rigged against most people who are participating in that system.

- Wealth is NOT a bad or evil thing. But the current mammon system is clearly rigged against most people.

- We need to divorce the mammon system and plug into God's provision. It protects against the ups and downs of the man-made and manipulated financial markets and systems.

DELIVERANCE FROM MAMMON IS A LINCHPIN TO REALIZING TRUE FREEDOM.

WHY WE SHOULD GRADUATE FROM MAMMON

- Mammon is a force over a whole menu of programs and systems that keeps people in bondage. To be truly free, it's time to graduate from mammon.

- Because this is a linchpin in the quest for total freedom.

- Mammon is both man-made and demon-made. We have mistakenly believed it is a normal part of life. It is *not* a system created or ordained by God.

- Mammon is a program that warps our sense of self worth and the worth of others.

- Mammon is a system that is designed to keep us limited and out of our true nature made in God's image.

- Because we need to be fully delivered from the grip of any spirits and forces operating in, through and out of money systems in order be trustworthy stewards of God's Kingdom wealth and *"New heavens and a new earth, in which righteousness dwells.*"[12]

- Luke 16:11-12 affirms: "*Therefore if you have not been faithful in the use of earthly wealth, who will entrust the true riches to you? And if you have not been faithful in the use of that [earthly wealth] which belongs to another [whether God or man, and of which you are a trustee], who will give you that which is your own?*"

KEYS TO DIVORCING AND OVERCOMING THE GRIP OF MAMMON

- Seek security in God, not money or the systems of this world. God can bring money and sustenance from all kinds of sources and ways that the linear and limited mind cannot foresee or imagine.

- Seek the "*wealth of righteousness*" in Luke 16:9. Seeking the Kingdom of God *first* as a priority, syncs us up with God's heart and will, puts us in the right relationship with God, which then brings His blessings to us.

- Recognize that *aversion* to money can also be a grip. A vow of poverty does not bring holiness in and of itself. Poverty is not holiness. Inflicting self-suffering is not holiness. Holiness comes from right relationship with God.

- Identify the ways it has become an idol (e.g. 401 K, needing the latest model car or iPhone).

- Repent and plead guilty of money sins.

- Renounce ancestral mammon oaths, contracts, covenants, money issues and conditions that come through the bloodlines.

- Seek to become a partner, partaker of God's divine nature, yoking to the source of eternal sustenance.

> *"Through these things He has given us*
> *His precious and magnificent promises*
> *so that through them you may become*
> *partakers of the divine nature,*
> *since you have escaped the corruption*
> *that evil desires have brought into the world."*
> 2 Peter 1:4

COURTS OF HEAVEN PROTOCOL TO BE DELIVERED FROM THE MAMMON SPIRIT

1. Preparation.

Before you go into the Courts of Heaven, take the time to identify your petitions and purposes, what remedies you are seeking, what in your life and character require repentance and what in your family lineage requires renunciation. Ask the Holy Spirit to reveal to you these things before you go in to the Courts of Heaven. Often times, when you are in the Courts of Heaven, the Holy Spirit will bring other things to mind for which to repent.

. . .

You may receive information about specific family members who have already passed on. This can include activities they engaged in such as crimes, rituals, oaths, covenants, contracts and curses. You renounce, repudiate, and disavow the sins, transgressions and iniquities of your ancestors to remove any legal cases against yourself.

We repent and plead guilty for all personal sins, transgressions and iniquities, present the Blood of Jesus as our atonement, and then ask God to pass judgements on our behalf. The adversary operates through legality, which is why we go to God's Court-room to remove any legal cases the enemy is using against us or our family.

Remember to speak the entire protocol OUT LOUD!

2. Presentation of Purpose.

Dear God Adonai, Just Judge, I come before your Court of Mercy and Grace and ask that the courts be seated and the books be opened, according to Daniel 7:10. I ask for the Holy Spirit and Lord Jesus Christ Yeshua to be my Holy Advocates to represent me in your Court. I give them full permission to speak on my behalf.

I put on robes of righteousness and I loose the Blood of Jesus over myself so that satan has no access to me. I come into your Court right now and thank you that I am accepted here. Thank you for the privilege of being able to bring my petitions to your Court.

LORD God Adonai, I come before your Court to seek relief from the mammon spirit; to renounce, repent of and shed all mammon traits and programs in myself; to receive your forgiveness, grace and help to be free from all mammon influences and oppression over my life once and for all. To renounce all ancestral mammon oaths, contracts, covenants, money issues and conditions that have come through my bloodlines. I am ready to be truly free!

I ask LORD God that You release your Notification Angels, your Enforcement Angels and Hosts of Heaven to all those humans and non-humans who will be affected by your Court decisions to duly inform them of and immediately enforce all of your decisions in my case today.

3. Renounce & Repent.

Father God, I come in the name of Jesus Christ Yeshua to repent of all my sins, iniquities and transgressions, and renounce, repudiate, and disavow all the sins, transgressions and iniquities of my ancestors back to Adam and Eve, having to do with engaging in and with the spirit of mammon and all mammon bondage programs and systems.

I understand that *repent* means to turn away from, to change and transform my mind and way of living, to transmute flaws into virtues. It is a commitment to course correct, to cease and turn away from activities and habits that are detrimental to my spirit which was made in your image. I commit to becoming a new creation in Christ Jesus.

I repent for all disobedience to your commands; for turning away and listening to the enemy and to other people instead of listening to You and your Will, instead of waiting on You to know and do what is best. I repent for engaging in the misuse of and wrong relationship with money. I repent for any time promises or obligations to pay, give, support or tithe have been broken, and therefore created hardship for others and given the adversary a legal case to steal from me and my family.

On behalf of my family lineage, I apologize and am truly sorry for all those who did not properly care for their family, including fathers and mothers who deserted their children, failed to rightly provide for them, or kept money or goods for themselves or others. I renounce all mammon seeds and fruits from all of my bloodlines back to Adam and Eve.

I renounce all the ways that I and my bloodlines have operated in mammon systems; for the avarice, greed, misuse and abuse of money. I repent for in any way knowingly or unknowingly having worshiped, fed, empowered, supported, strengthened, honored, idolized, depended upon the spirit of mammon and mammon systems and put them above or in place of *your* systems of provision.

. . .

I repent for having a lack, debt and poverty mentality. I repent for living in fear of provision and survival, which is a rejection of faith in You and a repudiation of You as my provider. I now realize that fear chokes off the flow of grace and blessings.

I repent for all the ways I have tied social status, self worth, standing in society, respectability, recognition, honor and accomplishments to the amount of money made and material items owned. I repent for pride, snobbery, superiority; classism by owning good things, living in self-aggrandizing affluence and showing off.

I repent for putting a priority on identity in wealth and accompanying social status instead of identity and true self worth in relationship with You LORD God. I reject and renounce the normalization of traits which have been passed down through my bloodlines.

I repent for allowing the pursuit of money to take me out of balance and therefore out of alignment with your Will, values and statutes. I repent for using money and the finer things in life to define me, to win over others, to attain places of honor from others, rather than using it to serve You in charity to others.

I repent for all lying, cheating, and stealing money and other things for ANY reason. I repent of all unethical business practices including graft, embezzlement and fraud, that took advantage of others and that caused loss and suffering to others. I repent for irresponsible and reckless handling and mismanagement of money; for squandering, overspending money and creating debt; for living beyond my means and not honoring debt repayment. For those in my bloodline guilty of these sins and crimes, I apologize and ask for your forgiveness Lord God.

I repent for pursuing and buying information, consultation, advice about gaining money and favor through occult channels including psychics and fortune tellers. I repent for the use of occult practices, rituals and practitioners for gaining financial, material and vocational favor, any favor.

I repent for any forms of witchcraft, sorcery and divination used as a means to make money, gain assets and in general get ahead. I repent for yoking to practitioners of occult, witchcraft and sorcery in business and personal affairs. For those in my bloodline guilty of these sins and crimes, I apologize and ask for your forgiveness Lord God.

I repent for poor judgement in the choice of business partners, partners who were not godly and did not have good ethics and morals. I repent for being unequally yoked in business, finances and other relationships, which caused me to be out of alignment with your Will for my life. I repent for little hidden acts that weren't your standard of ethics, for thinking I could get away with small transgressions and shortcuts. You are a witness to every little action and choice that we make.

· · ·

I repent for the iniquities and character flaws of greed, avarice, stinginess, money and material lust, materialism, mis-spending and overspending, and for creating debt.

I repent for believing that being part of mammon systems is right, godly, necessary and your Divine Will, and that it is actually superior to or more reliable than *your* systems of provision, prosperity and security. I repent for the love of money.

I renounce, denounce and divorce all mammon oaths, contracts, covenants, agreements, curses, rituals, witchcraft, sorcery, occult practices, activities, beliefs, hexes, vexes, voodoo and money magic committed by my bloodlines; and all related demonic mammon strongholds and iniquities passed down and affecting my life.

I renounce and repent of all traits, habits, character flaws and inclinations that I have inherited, indulged in and expressed on account of these ancestral iniquities and having to do with the mammon spirit and programs. I recognize that they are wrong, hurtful to myself, others and You Heavenly Father. Please forgive me.

Father God, I renounce, denounce, divorce, nullify and cancel all oaths, contracts, covenants, agreements and curses having to do with:

- Exchange of funds done in ungodly ways, for ungodly purposes

- Not tithing sufficiently or to the right parties
- Greed, stinginess, and stealing money and goods
- Not caring for the poor, widows, orphans or homeless
- Oppression and other unjust treatment of the poor
- Excessive, reckless and/or irresponsible spending of money, including indebtedness
- Masons and others who created curses through idolatry and wrong spending, wrong means of making monies
- Godly vows of poverty that were broken or violated
- Ancestors who put money and other related curses on ensuing generations
- Usury including all corrupt, criminal, unethical banking and money practices
- Ungodly and/or criminal ways of making money
- Relying on monies from the government for survival
- Extortion and exploitation of people, monies, businesses and other unethical activities
- Those who stole, including cheating and fraud, through business and other deals
- Drug trafficking, human trafficking, all criminal trafficking
- Anyone in my lineage who cursed or blasphemed God, the Holy Spirit and/or Jesus Christ
- Blackmail taken against innocent people; all bribes and blackmail
- Mercenary acts and gambling
- Money spent on prostitutes and mistresses
- Giving money to ungodly people, purposes and parties
- Worship of money and "the love of money"

- Trusting in money and self-effort above trusting in God
- Leprechaun spirits including trickery and false promises of money through demons
- Funding of KKK, pro-abortion and other ungodly organizations and activities
- Unpaid wages and underpaying workers, undervaluing others and their worth
- Not forgiving debts and all related vindictive and punitive behaviors and actions
- Being guilty of 1 Timothy 5:8: *"But if anyone does not provide for his own family, especially for his own household, he has denied the faith and is worse than an unbeliever."* I apologize for all those in my lineage who neglected to provide for their own family first and foremost. I pray for this iniquity to stop with me now. I commit to penance for this.
- Those who shed innocent blood
- Witchcraft curses against finances, all sorcery and divination including santeria, santa muerte and voodoo
- All forms of witchcraft, sorcery, divination and money magic used as a means to make money, gain assets and in general get ahead
- All curses of bankruptcy and mismanagement of money
- Ungodly agreements with the enemy in obtaining finances
- Those who sold their souls to get ahead
- Those who did not serve God joyfully and gladly in the time of prosperity[13]
- Those who sold Christian relics for money or used religion for personal and monetary gain

- Violations to not honoring parents
- Curses placed on actual money given to me and/or my bloodlines
- Giving to a person, ministry, organization or party NOT operating in God's Will
- All other curses like the Scottish curse (i.e. "being Scotch", frugal or penny-pinching that often leads to a stinginess or lack of flow of money that is not as God desires)
- Any indigenous curses on or from people, tribes, nations
- Curses from masonic and other cults
- Any ungodly sacrifices and rituals
- All money given to ungodly or corrupt people, organizations, musicians, artists, actors, entertainers, celebrities, businesses, priests & prophets
- Religious or other programs, curses and spirits that have caused chronic lack, debt, poverty, struggle and strife
- All other violations of the 10 Commandments

I repent for any withholding of the first fruits and the best portions, for not tithing rightly, and for all wrong motives and attitudes in the heart regarding money, giving, sharing and receiving.

I repent for all anger, resentment, victimhood and greed. I repent for all habits of worry, anxiety, fear and lack, and believing the enemy's lies about poverty, struggle and strife. I repent for lack of situational awareness, not staying on top of financial responsibilities, for avoidance and shirking of proper financial stewardship.

LORD God, I repent for ungodly loaning of money. I repent for all the times and ways I have undervalued myself in the marketplace and have therefore unwittingly allowed others to underpay me and take advantage of me. As a son/daughter of the Most High God, I hereby divorce and renounce all mammon systems, programs and strongholds now!

4. Plead Guilty.

I plead guilty for everything I have just repented and renounced to remove all cases that satan and his demonic powers have held against me. I present the Blood of the Lamb of God, Jesus Christ as atonement. I present the Voice of the Blood of Jesus which speaks "paid in full" to clear these transgressions from my record and bloodline.

Father God, I ask for redemption from the curse by the Blood of Jesus and ask You to break off ALL curses of poverty, debt, lack, struggle and strife, mammon, and mammon programs and systems over me according to the promises in Corinthians 2:14. That is, all ordinances (cases) against me have been nailed to the Cross by the shed Blood of Jesus Yeshua. Let the shed Blood of Jesus break all of these curses now!

I ask You to release me from the consequences of my and my bloodlines' transgressions and iniquities regarding money and the pursuit of money, the grips and programs of mammon; as I commit to the penance and reparations You call me to do. Let the Blood of Jesus break off from me now all ungodly yokes, hooks, cords, curses, oaths, vows, covenants and contracts with ungodly people, entities and demons accordingly.

Father God, your Word in 2 Corinthians 10:5 teaches us that we are to cast down every evil imagination, bringing into captivity every contrary thought of disobedience to the distribution of God's good supply to meet the needs of the saints. Therefore I cast down every high thing of the spirit of mammon; and every high thing that exalts itself against the knowledge of You.

Cleanse, Clear & Release.

LORD God, pour your healing balm of Gilead into all my places of stored habits, traits, filters, beliefs, memories, imprints and traumas having to do with mammon and mammon programs. Clear them out now. Purify and cleanse my body, brain, mind, heart, soul, conscience, subconscious and unconscious minds, and restore me to "factory settings", your design for me.

1 John 4:4 tells me that I am from God and *"Greater is He who is in me than he who is in the world."* LORD God, I recognize, honor and accept that your potential for holiness in Christ Jesus dwells in me, that I am born of your seed of divinity, created in your image, and that You are healing, blessing and restoring me, my body, mind, heart, soul and life. Thank you for transforming me through your anointing, grace and love.

. . .

5. Reparations ~ Penance.

Dear Heavenly Father, please guide me to right reparations and/or penance for all the violations I have committed regarding the mammon spirit and its accompanying character traits, habits, personality flaws and behaviors; as well as any reparations on behalf of my family lineage for any mammon-related oaths, contracts, covenants and curses.

Speak to me through your Holy Spirit. Convict me in mind and heart of right restitution to make through my actions, relationships, charity, teaching, sharing, giving, sacrifices, prayers and fasting.

6. Plead Your Case.

Because I am in your courtroom LORD God Adonai, I am presenting my legal case to You through your legal document, your Word. Please receive your Word as the key to my freedom from the bondage of the mammon spirit, programs and its cohorts.

I Can Only Serve One Master.

- Matthew 6:24 *says: "No one is able to serve two masters: for he will hate the one and will love the other, or he will be devoted to one and he will despise the other. You are not able to serve God and mammon."*

- Father God, I commit to leaning on You, to looking to You for my provision; and breaking the fear and bondage programming that I must know how and where I shall be provided from the mammon systems, without considering or involving Your Will for my life.
- I understand that by following your perfect Will for my life and lifework, I will be provided for and You will bring to me the sources and kinds of provision that YOU desire for me, in the vocation to which You call me.

I Am to Lend But Not Borrow.

- In Deuteronomy 15:6, You tell us that we *"Are to lend to many nations, but not borrow."*
- Father God, the mammon systems set me up to always be a borrower and in debt. They work completely counter to your plans and Will for me. Help me as I commit to financial responsibility and honoring your laws for how to manage money, to live not by credit but responsibly by your provision LORD God.
- Father God, break the yoke of all debt off of me now! I ask You for supernatural debt cancellation in Jesus' name. Just as your Word directs people to forgive debts every seven years, I ask You to forgive mine now; as I commit to responsible situational awareness and management of my finances.
- As your Word in Matthew 6:12 instructs us to forgive our debtors, I release all unforgiveness

towards anyone who has owed me monies or other things. I release all offense, unforgiveness and bitterness that I have harbored. I release all debts to me, as I come to You and ask for all my debts, spiritual and financial, to be forgiven.

The Tithe is Yours.

- Malachi 3:10 reminds me that the tithe (10%) is yours: *"Bring the whole tithe into the storehouse, so that there may be food in My house, and test Me now in this," says the Lord of hosts, "If I will not open for you the windows of heaven and pour out for you a blessing until it overflows."*
- Father God, I commit to giving 10% of my income to your kingdom works, to honor You first. I will wait on You to hear where You want me to tithe.
- Thank you Father God, for opening the windows of heaven and pouring out your blessings upon me; as I recognize that blessings can include grace supports to cultivate godly virtues and strength.

My Prosperity is in Your Hands.

- Heavenly Father, help me to internalize your Word in Deuteronomy 8:17-19, as I understand and commit to being in a Covenant relationship with You to receive your blessings: *"You may say to yourself, 'my power and my own ability have gained this wealth for me,' but remember that the Lord your God gives you the power to gain wealth, in order to confirm His covenant He swore to your fathers, as it is today. If you ever forget the Lord your God and go after other gods to worship and bow down to them, I testify against you today that you will perish."*

- Dear Father, <u>I commit to giving You my heart every day</u>, to not seeking after the gods of this world, to trusting in your ways for my life.

- In Proverbs 8:21 You said: *"That I may cause those who love Me to inherit wealth, that I may fill their treasuries."* Help me to be worthy to receive this promise.

- Father God, the mammon spirit, programs and systems constantly seek to separate me from your heart, and thereby disrupt our relationship. They defy and deny your Will for me to prosper and fulfill my God destiny. I reject them! I reject their lies and programs. Free me, that I may fulfill my destiny with your provisions and support.

- Remove any remaining internal blockages or hindrances to my reliance on You.

- Jesus proclaims in John 10:10 that He has come to give us life and life more abundantly. Open the eyes of my heart dear Heavenly Father, that I may conceive of and receive this kind of abundant life. It surely is a life abundant in love, joy and peace — the fruits of your spirit.

God is My Provision.

- I take hold of Philippians 4:19 that promises: *"And my God will supply all your needs according to His riches in glory in Christ Jesus."*
- Matthew 6:26 assures me: *"Look at the birds of the air, that they do not sow, nor reap nor gather into barns, and yet your heavenly Father feeds them. Are you not worth much more than they?"*
- Psalm 81:10 says: *"I, the Lord, am your God, who brought you up from the land of Egypt; open your mouth wide and I will fill it."*
- Father God, I accept your Word that I am worthy and of worth to You. I release to You now any remaining feelings or beliefs of unworthiness. I lay them at the feet of Jesus.
- Father God, I release now my habits of worry, fear and anxiety over money and income.
- Father God, deliver me from the Egypt of financial bondage. I commit to looking to YOU as the source of my provision, my security and my peace. Thank you for setting me free!

Your Covenant Promise is to Prosper Me.

- I take hold of your promise in Jeremiah 29:11 which says: *"For I know the plans I have for you, plans to prosper you, to give you hope and a future."*
- Father God, the mammon slave spirit and systems attack and attempt to steal my hopes and dreams, by denying the spiritual freedom and prosperity

You have promised me as your covenant son/daughter. But You, Father God, are not a man that You should lie.[14] In God I trust, to leave the slave system and enter into true freedom lived in the fullness of faith!

- I understand this does not mean I quit my job without your guidance to do so. I understand this does not mean I should be lazy. I understand this means to listen with my heart to where You want me to be, even in a job or assignment I may not want, but You may have me there for a reason and a season. I understand that my covenant relationship with You means yielding to your Will, to trust in You and your plans for me and my life and vocation; that by serving You and your Will, I will be provided for.

- I understand that prospering is not all about money, but also spiritually prospering, prospering in inner shalom peace, prospering in health, prospering in healthy and happy relationships, prospering in joyful service, prospering in inner joy and faith. I ask You Father God, to bless me in these forms of prosperity.

There is Provision Resting in the Lord.

- Matthew 11:28 comforts me: *"Come to Me, all who are weary and heavy-laden, and I will give you rest."*
- Psalm 140:12 calms me: *"I know that the Lord will maintain the cause of the afflicted and justice for the poor."*

- Father God, You comfort me in the secret place, El Shaddai. In that place of peace and comfort, my problems dissolve and your lovingkindness fills me with blessed assurance that I am cared for. Thank you, that there is ALWAYS a solution in YOU.
- I commit to taking time in my day and life to rest in You. In this rest, I shall experience peace. In this peace, your provision can more easily flow to me, unobstructed by fear, anxiety and worry.

GOD'S PROVISION CAN FLOW MORE EASILY TO US WHEN IT IS UNOBSTRUCTED BY FEAR, ANXIETY AND WORRY.

Father God, it is indisputably clear throughout your Word which is your record of law and your covenant with me, that You have destined me to prosper in *your* ways and in *your* systems of abundance.

I understand by your Word that You have called me to disciple nations and to build your kingdom here on earth, which requires money and other resources to accomplish. It is clear that if I am not granted these requests from your Court, I will not be able to fulfill your plans for me to serve You in these ways.

7. Petitions.

The judgements I am requesting from your Court of Mercy and Grace are:

- Grant all of my petitions in the case I have presented to You here.
- Grant me a divorce decree from and a Divine Restraining Order against all mammon systems, programs and their cohorts and minions, including spirits of poverty, lack, struggle and debt from operating in my life, so that I will no longer be dependent on any mammon system. Break the devourer off of me and my bloodline now Father God! As Malachi 3:11 proclaims: "'Then I will rebuke the devourer for you, so that it will not destroy the fruits of the ground; nor will your vine in the field cast its grapes,' says the Lord of hosts."
- Break the stronghold and stranglehold of debt on me and my life. It is a lie and program from satan and his minions and defies your Will.
- Grant me a Divine Restraining Order against all mammon spirits, systems and programs operating in my life that are designed to control and limit my prosperity, my vocational, financial and relational success, to keep me under a glass ceiling of success and freedom, to keep me from fulfilling my God destiny.
- Grant me a Divine Restraining Order against all territorial spirits [name your area] working against my financial and material wellbeing and prosperity.
- Command satan, lucifer, mammon and all of their cohorts and minions, including regional and governmental demonic principalities, to loose the

holds that they have had on my supplies and return seven-fold all that is owed to me, including everything stolen from my bloodlines through manipulated markets, market crashes, recessions and depressions.

- Restore and release all provisions that You have allocated for me, as well as a seven-fold recompense for everything that satan, mammon and others, both human and non-human, have stolen from me that has not been on account of my own actions and choices, according to your Word in Proverbs 6:31, which says that when the thief is caught he must repay seven-fold all he has stolen. The thieves have been caught LORD God!
- Yoke me fully, eternally and exclusively to You and your provisions for my life.

8. Wait on the Lord's Response.

This is a pause, allowing for stillness and silence to respect God's response to our petitions. This is cultivating an awareness and sensitivity to our relationship with God, just as we would communicate with someone sitting right in front of us.

9. Thanks and Gratitude.

[Let this be dedicated time to thank God for receiving and answering your petitions. You may want to play or sing praise music, dance, whatever is your personal way to express thanks to God.]

- Thank you for your mercy, grace and love!
- Thank you God for granting all of my petitions!
- Thank you LORD God for delivering me from all mammon, money, financial and materialism bondage once and for all!
- To You alone be all the glory in Heaven and upon the Earth forever and ever! AMEN!!!

"For you are a holy people [set apart]
to the LORD your God;
The LORD your God
has chosen you out of all the peoples
on the face of the earth
to be a people for His own possession."
Deuteronomy 7:6

———

CHAPTER 13
DELIVERANCE FROM THE PYTHON SPIRIT

"And if there be a man or a woman in whom is
a spirit of Python or of divination,
they shall certainly be put to death:
they shall stone them with stones;
their blood is upon them."
Leviticus 20:27

WHAT IS THE PYTHON SPIRIT

THERE WAS a time when I believed these demons-spirits were more metaphorical, not actually real, but I have seen physical evidence of their existence. This python spirit is known for choking its victims, like certain species of snakes are known to do.

Our prayer group was working with this protocol and one member began to have physical experiences of having his breath cut off. We did the python protocol again and the symptoms broke off of him for good. What essentially happened was that this man was breaking free of the python spirit and it began to fight back, or just kick him on the way out the door. Once he repeated the protocol, the spirit left.

Even though the python spirit is considered a principality that has authority over large regions, it absolutely affects people personally. As the above verse from Leviticus indicates, python is associated with witchcraft and other various forms and practices of divination. If you have ever engaged in such activities or have people close to you that have done so, this python spirit has likely gained a foothold into your life.

If you leave doors open through occult, witchcraft, sorcery and divination activities, objects in your home and entertainment, then you have opened the door to this python spirit. It can also enter through various "healing" modalities, so be careful who you choose to work with for your healing. In some regions, it is very common for massage therapists to also practice Reiki.[1] Often times, they will not ask or tell their client that they are including or incorporating Reiki into their massage. Make sure you ask and screen accordingly.

The only way to be truly free of these demonic powers is to completely and permanently divorce them, renounce them and cut all ties to them; and also not to feed them with certain activities, behaviors and traits. The most effective results come from making a very thoughtful and thorough review of your life; what you've done, with whom, where, etc. Don't worry about not remembering everything the first time you do this protocol. You can always come back and do it again as you remember other things or events to clear. Life is a process!

WHAT TO KNOW ABOUT THE PYTHON SPIRIT

- It acts as a counterfeit Holy Spirit. Acts 16:16[2]
- It can be a territorial spirit, seeking authority over regions, governments, organizations and practices.[3] Tho it is territorial, it also affects and targets individuals.
- As a territorial spirit, it gathers and communicates information about the destiny, activity, calling, anointing, mission and level of spiritual authority of those given charge by God over a region.
- It targets worship, intercession, intercessors, money and governmental authority including Apostolic governments.
- It often gives the deceptive appearance of revelation, discernment and prophecy. (Mistaking second heaven information and authority, or familiar spirits, for the Holy Spirit.). This is very common in Christian circles.
- It operates within the Body of Christ, as well as New Age practices, such as channeling, psychics and fortune-telling.[4] It is equal opportunity with regards to spiritual or religious denominations.[5]
- It is a high power - not a random snake/demon/minion - whose position is over the Body of Christ at large. It is often associated with the serpent spirit called nahash.
- Its assignment is to keep God's children from operating in or coming into the manifest power of God.
- It does this by orchestrating his forces very strategically against every individual who has

received (or will receive) Christ; every group,
church and ministry large or small, and the entire
corporate body as a whole.

- It seeks to hinder God's sons and daughters from
  realizing and implementing their full authority,
  power and destiny in Jesus Christ.
- It loves to stir up gossip, rebellion, slander, lies,
  strife, manipulation; ungodly authority, control and
  manipulation.
- It is infamous for being brutal and unmerciful
  towards godly leaders.
- It squeezes, strangles, cuts off life breath or life
  force to prevent people from being able to carry out
  God's Will.
- It seeks to squeeze the life breath out of churches
  and ministries doing the will of God.

WHY WE NEED TO BE DELIVERED FROM THE PYTHON SPIRIT

- It blocks the redemptive promises and blessings of
  individuals, families, businesses, churches and
  nations.
- It hinders people from realizing their God calling,
  anointing and ability to possess all that Jesus Christ
  has availed for them.
- It squeezes the anointing out of already effective
  vessels.
- It seeks legal entry and ground into a person's life
  through false beliefs, idolatry, doubt, murmuring,
  gossip and unbelief to hinder God's purposes for an
  individual, group, family or church community.

- It strives to slither into a person's or ministry's life by acquiring ground and gradually crushing the life and God anointing out of it.
- It seeks to thwart, skew, hide or veil anointings, revelations, truth, blessings, provisions, healthy relationships, anointed opportunities; and most importantly, God's love for us.

WHAT TO DO BEFORE GOING TO THE COURTS OF HEAVEN FOR THE PYTHON SPIRIT

It is essential to do a clean sweep of your home for occult objects.

By clean sweep, I mean get rid of these objects! These can include pictures, art work, crafts, photographs, music (CDs) and books. This can also include objects that were gifted to you or that you acquired second-hand. That is, someone owned the objects prior to you. Even if the objects are not occult in and of themselves, they may have been used in witchcraft rituals or owned by someone who was a practitioner of witchcraft, sorcery or divination and placed hexes, vexes, incantations etc. into the object.

If you ever acquire objects through gifts or second-hand, make sure that you clear them, bless them and anoint them before bringing them into your home. If you are not sure, 'when in doubt, throw it out.' We recommend doing this for brand new objects as well — cleanse and bless them. I've done this purging process several times and did not get everything the first or even the second time I swept through my home.

. . .

Purging Check List:

- Check all the boxes and shelves in your closets, attic, basement, garage, even your car.
- Go through your bookshelves. There was one book that I just had to tear out one specific page, yet kept the rest of the book.
- Your music collection: this can include lyrics and artists having to do with sorcery, witchcraft or vulgar lyrics.[6]
- Gifts, second-hand items, brand new items.
- Check your car in the trunk and glove box.
- Check under your bed and sinks.
- Check your property as well.
- Cleansing your life of occult objects is critical to being free of any footholds these spirits can have into your life.

CLEARING YOUR LIFE AND HOME OF ALL OCCULT OBJECTS IS ESSENTIAL TO BEING FREE OF DEMONIC POWERS IN YOUR LIFE.

COURTS OF HEAVEN PROTOCOL TO BE DELIVERED FROM THE PYTHON SPIRIT

1. Preparation.

Before you go into the Courts of Heaven, take the time to identify your petitions and purposes, what remedies you are seeking, what in your life and character require repentance and what in your family lineage requires renunciation. Ask the Holy Spirit to reveal to you these things before you go in to the Courts of Heaven. Often times, when you are in the Courts of Heaven, the Holy Spirit will bring other things to mind for which to repent.

You may receive information about specific family members who have already passed on. This can include activities they engaged in such as crimes, rituals, witchcraft, sorcery, occult, oaths, covenants, contracts and curses. You renounce, repudiate, and disavow the sins, transgressions and iniquities of your ancestors to remove any legal cases against yourself.

We repent and plead guilty for all personal sins, transgressions and iniquities, present the Blood of Jesus as our atonement, and then ask God to pass judgements on our behalf. The adversary operates through legality, which is why we go to God's Courtroom to remove any legal cases the enemy is using against us or our family.

Remember to speak the entire protocol OUT LOUD!

2. Presentation of Purpose.

Father God, I come before your Court of Mercy and Grace and ask that the courts be seated and the books be opened, according to Daniel 7:10. I ask for the Holy Spirit and the Lord Jesus Christ to be my Holy Advocates to represent me in your Court. I give them full permission to speak on my behalf. I put on robes of righteousness and I loose the Blood of Jesus over myself so that satan has no access to me. I come into your Court right now and I thank you that I am accepted here.

As I stand before your Court, I thank you Jesus Yeshua for everything You've done for me, that when You died on the Cross, You gave your blood to redeem me, to deliver me from curses and demonic powers. That sacrifice is speaking for me right now. Thank you for your sin payment on my behalf.

LORD God Adonai, I come before your Court to seek relief from the python spirit; to renounce, repent of and shed python traits in myself; to renounce and divorce all python activities, curses and connections from my bloodlines; to receive your forgiveness, grace and help to be free of all python influence and oppression over my life once and for all.

I ask LORD God that You release your Notification Angels, your Enforcement Angels and Hosts of Heaven to all those humans and non-humans who will be affected by your Court decisions to duly inform them of and immediately enforce all of your decisions in my case today.

3. Renounce & Repent.

Father God, I come in the name of your Son Jesus Christ and repent of all my sins, iniquities and transgressions, and renounce, repudiate, and disavow all the sins of my ancestors back to Adam and Eve, having to do with satan, the python spirit, the nahash spirit, any and all of their cohorts and minions

including witchcraft, divination, sorcery, occultism, necro-
mancy, familiar spirits, seducing spirits, beguiling spirits, critical spirits, incubus and succubus, jezebel and leviathan spirits;
and the spirits of controlling, domination, manipulation, delu-
sion, deceptiveness, gossip, slander, heaviness, weariness,
fatigue, frustration, confusion, depression, oppression, and
destiny-suppression and sabotage.

I renounce, denounce, divorce and break all oaths, vows,
contracts, covenants, agreements, soul ties, hooks, cords,
connections to, relationships with all of these spirits that I or
anyone in my bloodline established or participated in. I
renounce and repent of all activities, rituals, vocations, avocations, beliefs I have engaged in, having to do with python and
these other demonic spirits.

I renounce all python seeds and fruits from all of my bloodlines
back to Adam and Eve. I reject and renounce the normalization
of these spirits and traits which have been passed down
through my bloodlines.

I understand that *repent* means to turn away from, to change
and transform my mind and way of living. It is a commitment
to cease and turn away from activities, relationships and habits
that are detrimental to my spirit which was made in your
image.

LORD God, on behalf of myself and all of my paternal and
maternal bloodlines back to Adam and Eve, I reject, refuse,

renounce and divorce all demonic spirits including familiar, perversity, incubus, mare, succubus, lust, pornography, pedophilia, mischievous, trouble-making, double-mindedness; all sexual perversion including rape, assault, abuse, voyeurism, domination, brutality, confusion; astral projection and spirit travel; all witchcraft, sorcery, divination, idolatry; all hard-heartedness, unbelief, anger, rage, bitterness, unforgiveness, pride, rebellion, death, murder and destruction; lilu, lilith and all offspring of satan and his demons, and any satan seed implanted in me.

Father God, I repent of all the times and ways I have compromised and/or turned away from your Will and purposes; chickened out or compromised as an intercessor; lived in spiritual dryness, rebelliousness and selfishness, not doing what You wanted and needed, as and when You wanted and needed.

I repent for surrendering ground to the enemy, including my city, state and country (name them specifically), and allowing evil to proliferate, abide, reside and operate on our lands.

I repent for all the times and ways the python spirit has been operational through me to control, manipulate or damage other human beings and their relationship with You; that have in any way choked others off from You. I repent for ever believing python lies and for perpetuating them by sharing them with others.

· · ·

I forgive all those who contributed to my beliefs and behaviors connected to python and these other demon spirits. I am truly sorry for all the divisiveness and strife within the Body of Christ and your Holy Church; and any way that I may have contributed to it.

I renounce, denounce and divorce all ungodly oaths, contracts, covenants, agreements, curses, rituals, witchcraft, sorcery, occult practices, activities, vocations, avocations, beliefs, hexes, vexes, voodoo having to do with the python spirit and its programs committed by my bloodlines; and all related demonic strongholds and iniquities passed down and affecting my life.

I renounce and repent of all traits, habits, character flaws and inclinations that I have inherited, indulged in and expressed on account of these ancestral iniquities and having to do with the python spirit and its programs. I recognize that they are wrong, hurtful to myself, others and You Heavenly Father. Please forgive me.

I renounce, divorce and cut all ties, including all soul ties, with python and python-related spirits, people, relationships and seeds implanted in me, my belief systems and body, now and forever more; as well as former spouses, lovers and others that have been tied to me in the spirit. I return all soul parts to them now.

4. Plead Guilty.

Father God, for everything I have repented and renounced

here, I plead guilty to remove all the cases that satan and his demonic powers have held against me. I present the Blood of the Lamb of God, Jesus Christ Yeshua as atonement. I present the Voice of the Blood of Jesus which speaks "paid in full" to clear these transgressions from my record and bloodline.

Lord God, let the speaking Blood of Jesus deliver me from every judgement against me and my genetics. Let them all be revoked now. Let every agenda and curse against me be now silenced; that the enemy no longer has a right to bring any python and python-related case against me because of what the Blood of Jesus speaks, because of the finished work of Jesus on the Cross according to Corinthians 2:13-15.

Father God, I present your Word in Colossians 2:13-15 to release me from any python and python-related bondage: *God made me alive together with Christ, having forgiven me all my sins, having canceled out the certificate of debt consisting of legal demands [which were in force] against me and which were hostile to me. And this certificate He has set aside and completely removed by nailing it to the cross. When He had disarmed the rulers and authorities [those supernatural forces of evil operating against me], He made a public example of them [exhibiting them as captives in His triumphal procession], having triumphed over them through the cross.* What grace! What a profound gift of mercy! Thank you Jesus!

Therefore Father God, I ask for redemption from the curse, by the Blood of Jesus, and ask You to break off all curses from python, nahash and all other related demonic spirits, systems and agendas over me now! Let the Blood of Jesus break all these curses now.

Cleanse, Clear & Release.

LORD God, pour your healing balm of Gilead into all of my stored memories, imprints and traumas; my body, brain, mind, heart and soul; my conscience, my subconscious and unconscious minds; my beliefs, habits, traits and traumas having to do with python; to dissolve them all now. Erase all damage and confusion in the chambers of my mind.

Let all stolen or scattered parts or fragments of my soul be fully healed with the Blood of Jesus and be returned to me now.

Father God, cleanse me now with your Holy healing love, from all shame, guilt, self-hatred, self-condemnation, resentment, offense, bitterness, fear, anxiety, worry, insecurities, inferiority, prejudice, bigotry, slander, poisonous tongue and anger. Heal the source and cause of these disordered emotions now.

I receive by faith cleansing, clearing and healing, including my relationship with You LORD God, myself and others. 1 John 4:4 tells me that I am from God and *"Greater is He who is in me than he who is in the world."*

LORD God, I recognize, honor and accept that your holiness in Christ Jesus dwells in me, that I am born of your seed of divinity, created in your image, and that You are healing, blessing and restoring me and my life through your mercy, grace and love. Thank you Heavenly Father Abba!

~ *Pause in Silence to Receive God's Healing* ~

5. Reparations ~ Penance.

Dear Heavenly Father, please guide me to right reparations and/or penance for all the violations I have committed regarding the python spirit and its accompanying character traits, habits, personality flaws and behaviors; as well as any reparations for any rituals, oaths, contracts and covenants on behalf of myself and my lineage.

Speak to me through your Holy Spirit. Convict me in mind and heart of right restitution to make through my actions, relationships, charity, teaching, sharing, giving, sacrifices, prayers and fasting.

6. Plead Your Case.

Lord God Adonai, Righteous Judge, I am presenting You my legal case through your legal document, your Word. Please receive your Word as the key to my freedom from bondage to the python spirit and its cohorts. LORD God, your Word declares the following:

I Am Made in Your Image.

- Your Word in Genesis 1:27 says: *"So God created man in His own image, in the image and likeness of God He created him; male and female He created them."*
- Father God, python seeks to deceive me into believing I am not made in your image and am not worthy of being your son/daughter and part of Your kingdom. He seeks to cloud my judgement of myself and others.
- Father God, I reject the lies of python and forbid them from continuing to wreak havoc in my life and family.
- Father God, please bind the python that has been strangling my life and destiny, and the life and destiny of my family, that has been strangling your truth and your Word in us.

No Weapon Formed Against Me Shall Prosper.

- Your Word in Isaiah 54:17 promises: *"'No weapon that is formed against you will succeed; and every tongue that rises against you in judgment you will condemn. This [peace, righteousness, security, and triumph over opposition] is the heritage of the servants of the LORD, and this is their vindication from Me,' says the LORD."*
- Father God, python wants me to believe I am always subservient to and victim to his agendas. I say, no more!

- Father God, condemn the weapons and lies of the python spirit. Let his condemning voice against me be silenced for good.

YOU Lord God are My Protector.

- Your Word in Psalm 139:5 says that: *"You have enclosed me behind and before, and placed your hand upon me."* I receive Your Word into my spirit.
- Father God, python strives to strip me of your protection and instill fear and anxiety in me. I reject this.
- Father God, I reject the harassment and taunts of python that have been projected against me.
- Father God, enclose me all around, enclose my family all around, from the encroaching, sneaky, slithering ways of python. Protect us LORD God!

I Am Pre-Destined to Godliness.

- Your Word in Psalm 139:16 says: *"Your eyes have seen my unformed substance; and in your book were all written the days that were appointed for me, when as yet there was not one of them [even taking shape]."* I receive this beautiful passage as my hope and healing.
- Father God, python whispers in my ears false prophecies about doom and failure. He tries to

keep me from my God destiny that You have
established and pre-ordained.

- Father God, as I choose to stop believing the lies, I
ask You to loose your hand of justice on the python
spirit slithering through my life and cut off his
head.

You Have Plans to Prosper Me.

- Your Word in Jeremiah 29:11 promises: *"For I
know the plans I have for you, plans to prosper you,
to give you hope and a future."*
- Father God, python has stolen blessings, hopes,
health, morale, time, resources, reputations and
relationships. Let it all end here and now! Fulfill
your Word to prosper me in the ways You desire
me to prosper. Prosper me in Christ Jesus living in
and through me. Do this so that your own glory
shall be revealed!

Father God, it is indisputably clear throughout your Word,
which is your record of law and promises for me, that You have
created me in *your* image for *your* purposes. It is clear that if
this python spirit, its cohorts and minions are allowed to
continue to control, steal or compromise any part of me or my
life, I will not be able to fulfill *your* Will and destiny for my life.
It is clear that if I am not granted these requests from your
Court, I will not be able to fulfill your plans for me.

· · ·

7. Petitions.

Therefore, the judgements that I am requesting from your Court of Mercy and Grace are:

- Grant all of my petitions in the case I have presented to You here.
- Bind the spirit of python operating in, through and out of my life.
- Grant me a divorce decree from and a Divine Restraining Order against python and all python cohorts, minions, entities, operations, agendas and systems from operating in my life, so that I will no longer be tormented, so that I may be the strong, effective son/daughter of God that You have created me to be.
- Loose the holds that satan, lucifer, python and their cohorts and minions have had on my destiny, lifework and provisions.
- Replace every lie in my belief system with your Truth that shall set me free, including revelation of my true identity in Christ Jesus; so that I may fully operate from the indwelling spirit.
- Fulfill Ezekiel 36:27 in me: "*I will put My Spirit within you and cause you to walk in My statutes, and you will be careful to observe My ordinances.*" Let your Spirit in me be so impenetrable that no other spirit can co-exist with it or harm me ever again.
- Frustrate the plans of the wicked including all spirits of divisiveness, false discernment, backbiting, slander, badmouthing; and strife against me and within my family.

- Restore to me seven-fold everything python, his minions and cohorts have stolen from me that has not been on account of my own actions and choices, according to your promises in Proverbs 6:31, that when the thief is caught he must repay seven-fold all he has stolen.
- Direct your supports to be forthcoming so that my work and life may go on unhampered and I may fulfill my God destiny completely now, including all collaborative work and destiny with others You have so destined and appointed for me.
- Yoke me fully, eternally and exclusively to You Father God.

8. Wait on the Lord's Response.

This is a pause, allowing for stillness and silence to respect God's response to our petitions. This is cultivating an awareness and sensitivity to our relationship with God, just as we would communicate with someone sitting right in front of us.

9. Thanks and Gratitude.

[Let this be dedicated time to thank the Lord after all of your petitions. You may want to play or sing praise music, or other ways that you express thanks and praise.]

- Thank you LORD God for granting my petitions!
- Thank you LORD God and Jesus Christ for healing, restoring and redeeming me!
- Thank you LORD God for delivering me from all of these demonic powers once and for all!

- To You alone be all the glory in Heaven and upon the earth forever and ever! AMEN!!!

———

But you are A CHOSEN RACE,
A royal PRIESTHOOD,
A CONSECRATED NATION,
A [special] PEOPLE FOR God's OWN POSSESSION,
so that you may proclaim the excellencies
[the wonderful deeds and virtues and perfections]
of Him who called you out of darkness
into His marvelous light.
1 Peter 2:9

———

CHAPTER 14
DELIVERANCE FROM THE BAAL SPIRIT

"So they abandoned the Lord and served Baal
[the pagan god of the Canaanites]
and the Ashtaroth."
Judges 2:13

WHAT IS THE BAAL SPIRIT

BAAL IS the kingpin of all the demon-gods. It is an ancient pagan deity that was worshiped thousands of years ago. Incredibly, baal worship is alive and well in today's elite circles. You will see from the descriptions below how baal worship has been injected into every sector of modern society, and how its symbols and agendas have been infused into our culture. Why should it matter to you?

Rituals and practices that propitiate and give power to this demon deity are affecting and infecting our lives. It is witchcraft and sorcery at the highest levels. The reason that people worship baal and its cohort moloch is because they believe that these dark entities give them power, advantages and control over the peon masses. At its worst, the practices are truly evil and horrific. No truly civilized society should be ok with them.

WHAT TO KNOW ABOUT THE BAAL SPIRIT

Kingpin Demon.

- Baal was the kingpin 'god' of the Canaanite people and religion.
- It is considered the ruler and highest authority of demons, and is also known as Beelzebub.
- It is referred to in Mark 3:22, *"He is possessed by Beelzebub,"* and *"He casts out the demons by the ruler of the demons."*

Key Rival to God.

- Baal was constantly a rival of the Most High God with God's people, who were repeatedly drawn to it, betraying their relationship with Father God.
- 1 Kings 18:21 says: *"How long will you hesitate between two opinions? If the LORD is God, follow Him; but if Baal, follow him."*
- Deuteronomy 32:16-17 says: *"They provoked Him to jealousy with strange gods [by denying Him the honor and loyalty that is rightfully and uniquely His]; and with repulsive acts they provoked Him to anger. They sacrificed to demons, not to God, to gods whom they have not known, new gods who came lately, whom your fathers never feared."*

. . .

Enslaver.

- 'Baal' means lord, master, husband, or owner. It
  seeks to enslave people, to own and control them.
- It does not tolerate competition.

Child Sacrifice & Death.

- Baal worshipers sacrifice their children,
  traditionally the first born, to gain favor with baal.
- Jeremiah 19:5 describes: "...*And have built the high
  places of baal to burn their sons in the fire as burnt
  offerings to baal, which I never commanded or spoke
  of, nor did it ever enter My mind (heart)."*
- Moloch is a cohort of baal. Moloch worshipers are
  also known to sacrifice children. Statues of Moloch
  show him eating children.
- 2 Kings 17:17 records: "*Then they made their sons
  and their daughters pass through the fire, [killed
  them as a sacrifice to moloch or baal] and they
  practiced divination and interpreting omens, and
  gave themselves over to do evil in the sight of the
  LORD, provoking Him."*
- "*Made their sons and their daughters pass through
  the fire*" means sacrificing them by burning them
  alive. Killing their own children by offering them to
  baal or moloch was considered a way to gain favor
  with these gods. It is still happening today in
  various forms of child sacrifice. Even cartels who

engage in Santa Muerte ("holy death" cult) will steal babies and kill them in a satanic ritual for power and favor.

- There is archeological evidence of both animal and human infant sacrifices to these gods.
- Baal practices and worshipers are more prevalent today than ever before. Their actions show up in the form of child trafficking, child ritual abuse (rape, torture and murder) and fetal abuse (abortion and trafficking of aborted fetal parts). [1]

Self-harm.

- Baal is a demon god associated with self-harm, cutting and mutilation; perhaps connected to tattooing and mutilation of body parts. This is not to say that all those who engage in these activities are aware the practice is associated with this demon god. Those that promote it however, may be aware of it. Demons can act on a person to drive them to actions unbeknownst to that person. Why? To give the demon an entryway into the person's life, to use that person and their body for the demon's agendas.
- 1 Kings 18:28 says: "*So they cried out with a loud voice [to get baal's attention] and cut themselves with swords and lances in accordance with their custom, until the blood flowed out on them.*"
- Self-harm, including cutting until there is blood flow, is a way of propitiating, gaining favor with baal. Baal and other demon gods love bloodshed.

- God speaks against this self-damaging practice in Leviticus 19:28: "*You shall not make any cuts on your body for the dead, nor make any tattoo marks on yourselves; I am the* LORD."

God of Weather & Fertility.

- Baal was called the "son of Dagon", who was in turn the god of grain. By this association, baal was considered to rule over grain and crops.
- Baal worshipers believed baal also controlled rain and lightning. However, when Queen Jezebel's baal prophets attempted to call down lightning in a showdown with the Prophet Elijah, they failed.[2]
- A lot of strange and intense weather patterns and events have been escalating in recent times believed to be engineered with advanced weaponry.[3]
- GMO[4] food grains have been engineered to control the food supply & are believed to contribute to decreased human fertility.

Sensuality, Sexual Promiscuity, Consort of Jezebel.

- Baal is the 'god' that Queen Jezebel worshiped. She brought 450 prophets of baal & 400 prophets of the goddess asherah (a consort of baal) into the Kingdom of Israel when she married King Ahab.[5]

- Jezebel was a chief priestess of baal worship, which is why baal is often associated with a female demon such as jezebel or asherah. Worshipers engaged in temple prostitution and sex magic; which is why baal worship typically has elements of sex magic, distortions of sexuality and vulgar sex acts.
- Sex magic is very prolific in our culture, practiced and spread throughout media and entertainment, especially via pop divas. Seduction, mesmerizing and symbology are pouring out of entertainers' concerts, costumes, music videos, lyrics, sets and other visuals. Controlling and manipulating through seduction and satanic symbology are very powerful ways to bring someone under demonic control and influence. It opens people up to attacks in their sleep, attaches demons to a person, normalizes and propagates addiction to pornography, and degrades human sexuality, to name just a few effects. It's all about control. Control of a person's soul.

Distorts Governments & Exploits Legalism.

- Queen Jezebel set up temples to baal & asherah in Israel's two capital cities, Samaria & Jezreel, in order to manipulate and control the governments in those cities.
- Baal arches have been replicated thru 3D printing and placed in capitals of government and commerce around the world (DC, NYC, London

etc.). Baal worshipers are operating over the seats of government throughout the world.

- Baal controls through legalism and its systems by creating chaos, confusion and strife.
- It is the antithesis of 'law and order', yet works through legal and judicial systems to foment chaos via lawfare, using lawsuits to harass and pummel opponents. It makes a mockery of rule of law, and law and order.
- Think of all the events of violence and chaos occurring around the world and the puppeteers behind them.

The Elite's God.

- It is the kingpin demon of today's elites prevalent in all 'Seven Mountains' of society: media, entertainment, education, religion, government, family and business. Reading this list of features and traits of baal, can you now identify baal's footprint in each of these sectors of our culture?
- Baphomet is another cohort of baal and worshiped by the elites. It is the god of transgenderism. Hollywood has many rituals, symbols and architecture (arches etc.) to propitiate these demons. Many pop divas have worn baphomet or baal horns as part of their costumes in their shows. It's become so common, it's predictable as well as boring. Their garb, jewelry and symbology telegraph to each other and the world that they are 'in the club.'

. . .

A Bull & Lightning Bolt.

- Baal is often portrayed as a calf, bull or lightning bolt. See the bronze statue of a bull on Wall Street.
- The golden calf created by the Israelites whilst Moses was with God was a facsimile of baal.[6]
- Baal horns as bull's horns are frequently worn as costumes by baal worshipers.

WHY WE NEED TO BE DELIVERED FROM BAAL

Key to Full Deliverance.

- He is the kingpin demon that works with and over all the other strongholds and demonic powers.

- Therefore, deliverance from baal is "capturing the forte."

- Prophets have said that God and baal are currently in an epic battle on earth.

Infused Into Society.

- Baal has the strongest foothold into our lives on account of it being so infused into our culture.

- Baal programs and agendas are subliminally transmitted through media, music and entertainment industries (e.g. costumes, sets and lyrics).

- Because baal worship has been inculcated into our lives, <u>we have unwittingly normalized baal worship and its presence</u>.

- It's virtually impossible not to be in some way influenced by baal, and therefore not require deliverance from it.

Steals Our Destiny.

- Baal hinders or stops God's people from realizing their calling and ability to possess all that Jesus Christ redeemed for them. From its inception, it has been in competition with the Most High God.

- It is not the true Light; it is the counterfeit light. As such, it must steal and syphon life force energy from human beings. It steals our God destiny in order to do this.

- It distorts and steals self-worth and gifts to prevent us from fulfilling our destiny.

- It profanes the holy. It mocks God. It mocks and steals sacred destiny given by God.

- It turns people on paths that are a mockery and distortion of their true purpose. For example, someone who is called to create sacred art to uplift humanity becomes used by baal and satan to make profane art that mocks the beauty of man created in God's image.

- It breaks up marriages, families, societies, ministries and kingdom missions. It mocks and distorts these institutions, thereby stealing their destiny and higher purposes. Whole lives have been stolen by it.

Operates Thru Legal Entry.

- Through our family, our own actions and choices, the culture we are immersed in, baal has legal entry and ground into our life.

- If we attend a concert that is essentially a baal satanic ritual, we have unwittingly given permission for its entryway into our life. Many music concerts and shows are essentially rituals for baal and its demon cohorts. Pay attention!

- Because it is a kingpin strongman, it is imperative to remove its hold on us!

Theft of Our Governing ~ Lawlessness.

- Baal and its accomplices are the key thieves of our governments, and law and order.

- It is the spiritual cause of chaos and lawlessness at our borders, in political systems, and throughout nations and our world.
- Baal and his accomplices are at the command center fueling the chaos and evil on earth.

We Are Responsible for the Children.

- Human trafficking, especially of children, feeds the baal spirit. Millions of trafficked children have been repeatedly raped, tortured and eventually murdered. What civilized society allows children to be treated so horrifically?
- Aborting babies at nine months? Killing babies right after they have been born?[7] Seriously?

Why be delivered of the baal spirit? Do it for the children. <u>Do it for the children.</u>

WALK AS CHILDREN OF LIGHT

"For once you were darkness,
but now in union with the Lord you are light.
Walk as children of light."
Ephesians 5:8

We are here to walk as Children of Light, in union with the Lord Jesus Christ. We are here to bring others to the Light. Jesus Christ exhorts us that we are the light of the world. Only light can dispel the wicked darkness of this world. BE the light that dispels evil!

"You are the light of the world.
A town built on a hill cannot be hidden.
Neither do people light a lamp and put it under a bowl.
Instead they put it on its stand,
and it gives light to everyone in the house.
In the same way, let your light shine before others,
that they may see your good deeds
and glorify your Father in heaven."
Matthew 5:14-16

COURTS OF HEAVEN PROTOCOL TO BE DELIVERED FROM THE BAAL SPIRIT

1. Preparation.

Before you go into the Courts of Heaven, take the time to identify your petitions and purposes, what remedies you are seeking, what in your life and character require repentance and what in your family lineage requires renunciation. Ask the Holy Spirit to reveal to you these things before you go in to the Courts of Heaven. Often times, when you are in the Courts of Heaven, the Holy Spirit will bring other things to mind for which to repent.

You may receive information about specific family members who have already passed on. This can include activities they engaged in such as crimes, rituals, oaths, covenants, contracts and curses. You renounce, repudiate, and disavow the sins, transgressions and iniquities of your ancestors <u>to remove any legal cases against yourself.</u>

We repent and plead guilty for all personal sins, transgressions and iniquities, present the Blood of Jesus as our atonement, and then ask God to pass judgements on our behalf. The adversary operates through legality, which is why we go to God's Courtroom to remove any legal cases the enemy is using against us or our family.

Remember to speak the entire protocol OUT LOUD!

. . .

2. Presentation of Purpose.

Father God, I come before your Court of Mercy and Grace and ask that the courts be seated and the books be opened, according to Daniel 7:10. I ask for the Holy Spirit and the Lord Jesus Christ Yeshua to be my Holy Advocates to represent me in your Court. I give them full permission to speak on my behalf.

I put on robes of righteousness as an officer in your Court and loose the Blood of Jesus over myself so that satan has no access to me. I come into the Courts right now and I thank you that I am accepted here. Thank you for the privilege of being able to bring my petitions to your Court.

As I stand before your Court, I thank you Jesus Christ for everything You've done for me, that when You died on the Cross, You gave your blood to redeem me, to deliver me from curses and demonic powers. That sacrifice is speaking for me right now. I thank you for this profound gift of divine mercy and grace.

LORD God Adonai, I come before your Court to seek relief from the baal spirit and its cohorts; to renounce, repent of and shed all baal elements and traits in myself; to receive your forgiveness, grace and help to be free of all baal influence and oppression over my life once and for all.

I ask LORD God that You release your highest ranking Notification Angels, Enforcement Angels and Hosts of Heaven to all those humans and non-humans who will be affected by your Court decisions, to duly inform them of and immediately enforce all of your decisions and judgements in my case today.

3. Renounce & Repent.

Father God, I come in the name of Jesus Christ Yeshua to repent of all my sins, iniquities and transgressions, and renounce, repudiate, and disavow all the sins of my ancestors back to Adam and Eve, that have engaged, fed, collaborated or participated with, endorsed, worshiped, advocated, used, and opened doors to satan, lucifer, baal, moloch, baphomet and any of their cohorts, minions, accomplices and representatives, including all spirits, practices and programs of ritual abuse, satanic rituals, witchcraft, sorcery, divination, occult, idolatry, beguiling, seduction, sensuality, prostitution, pornography; sexual perversion including rape, assault and abuse, promiscuity, voyeurism, domination, brutality, sadism, masochism; confusion, gender confusion, human trafficking, self-harm, child-sacrifice, manipulation, controlling, mesmerizing, pharmakeia, jezebel, asherah, anath, nahash; death, murder and destruction; genetically engineered foods, people and animals; any distortion of God's creation and purposes here on earth. I renounce all baal seeds and fruits from all of my bloodlines back to Adam and Eve.

I understand that *repent* means to turn away from, to change and transform my mind and way of living. It is a commitment to cease and turn away from activities, traits and habits that are detrimental to my spirit which was made in your image.

. . .

I renounce, repent of, divorce and break all soul ties, oaths, vows, contracts, covenants, agreements and programs with all of these spirits and any person or party that I or anyone in my bloodline has established with baal and any of these other spirits, practices and programs.

I renounce and repent of all activities, words, music, music videos, lyrics, concerts, movies, any entertainment, rituals including satanic rituals, vocations, avocations and beliefs having to do with baal and these other demonic powers.

I repent for all the times and ways I have used the baal spirit and its cohorts and minions to control, manipulate or damage other human beings, and my relationship with You. LORD God, I forgive all those who contributed to my beliefs and behaviors connected to baal and these other demon spirits.

I renounce, denounce and divorce all ungodly oaths, contracts, covenants, agreements, curses, rituals, witchcraft, sorcery, occult practices, activities, vocations, avocations, beliefs, hexes, vexes, voodoo having to do with the baal spirit, its programs and cohorts committed by my bloodlines; and all related demonic strongholds and iniquities passed down and affecting my life, my character and personality.

I renounce and repent of all traits, habits, character flaws and inclinations that I have inherited, indulged in and expressed on account of these ancestral iniquities and having to do with the baal spirit, its programs and cohorts. I recognize that they are wrong, hurtful to myself, others and You Heavenly Father. Please forgive me.

I renounce, divorce and cut all ties with all ungodly relationships, all baal and baal-related spirits, and every seed implanted in me, my belief systems and body, now and forever more. I renounce, sever, divorce, and close all doors permanently to all ungodly sources, parties, and soul ties with former spouses, lovers and others that have been tied to me in the spirit on account of baal. I return all soul parts to them now.

Father God, I repent for surrendering ground to baal and all its cohorts and minions, including my city, state and country [name them]. I repent for all the ways my city, state and country have given over to these demonic powers and have been allowed to abide, reside and operate on our lands and against me and my family.

4. Plead Guilty.

Father God, for everything I have repented and renounced here, I plead guilty to remove all cases that satan and his demonic powers have held against me. I present the Blood of the Lamb of God, Jesus Christ Yeshua as atonement. I present the Voice of the Blood of Jesus Yeshua which speaks "paid in full" to clear these transgressions from my record and my bloodline.

Father God, I ask for redemption from the curse by the Blood of Jesus, and ask You to break all baal and baal-related curses, programs and agendas off of me and my family line now! Let the Blood of Jesus break all these curses now!

Lord God Adonai, let the speaking Blood of Jesus deliver me from every judgement against me, my lineage and genetics. Let them all be revoked now; every agenda, curse and access point.

Father God, I present your Word in Colossians 2:13-15 to release me from all baal and baal-related bondage: *"God made me alive together with Christ, having forgiven me all my sins, having canceled out the certificate of debt consisting of legal demands [which were in force] against me and which were hostile to me. And this certificate He has set aside and completely removed by nailing it to the cross. When He had disarmed the rulers and authorities [those supernatural forces of evil operating against me], He made a public example of them [exhibiting them as captives in His triumphal procession], having triumphed over them through the cross."*

Thank you LORD God, for bringing me triumph over baal once and for all!

Cleanse, Clear & Release.
LORD God, pour your healing balm of Gilead into my body, brain, mind, heart and soul, my conscience, my subconscious and unconscious minds, my memory bank and everywhere in me where programs, imprints, beliefs, traumas and traits having to do with baal and its accomplices have been operational, to dissolve them now; dissolve all damage and

distortions, and heal me. Purify and cleanse all of me and restore me to "factory settings", your design for me.

Father God, cleanse me now with your holy healing love. Convict me of any acts of atonement to do in this regard.

Let all stolen, damaged, scattered parts or fragments of my soul be fully healed with the Blood of Jesus and returned to me now.

1 John 4:4 tells me that I am from God and *"Greater is He who is in me than he (the adversary) who is in the world."* Heavenly Father, I recognize, honor and accept that your holiness in Christ Jesus dwells in me, that I am born of your seed of divinity, created in your image, and I commit to a new life in Christ Jesus. Thank you for transforming me through your mercy, grace and love.

~ *Pause in Silence to Receive God's Healing* ~

5. Reparations ~ Penance.

Dear Heavenly Father, please guide me to right reparations and/or penance for all the violations I have committed regarding the baal spirit and its accompanying character traits, habits, personality flaws and behaviors; as well as any reparations for any oaths, contracts and covenants on behalf of myself and my family.

. . .

Speak to me through your Holy Spirit. Convict me in mind and heart of right restitution to make through my actions, relationships, charity, teaching, sharing, giving, sacrifices, prayers and fasting.

6. Plead Your Case.

God, Righteous Judge, I am presenting my legal case through your legal document, which is your Word. Please receive your Word as the key to my freedom from bondage to the baal spirit and its cohorts. Father God, your Word declares the following:

YOU are the Creator of Earth.

- LORD God, your Word in 2 Kings 19:15 clearly states that: "*You are the God, **You alone,** of all the kingdoms of the earth. You have made heaven and earth.*"
- In Isaiah 45:12 You say: "*It is I who made the earth, and created man upon it. I stretched out the heavens with My hands and I ordained all their host.*"
- Your Word in Amos 4:13 clarifies: "*For behold, He who forms mountains and creates the wind and declares to man what are His thoughts, He who makes dawn into darkness and treads on the high places of the earth, the LORD God of hosts is His name.*"
- Father God, baal and his accomplices have damaged, distorted and disrespected your creations

of earth and humanity. They have manipulated our
bodies, weather, climate, food, seasons, even our
sexuality.

- They have genetically engineered our food supply
  and introduced genetic manipulation into humans
  and mammals. This is an abomination and blatant
  disrespect and violation of your creation and your
  Will!
- Furthermore, baal and his accomplices have tried to
  usurp your power, purposes and place as the One
  True God over all of humanity and your creation
  on earth.
- Father God, only You can have complete authority
  over baal. I stand before You and ask You to forbid
  this monstrosity from wreaking anymore havoc in
  my life and within my family. Have mercy on us
  LORD God.
- Release your mighty warring angels and justice
  angels to bind baal and his cohorts.
- Heal our lands and people of the genetic
  abominations. Restore them to your factory
  settings.

The Sanctity of Children.

- Your Word in Jeremiah 32:35 says: *"They built the
  high places [for worship] ... to make their sons and
  their daughters pass through the fire to [worship and
  honor] Moloch—which I had not commanded them
  nor had it entered My mind that they should do this
  repulsive thing."*

- Baal, moloch and baphomet have perverted childhood, children and sexuality to distort and destroy humanity, and your kingdom design and destiny for your sons and daughters here on earth. They are using child sacrifice to gain power, control and domination over humanity.
- Father God, no more! We do not consent! In Jesus name, put an end to this! Save the children! Bring the perpetrators to justice! Heal the soul of our people. Heal the children.
- Father God, as your Presence in the Ark of the Covenant knocked down dagon, pour out your power and might, and take out all of the baal temples, altars and forces in my life, family and community. Close his wicked portals with your Mighty Rushing Wind!

My Body is Your Temple.

- Lord God, your Word in 1 Corinthians 3:16-17 tells us: *"Do you not know and understand that you are the temple of God, and that the Spirit of God dwells [permanently] in you? If anyone destroys the temple of God [corrupting it with false doctrine], God will destroy the destroyer; for the temple of God is holy (sacred), and that is what you are."*
- Father God, baal works on so many fronts to assault and destroy my body temple with messages, foods and activities to deny and deprive my body of being in the purity and holiness You designed it to be. Defend and protect me God!

- Father God, according to your own Word in 1 Corinthians 3:17, destroy the destroyer of my body temple.
- Heal and restore my body temple now, as I commit to treating it with the reverence and respect it deserves.

YOU Lord God are My Protector & Liberator.

- Heavenly Father, *"Lead me to the rock that is higher than I [a rock that is too high to reach without your help], for You have been a shelter and a refuge for me, a strong tower against the enemy,"* according to your Word in Psalm 61:2-3.
- John 8:36 says: *"So if the Son makes you free, then you are unquestionably free."* I take hold of this freedom now!
- Father God, baal strives to strip me of your protection and instill fear and anxiety in me, when the Truth is that You are my fortress, protection and safety. YOU are my liberator. Set me free now I pray in Jesus' name.
- Father God, loose your holy fire into the baal strongholds, altars and portals over my life and my family to burn them to ashes now. Send your angel armies to remove these wicked strongholds now.

You Will Destroy Your Enemies.

- Lord God, your Word in Psalm 68:21 says: *"God certainly will shatter the heads of His enemies."*
- Father God, shatter the heads of baal and all his accomplices operating over my life and family!
- Destroy your baal enemies with your angel armies!

Your Plans to Prosper.

- Your Word in Jeremiah 29:11 promises: *"For I know the plans I have for you, plans to prosper you, to give you hope and a future."*
- Father God, hope deferred makes the heart sick. Restore to me all that baal has stolen – my blessings, hopes, morale, health, time, energy, resources and relationships.

Our Government Shall Rest Upon Your Shoulders.

- Father God, the earth is your creation and furthermore, your Word in Isaiah 9:6-7 clearly states that: *"The government shall be upon His shoulders, and His name shall be called Wonderful Counselor, Mighty God, Everlasting Father, Prince of Peace. There shall be no end to the increase of His government and of peace, [He shall rule] on the throne of David and over His kingdom, to establish*

it and to uphold it with justice and righteousness from that time forward and forevermore."
- Heavenly Father, baal and his accomplices continually strive to overthrow your Will and governance. He seeks to instill his perverse version of legality, legalism and governance with his wicked puppets. Bind them now Lord God!
- Father God, establish your throne of governance over my life and family, upheld with your justice and righteousness.

Father God, it is indisputably clear throughout your Word, which is YOUR record of law and covenants, that You have created me in *your* image for *your* purposes. It is clear that if this baal spirit and its accomplices are allowed to continue to control, steal or compromise any part of me and my life, that I will not be able to fulfill your Will and destiny for my life.

It is clear that if I am not granted these requests from your Court, I will not be able to fulfill your plans for me. Your Word in Galatians 6:7 proclaims: *"God is not mocked [He will not allow Himself to be ridiculed, nor treated with contempt nor allow His precepts to be scornfully set aside]."* Father God, do not let baal mock you!

7. Petitions.

Therefore, the judgements that I am requesting from your Court of Mercy and Grace are:

- Grant all of my petitions in the case I have presented to You here.
- Grant me a divorce decree from and a Divine Restraining Order against baal and all baal cohorts, minions, entities, operations, agendas, programs and systems from operating in my life, so that I will no longer be tormented by anything having to do with them.
- Grant me a Divine Restraining Order against baal and all his accomplices purposing to create disunity, disharmony and strife amongst me and my loved ones.
- Burn to ashes all seeds of the union between baal and asherah, and baal and anath. Let all the fruits of baal's unions with all demon gods be aborted and dead-on-arrival.
- Burn to ashes all the harvests of baal, asherah and anath. Lay waste to all their crops, fruits and seeds.
- Close all portals and destroy all altars and temples opened, created, utilized, inhabited, appropriated and exploited by baal and all his cohorts and minions, over me, my family and community.
- Loose the holds that satan, lucifer, baal and all their accomplices have had on my health, destiny and provisions.
- Release all supports and resources for me to fulfill my God destiny now.
- Restore to me seven-fold everything baal and his accomplices have stolen from me that has not been on account of my own actions and choices, according to your Word in Proverbs 6:31; that when the thief is caught, he must repay seven-fold

all that he has stolen. He has been caught
LORD God!

- Send your Retrieval Angels to collect what has
  been stolen from me so that my work and life may
  go on unhampered and I may completely fulfill my
  God destiny, as well as all collaborative work and
  destiny with others You have so destined and
  appointed for me.
- Yoke me fully, eternally and exclusively to YOU
  Heavenly Father; that nothing shall wedge
  between us ever again.

8. Wait on the Lord's Response.

This is a pause, allowing for stillness and silence to respect God's response to our petitions. This is cultivating an awareness and sensitivity to our relationship with God, just as we would communicate with someone sitting right in front of us.

9. Thanks and Gratitude.

[Let this be dedicated time to thank the Lord after all of your petitions. You may want to play or sing praise music, or other ways that you express thanks and praise.]

- Thank you God for granting my petitions!
- Thank you for your divine mercy, love and grace!
- Thank you LORD God for delivering me from
  these wicked demonic powers once and for all!
- To You alone be all the glory in Heaven and upon
  the earth forever and ever! AMEN!!!

NEXT STEPS

We have been emptying out a lot of programs, ancestral imprints and iniquities, and personality flaws and traits. We have peeled back to now heal soul wounds that have hindered our gifts and joy. Deliverance also includes healing from soul wounds that have bound and held us captive emotionally, relationally and spiritually.

In the next chapter, we offer healing for the soul. When soul wounds are healed, we can truly experience inner love, joy and peace. Let us be truly free from the inside out!

———

CHAPTER 15
HEALING SOUL WOUNDS

SOUL WOUNDS COME from major traumatic events that have happened either in our childhood or adulthood. It could be your or your parents' divorce, losing a child, molestation, abandonment or rejection by a parent or spouse. It could be something someone said to you that cut you to your core, effectively a word curse over you and your life. Some soul wounds are inherited through our bloodline. Love can heal our soul.

As Love Incarnate, Jesus can truly heal our soul wounds. His love wipes away the sting and the scars. He actually holds a special place in His heart for the brokenhearted and the downtrodden.

> *"The Lord is near to the brokenhearted*
> *and saves those who are crushed in spirit."*
> Psalm 34:18

Soul wounds keep us from the fullness of life that God designed us to express. They keep us from the fullness of love and loving, receiving and giving love. They keep us from the fullness of relationship with God and others, as well as with our own spirit.

SOUL WOUNDS KEEP US FROM FULLY LOVING.

Soul wounds become normalized because life grows over them, like ivy covering a brick house. We habituate and move on with our life. Nonetheless, they are there beneath the surface and they keep heartache running in the background of our life.

SOUL WOUNDS KEEP HEARTACHE RUNNING IN THE BACKGROUND OF OUR LIFE.

God wants us free. Jesus came to heal the broken-hearted, to bind up our wounds, to give us new life. We can be functioning in this world, yet have these soul wounds still nesting in the deepest part of our being, keeping us from the fullness of life.

Even if you don't think you need this prayer protocol, take the time to reflect and write down events, experiences and words of hurt, pain and trauma that you have incurred. Search your life and heart for any deeply wounding events, experiences and words. Write them down if that helps.

> *"The Spirit of the Lord GOD is upon me,*
> *Because the LORD anointed me*
> *To bring good news to the humble;*
> *He has sent me to bind up the brokenhearted,*
> *To proclaim release to captives and freedom to prisoners."*
> Isaiah 61:1

SOURCES AND CAUSES OF SOUL WOUNDS

Search your life and heart for any deeply wounding events, experiences, relationships, choices, actions and words. It's helpful to write down your insights and feelings. This can help in being able to identify patterns in your life experience.

Family and Early Childhood.

What are your earliest traumatic memories? Who was involved? How did that make you feel as a small child? What are your lasting impressions of those events or experiences? What emotions have you been carrying around from them?

. . .

Relationships: Romantic, Family, Friendships.

What have been your most significant relationships? Romantic or marriage, close friendships, close family ties, parents? List any where you incurred a traumatic or very emotionally damaging or upsetting experience. How exactly did they affect you? How did you change as a result of these difficult or traumatic or damaging relationship experiences? What unresolved or unexpressed feelings do you still have from them?

Major Life Events.

What major life events have shaped who you are? What traumatic events? How did they affect you? What changed in you as a result of that life event? How did it affect or change your personality, your emotions, your beliefs, your way of relating to others, your ability to trust? How did it wound you?

Spiritual or Religious Wounds.

Do you have any wounds or upsetting experiences from your spiritual or religious background? Write them down and include your feelings, perceptions and beliefs that arose from those experiences. How did these experiences change the way you view God or Jesus? How you view having a spiritual life? Your trust in others? Your trust in God?

Anything Else?

Is there anything else that has come up for you in the process of this self-reflection — other wounds to your heart and soul?

PRAYER TO HEAL SOUL WOUNDS

This is not a Courts of Heaven protocol, but a prayer petition to God to heal our soul wounds. Make sure to add your own personalized petitions from the worksheet in this chapter; this is just a template.

SPEAK THIS OUT LOUD.

. . .

Heal My Soul Wounds Lord Jesus.

Dear Abba, my Heavenly Father, I am ready for all of my deepest soul wounds to be healed. I do not even know all the ways these soul wounds have affected me and my life. I may not even be fully aware of all of them, but I come before You and Jesus today because I truly want to be healed and I am asking You to heal me now. I don't want to carry these soul wounds anymore.

Dear Lord Jesus, I place before You now all the events, experiences and words that have caused me pain, hurt and trauma throughout my life. [Name them to the Lord.]

I express to You now how they have hurt me, and what are my feelings and thoughts about them. [Share with God and Jesus your pain, your feelings and experiences regarding these traumas. Do not hold back. Do not hold back anger. Let it all out!]

I now realize that walking around with soul wounds for so long has caused me to believe these wounds are just a fact of life, a part of my nature, an appendage to my body, that I have just acclimated to, and have come to accept as my normal. I don't want this to be my normal anymore.

Dear Jesus Christ, You came to heal the broken-hearted. I now lay at your feet all of my brokenness, all of my soul pain and heartaches, my heartbreak, all of my hurts, traumas and disappointments; everything that I have buried in order to have a good and functioning life, yet these wounds still remain.

. . .

I don't want to carry them anymore. I want to be truly and fully free. I don't want anymore woundedness in my heart and soul. So I lay at your mercy feet all of my memories, sorrows and wounds I have just shared with You. I release to You all unforgiveness towards the people who have caused my pain and trauma. Lord Jesus, help me to fully forgive and let go once and for all. Help me to release all of my anger and bitterness.

Heavenly Father, I may have turned away from You or kept You at arm's length on account of my own traumas and woundedness, on account of being hurt and betrayed by people I love, even people in spiritual and other authority over me, such as my own parents. I may have even taken it out on You. I am truly sorry for that. I don't want these barriers between us anymore. I don't want to carry this trauma and hurt anymore. I don't want to hold this anger anymore. Please take this from me. I release it to you now. Jesus, please heal me now.

I forgive my parents, my family, my ancestors and all those who have hurt me and caused me trauma and woundedness. [You can name specific people.] I release any unforgiveness towards myself. I also forgive myself for my mistakes and transgressions and know that the Blood of Jesus has washed me clean and white as snow, according to Psalm 51:7, *"Purify me with hyssop, and I shall be clean; wash me, and I shall be whiter than snow."*

Heal Me by Your Word.
Dear Abba, my Heavenly Father, I receive your Word as

healing balm into my heart and soul; because You are pure Love and therefore your Word is Love. I receive it into every wound I have sustained and held on account of traumatic and deeply hurtful events, experiences and word curses.

Isaiah 53:4-6 comforts me: *"However, it was my sicknesses that He Himself bore, and my pain that He carried; yet I myself assumed that He had been afflicted, struck down by God, and humiliated. But He was pierced for my offenses, He was crushed for my wrongdoings; the punishment for my well-being was laid upon Him, and by His wounds I am now healed. All of us, like sheep, have gone astray, each of us has turned to his or her own way; but the Lord has caused my wrongdoing to fall on Him."* How profound Lord Jesus that You suffered in order to heal me! Thank you from the bottom of my heart. THIS is true love!

From Jeremiah 17:14 I cry out: *"Heal me, O Lord, and I will be healed; save me and I will be saved, for You are my praise."*

From Psalm 30:2-3 I say: *"Lord my God, I called to You for help, and You healed me. You, Lord, brought me up from the realm of the dead; You spared me from going down to the pit."* Thank you Jesus. Thank you Heavenly Father for answering my cry for help and healing me.

From Psalm 23:1-4 I declare that: *"The Lord is my shepherd, I shall not want. He makes me lie down in green pastures, He leads me beside quiet waters, He refreshes my soul. He leads me on the paths of righteousness for His name's sake. Even though I walk through the darkest valley, I will fear no evil, for You are with me; your rod and your staff, they comfort me."* Thank you Jesus, for being my comfort and my healer. Thank you for not forsaking me.

Thank you Lord God, that You have healed me, the brokenhearted, and bound up my wounds, according to Psalm 147:3.

Thank you Heavenly Father Abba, for giving me hope and comfort through Psalm 34:17-19 & 22 which I proclaim over myself: *"When I the righteous cry for help, the Lord hears and delivers me out of all my troubles. The Lord is near to the brokenhearted and saves the crushed in spirit. Many are the afflictions of the righteous, but the Lord delivers me out of them all. The Lord redeems the souls of His servants, and none of those who take refuge in Him will suffer for their guilt."* Thank you God, for delivering me out of all of my wounds and restoring my spirit. Thank you for redeeming my soul and being my refuge.

Heavenly Father, I receive the promises from your Word in Isaiah 40:29-31 which comfort me: *"He, the LORD, gives strength to the weary and increases the power of the weak. Even youths grow tired and weary, and young men stumble and fall; but those who hope in the Lord will renew their strength."* Thank you for renewing my strength my beloved Father.

. . .

I take hold of Jeremiah 3:22 which says: "*Return, all of you who have turned away from the Lord; He will heal you and make you faithful. You say, 'Yes, we are coming to the Lord because He is our God.'*" Yes Lord God, I am coming home to You now. I am coming home to You. Thank you for not giving up on me.

I Am Healed By the Empathy of Lord Jesus.

Dear Abba, my Heavenly Father, knowing that Lord Jesus also went through intense human suffering and therefore holds empathy and compassion for my suffering, helps me to receive His healing love. Jesus, I trust in You!

I am comforted by Hebrews 2:18 which says: "*For because He himself has suffered when tempted, He is able to help those who are being tempted.*"

I recognize that I *do not have a high priest who is unable to sympathize with my weaknesses, but one who in every respect has been tempted as I am, yet without sin,* according to Hebrews 4:15.

Knowing that Jesus also suffered yet triumphed encourages me: "*In the days of His flesh, Jesus offered up prayers and supplications, with loud cries and tears, to Him who was able to save him from death, and he was heard because of His reverence,*" Hebrews 5:7 affirms.

. . .

Hebrews 7:23-25 brings me hope, and <u>hope is a healing balm</u>: *"The former priests were many in number, because they were prevented by death from continuing in office, but Jesus holds His priesthood permanently, because He continues forever. Consequently, He is able to save to the uttermost those who draw near to God through him, since <u>He always lives to make intercession for them</u>."* Thank you Lord Jesus Christ, for interceding for me.

Dear Heavenly Father, I draw comfort knowing that Jesus always lives to make intercession for me, as I draw near to You. I am not alone on my healing journey. I receive now His intercession for my healing and deliverance. Thank you Lord Jesus.

The Former Things Pass Away.

Thank you Heavenly Father for making me a new creation, as the old things, wounds and traumas pass away, as 2 Corinthians 5:17 affirms: *"Therefore if anyone is in Christ, this person is a new creation; the old things passed away; behold, new things have come."* Thank you God for the new things to come, replacing my sorrows and wounds with hope and joy.

Thank you Lord Jesus that You *will wipe away every tear from my eyes, and death shall be no more, neither shall there be mourning, nor crying, nor pain anymore, for the former things have passed away*, according to Revelations 21:4. I embrace that the former things have passed away, as if they never happened. They are no longer a part of my identity. I embrace my true identity as pure love made in Your image.

. . .

Thank you Lord God, for wiping away the tears from my eyes. I rejoice that the former things have truly passed away and I am restored to wholeness in You, wholeness in Christ Jesus. I am truly a new creation in Christ Jesus, Love Incarnate. What profound power of true love!

Protect Me in Christ Jesus.

Dear Abba, your Living Word in John Chapter 17 reminds me that I am never alone, as I choose to be yoked to You, as I choose to be one with You. I am able to heal and grow stronger knowing that You will protect me in this world as I abide in You with Christ Jesus in me.

I take hold of Jesus' prayer to You in John 17:14-23 which says: *"I have given them your word and the world has hated them, for they are not of the world any more than I am of the world. My prayer is not that You take them out of the world but that You protect them from the evil one. They are not of the world, even as I am not of it. Sanctify them by the truth; your word is truth. As You sent me into the world, I have sent them into the world. For them I sanctify myself, that they too may be truly sanctified. My prayer is not for them alone. I pray also for those who will believe in me through their message, that all of them may be one, Father, just as You are in me and I am in You. May they also be in us so that the world may believe that You have sent me. I have given them the glory that You gave me, that they may be one as we are one— I in them and You in me—so that they may be brought to complete unity. Then the world will know that You sent me and have loved them even as You have loved me."*

.   .   .

Father God, I receive Your true and pure Love, as the unifying power that dissolves divisiveness, melts strife and triumphs over offenses; where I can meet others in the expanse of Your loving heart.

Heavenly Father, I receive your sanctification now. Sanctify me with your truth; your Word is truth. It is the healing balm for my soul. Let this sanctification make me a new creature in You, washed and cleansed of trauma and hurt, pain and humiliation, betrayal and loss. Thank you for restoring my hope. Thank you for renewing my life!

Heavenly Father, I take hold of Philippians 4:5-7 and declare, *The Lord is near. I shall not be anxious about anything, but in everything by prayer and pleading with thanksgiving let my requests be made known to God. And the peace of God, which surpasses all comprehension, will guard my heart and mind in Christ Jesus.*

Thank you Lord God, for guarding my heart and mind, for filling me with your peace, your Shalom, which is wholeness and a peace that surpasses all understanding from the flesh mind. Make your Shalom the operating system of my soul.

JESUS, MAKE YOUR SHALOM THE OPERATING SYSTEM OF MY SOUL.

. . .

My Recovery Springs Forth.
Dear Abba, Heavenly Father, I receive the promises from Isaiah 58:8 and declare: *Then my light will break out like the dawn, and my recovery will speedily spring forth; and my righteousness will go before me; the glory of the Lord will be my rear guard.*

Dear Lord God, I ask that You fill me with the fruits of your Spirit, according to Galatians 5:22: *love, joy, peace, patience, kindness, goodness, faithfulness.*

Dear Father God, pour out your healing balm of Gilead into my heart and soul, everywhere memories, imprints, beliefs, traumas, traits and habits having to do with traumatic and heartbreaking events and experiences have been engrained in me. Erase them now; erase all damage and trauma in me with your divine love, true love.

By Jesus' wounds, I have been healed and I receive this healing now. Let the Blood of Jesus heal me now. I receive by faith this healing in Jesus name. Thank you!

~ Pause in Silence to Receive God's Healing ~

MORE FOR OUR SOUL

This chapter has addressed healing our soul and soul wounds. In Chapter 19 we will sanctify our soul and in Chapter 20 we will provide remedies for repairing and strengthening our soul.

Sanctifying and strengthening our soul are essential for becoming inoculated against attacks from the kingdom of darkness and growing us in holiness which is the ocean of abiding peace and everlasting freedom .

———

PART THREE

INOCULATION, FORTIFICATION & SANCTIFICATION

CHAPTER 16

FILL WITH THE GOOD

"When an unclean spirit goes out of someone,
it roams through arid regions searching
for rest but, finding none, it says,
'I shall return to my home from which I came.'
But upon returning,
it finds it swept clean and put in order.
Then it goes and brings back seven other spirits
more wicked than itself who move in and dwell there,
and the last condition of that person
is worse than the first."
Luke 11:24-26

JESUS PROVIDES a guideline and a warning for deliverance in this passage. <u>It's not enough to say deliverance prayers to be free of problems.</u> The "house" in this passage from the Gospel of Luke is ourself. Jesus is telling His disciples that it is not enough to just cast out demons, because unless the inner part of the person has changed, the "empty house" will attract even more demons to it. Human flaws attract the demonic; godly virtues repel the demonic.

Human flaws attract and feed demonic powers. Godly virtues repel them.

Fill With the Good.

There is a fundamental tenet of healing and deliverance, that once there has been a removal of a negative element, it's important to then fill with the good. In this book of deliverance from demonic powers, we have been removing the presence and influence of key demonic power brokers. We have been shedding character traits and flaws that do not serve our highest best good, that feed and attract demonic powers.

Once we are delivered, we want to remain delivered. Once freedom is gained, we want to keep it. We do this by filling our house with the good, with God's holy presence, to strengthen our indwelling spirit. We fill with what will actually repel the demonic. This is why the Holy Spirit has structured these protocols the way they are.

Once we are delivered, we want to remain delivered.

As we've been repenting of and renouncing ungodly and unhealthy elements in ourself and in our life, we have utilized the purifying Word of God to edify us, to build us up and strengthen us from the inside out. Think of the Word, the Sacred Scriptures, as the new, strong foundation and building blocks for renovating our house.

We then re-furnish the rooms of our house with godly virtues. These virtues fill the space of our soul, heart and mind, i.e., our inner house, so that we are a mighty fortress and *"No weapon formed against us shall prosper."* Godly virtues are both the fruits of and fuel for our *SuperPower* prayers.

GODLY VIRTUES ARE THE FRUITS OF & FUEL FOR SUPERPOWER PRAYERS.

Virtues Become Our Inoculation.

Through these protocols and the five keys to purification, we have been cultivating foundational virtuous practices for our inoculation. These virtuous practices become the muscle that enable us to develop godly virtues. Godly virtues become our inoculation against the demonic.

GODLY VIRTUES BECOME OUR INOCULATION AGAINST THE DEMONIC.

. . .

This is because godly virtues are one with Divine Will, with God's Will and Heart. They repel the demonic because they are anathema, in utter opposition to, demonic operating systems and purposes. So this is a very practical reason for cultivating godly virtues: we are inoculating against demonic agendas. This brings spiritual health and freedom.

GODLY VIRTUES PRODUCE SPIRITUAL HEALTH & FREEDOM.

No Longer Slaves to Sin.

We have been crucifying, retiring our old self, in order to no longer be slaves to sin, no longer be bound and controlled by bad habits, traits and choices.

> "We know that our old self was crucified with him,
> so that our sinful body might be done away with,
> that we might no longer be in slavery to sin.
> For a dead person has been absolved from sin."
> Romans 6:6-7

So what comes next? After we have emptied out of the things that have been enslaving us and keeping us limited, then what?

What do we fill with? What do we become? What is our new identity and purpose?

Become an Instrument of Righteousness.

Apostle Paul explains this. We can actually become "instruments of righteousness". <u>We are no longer on the defense in life.</u> This is a profound shift. We walk as God's instruments, His ambassadors of good.

> *"Even so consider yourselves*
> *to be dead to sin,*
> *but alive to God in Christ Jesus.*
> *Therefore do not let sin reign in your mortal body*
> *so that you obey its lusts,*
> *and do not go on presenting*
> *the members of your body to sin*
> *as instruments of unrighteousness;*
> *but present yourselves to God*
> *as those alive from the dead,*
> *and your members*
> ***as instruments of righteousness to God.***
> *For sin shall not be master over you,*
> *for you are not under law but under grace."*
> Romans 6:11-14

"For sin shall not be master over you" — what greater freedom?

We have been walking as *"slaves to impurity"*, allowing demonic agendas to be master over us. No more! Now we choose to be *"slaves to righteousness."*

"I am speaking in human terms
because of the weakness of your nature.
For just as you presented the parts of your bodies
as slaves to impurity
and to lawlessness for lawlessness,
so now present them as
slaves to righteousness
for sanctification."
Romans 6:19

So through our purification, we become sanctified; that is, set apart. We are no longer part of the masses walking unconsciously through life, slaves to desires, programs and pop culture. We are awakening to the truth of who we are, as God created us to be. This awakening is strengthening and empowering.

"But now that you have been freed from sin
and have become slaves of God,
the benefit that you have leads to sanctification,
and its end is eternal life."
Romans 6:22

Purification and sanctification transform our house and establish it as a mighty fortress that demonic powers cannot shake and penetrate. It leads to eternal life. THIS is true freedom!

PURIFICATION & SANCTIFICATION MAKE US A MIGHTY FORTRESS.

Our House is Transformed: Eternal in the Heavens.

The marvel of this spiritual house of ours is that it is eternal! Again Saint Paul the Apostle describes our *"building from God"* in the following passage.

> *"For we know that if our earthly tent*
> *which is our house is torn down,*
> *we have a building from God,*
> *a house not made by hands,*
> *eternal in the heavens.*
> *For indeed, in this tent we groan,*
> *longing to be clothed*
> *with our dwelling from heaven,*
> *since in fact after putting it on,*
> *we will not be found naked."*
> 2 Corinthians 5:1-3

This last verse, *"we will not be found naked,"* refers to the nakedness of Adam and Eve that they experienced once they separated themselves from God. They were clothed in shame and the Law was then established to place guidelines in response to reckless human behavior that separated us from God.

. . .

Now the Law has been replaced with Grace, so nakedness has been replaced with heavenly clothing. This is the transformation and transmutation that is available to us! How profound!

Godly Ambition for Virtues.

"Therefore we also have as our ambition,
whether at home or absent,
to be pleasing to Him.
For we must all appear
before the judgment seat of Christ,
so that each one may receive compensation
for his deeds done through the body,
in accordance with what he has done,
whether good or bad."
2 Corinthians 5:9-10

So now we have another motivation for pursuing virtues: to be pleasing to God. Out of love for Him. Not out of some blind obedience, but out of love. Do it for love!

LOVE FOR GOD INSPIRES US TO GODLY VIRTUES.

Now may this passage that we have been using in our prayer protocols come more deeply alive in you; adapted here in first person. Declaring this aloud is empowering.

"And when I was dead in my wrongdoings
and the uncircumcision of my flesh,
He made me alive together with Him,
having forgiven me all my wrongdoings,
having canceled the certificate of debt consisting of
decrees against me, which was hostile to me;
and He has taken it out of the way,
having nailed it to the cross.
When He disarmed the rulers and authorities,
He made a public display of them,
having triumphed over them through Him."
Colossians 2:13-15

The Second Adam.

Remember that Jesus came as the progenitor for God's godly race, the restoration of our destiny *"made in His image"*. In this role He is called the Second Adam or the Last Adam.

"The first man, Adam, became a living person.
The last Adam was a life-giving spirit.
However, the spiritual is not first, but the natural;
then the spiritual.
The first man is from the earth, earthy;
the second man is from heaven."
1 Corinthians 15:45-47

The implications are that <u>Christ Jesus paved the way for us to</u>

return to being life-giving spirit, operating from an indwelling spirit operating system, enabled to "*do the greater works.*"

JESUS PAVED THE WAY FOR US

Jesus paved the way for us to be walking on earth spiritually reborn. He established our destiny following in His footsteps: "*Just as we have borne the image of the earthy, we will also bear the image of the heavenly,*" says 1 Corinthians 15:49.

WE "BEAR THE IMAGE OF THE HEAVENLY" THROUGH GODLY VIRTUES.

We "*bear the image of the heavenly*" through godly virtues. This is possible because Jesus came as a human man, Son of Man, to live out His ministry and perform miracles as a human. The Word encourages us, that we may live in a new operating system.

> "*Just as Christ was raised from the dead*
> *through the glory of the Father,*
> ***so we too may walk in newness of life.***"
> Romans 6:4

Jesus Has Our Back.

It may feel daunting to think of pursuing godly virtues, but that is the inclination of the flesh or ego-mind. There is so much richness to the Passion Gift that Jesus has given us. There are so many dimensions to it; one of which is that Jesus has our back in developing virtues and resisting the forces that seek to come against this goal.

> *"For since He Himself was tempted in that*
> *which He has suffered,*
> **He is able to come to the aid**
> **of those who are tempted."**
> Hebrews 2:18

In this regard, the sufferings that Jesus experienced in His Passion Gift actually paved the way for our being able to cultivate godly virtues in union with God's Heart. All roads lead back to God's Love. God's Will is the manifest expression of His Love for us, the guidelines and guide posts for how to fulfill our highest purpose in Him.

GOD'S WILL CONTAINS GUIDE POSTS FOR HOW TO FULFILL OUR LIFE PURPOSE.

Jesus' Sufferings Were Reparations for Our Flaws.

Jesus' sufferings were all very purposeful reparations for specific flaws in our humanity. These primordial flaws have been the portals through which demonic powers have attacked, influenced and controlled us in our fallen and wounded human state.

These core portals are through our soul, body, ego, character and will. The supreme antidote to the kingdom of darkness is love, God's love. Knowing this gives us a deeper understanding of and appreciation for God's supreme commandment:

> *"Love the Lord your God with all your heart*
> *and with all your soul and with all your mind*
> *and with all your strength."*
> Mark 12:30

When we love God with all of our heart, soul, mind and strength, we are closing up any portals from the demonic. We are repairing the breaches to our inner house. We are building ourselves up in the most holy of faith[1].

WHEN WE LOVE GOD WITH ALL OF OUR HEART, SOUL, MIND AND STRENGTH, WE CLOSE PORTALS FROM THE DEMONIC.

In the next chapters, we will learn how to close these portals and cultivate godly virtues in order to sustain our deliverance and deepen our inner joy and peace. We do this through sanctification, consecrating the elements of our free will to God.

SANCTIFICATION IS CONSECRATING OUR FREE WILL
TO GOD.

Sanctification is the foundation for inoculation and fortification against demonic powers. It is the cornerstone of true and abiding spiritual health and freedom.

———

CHAPTER 17
SANCTIFICATION
THE FOUNDATION FOR INOCULATION AND FORTIFICATION

WHAT IS SANCTIFICATION?

Sanctification is the state of being sanctified, which means to be set apart, designated as God's own. To sanctify involves a purification — a purification of body, mind, heart and soul. It is choosing to live in God's Will over personal will. It is choosing to release all that is not a part of God's plan and purposes and to live in His current of life.

SANCTIFICATION IS CHOOSING TO LIVE IN GOD'S CURRENT OF LIFE.

Sanctification brings inoculation against demonic influence. It does not mean there will never be an experience of the demonic or that demonic elements will never come against us, but that *"No weapon formed against us shall prosper."* This is fortification.

. . .

In Hebrew, the word "sanctify" is "*qâdash*" and shows up 175 times in the Holy Scriptures, which is indicative of its importance. "*Qâdash*" is variously translated as "sanctify", "consecrate", "be holy", "set apart" (to or for God). People, places, time and objects can be sanctified. God sanctifies, priests sanctify and people can sanctify themselves as well.

GOD HIMSELF IS SANCTIFIED AS HOLINESS

God is holiness itself. So when He exhorts us to be holy, sanctified, He is inviting us to himself, to a deeper intimacy and even union with Him.

> *"I am the Lord your God;*
> *consecrate yourselves and be holy,*
> *because I am holy."*
> Leviticus 11:44

SANCTIFICATION IS AN INVITATION TO UNION WITH GOD.

God himself is *qâdash* and we were created from him. We were created from holiness itself. How does this expand your understanding and revelation of your purpose and spiritual potential? How does this inspire you to reach higher? What might this stir in your heart? How willing are you to allow the implications of this truth to sink into your awareness and heart?

> *"Who is like You among the gods, Lord?*
> *Who is like You, majestic in holiness* (qâdash),
> *awesome in praises, working wonders?"*
> Exodus 15:11

Yoke Yourself to the Gold Standard.

God the Creator, source and author of Divine Love, is the gold standard of holiness. Not 'ascended masters' or gurus. Not demons or 'deities' of various spiritual traditions. Yoke yourself to the gold standard!

> *"There is no one holy like the Lord,*
> *indeed, there is no one besides You,*
> *nor is there any rock like our God."*
> 1 Samuel 2:2

This verse is part of "Hannah's Song". Hannah was barren but was given the miracle birth of a son, who became the great prophet Samuel. She not only consecrated her son to God, but gave him to the Lord when he was only two years old. What a sacrificial gift of love!

GOD SANCTIFIES

God sanctifies people. He does this when we choose to abide by

His teachings (Torah)[1], which are protections. They are protective fencing around our lives.

GOD'S TEACHINGS ARE PROTECTIVE FENCING AROUND OUR LIFE THAT LIBERATE US FROM THE EFFECTS & INFLUENCES OF DEMONIC POWERS.

God's ways are not to confine us, but to *liberate* us from the effects and confines of demonic powers. God sanctifies us to mark and keep us as His. This is a 'keep out' sign to demonic powers.

SANCTIFICATION IS A 'KEEP OUT' SIGN TO DEMONIC POWERS.

God's love is at the core of all of His teachings. They are not for the sake of control as we humans are programmed to understand; that is, ways to limit enjoyment of life. Choosing God's current of life puts us into alignment with His Heart, able to receive and experience more of His love, blessings and protection.

SANCTIFICATION IS CHOOSING GOD'S LOVE AS THE CURRENT OF LIFE.

. . .

"You must keep My Sabbaths; for this is a sign
between Me and you throughout your generations,
so that you may know that
I am the Lord who sanctifies you.
Therefore you are to keep the Sabbath,
for it is holy to you."
Exodus 31:13-14

God set apart, sanctified, one day a week called the Sabbath, to be a day of rest. A day of rest that says, 'I want you to enjoy resting in Me', to fill up on love, to enjoy stillness, to re-create and rejuvenate. If you understand that the Sabbath is a love letter to you personally, how does that change your view of it?

"Also I gave them My Sabbaths to be
a sign between Me and them,
so that they might know that I am the Lord
who sanctifies them."
Ezekiel 20:12

SANCTIFICATION IS A LOVE AGREEMENT BETWEEN YOU AND GOD.

WE CAN SANCTIFY OURSELVES

The Sacred Scriptures tells us that we can also sanctify ourselves. One of the most repeated exhortations from God is to *"Be ye holy as I AM holy."*[2] Apostle Peter shares God's exhortation to holiness, with an add-on, to be holy in all that we do.

"But, as he who called you is holy,
be holy yourselves in every aspect of your conduct,
for it is written,
'Be holy because I [am] holy.'"
1 Peter 1:15-16

This exhortation tells us:

- We have *free will* to be holy (sanctified, set apart). It is a personal choice.
- We have *the ability* to become sanctified.
- We *take an active part* in becoming sanctified.
- We *become more like* our Heavenly Father in whose image we were made, when we choose to be sanctified.

BENEFITS TO SANCTIFICATION

Sanctification brings blessings including miracles, provision and protection.

Sanctification Precedes Blessings from God.

There are various instances in the Scriptures where the people are invited to consecrate themselves prior to a blessing.

"Then Joshua said to the people,
'Consecrate yourselves,
for tomorrow the Lord will do miracles among you.'"
Joshua 3:5

Sanctification Brings Protection from God.

The following passage from Joshua, the great warrior of God, demonstrates the protective element to consecration.

"I will not be with you anymore
unless you eliminate from your midst
the things designated for destruction.
Stand up! Consecrate the people and say,
Consecrate yourselves for tomorrow,
because the Lord, the God of Israel, has said this:
'There are things designated
for destruction in your midst, Israel.
You cannot stand against your enemies until you have removed
the designated things from your midst.'"
Joshua 7:12-13

God is telling us:

- Remove the detrimental elements from your midst.
- Consecrate (sanctify) yourselves.

- You cannot be victorious against your enemies (demonic powers) until you have removed (been delivered of) detrimental elements.

This is what we have been doing in this book.

PRAYERS FOR SANCTIFICATION

Psalm 119 offers some beautiful prayers as proclamations for sanctification. A precursor to the Beatitudes, it presents and celebrates the Word as a means to holiness. It is structured in 22 stanzas corresponding to each of the 22 letters of the Hebrew alphabet, with each letter expressing a way of connection between God and us.[3] Here are some select verses from Psalm 119 to begin our sanctification. The translation here uses "Law" where you can also use "teachings."

I proclaim:

- *"I will keep your statutes; do not utterly abandon me!"* Psalm 119:8
- *"I will meditate on your precepts and regard your ways."* Psalm 119:15
- *"Open my eyes, that I may behold wonderful things from your Law."* Psalm 119:18
- *"Remove the false way from me, and graciously grant me your Law."* Psalm 119:29
- *"Incline my heart to your testimonies, and not to dishonest gain."* 119:36
- *"I sought your favor with all my heart; be gracious to me according to your word."* Psalm 119:58

- *"Teach me good discernment and knowledge, for I believe in your commandments."* Psalm 119:66
- *"May your compassion come to me so that I may live, for your Law is my delight."* Psalm 119:77
- *"Revive me according to your faithfulness, so that I may keep the testimony of your mouth."* Psalm 119:88
- *"I am yours, save me; for I have sought your precepts."* Psalm 119:94
- *"How sweet are your words to my taste! Yes, sweeter than honey to my mouth!"* Psalm 119:103
- *"I have inclined my heart to perform your statutes forever, even to the end."* Psalm 119:112
- *"Redeem me from oppression by man, so that I may keep your precepts."* Psalm 119:134
- *"Let my soul live that it may praise You, and let your ordinances help me."* Psalm 119:175

Now let's sanctify our soul, body, ego, character and will for inoculation and fortification against demonic powers! True and abiding health and freedom are realized through inner strength, peace and joy of the LORD.

———

CHAPTER 18

5 AGONIES, 5 REPAIRS

JESUS EXPERIENCED five major sufferings in His Passion Gift for humanity. These were all reparations for the primordial sins of humanity: sins or breaches against our soul, our body, our ego, our character and our will.

He also incurred five major wounds: a nail wound in each hand and each foot, and a spear wound in His side.

Jesus became the template for repairing our own core wounds. We follow the same redemption path that Christ took: five fundamental breaches, five fundamental repairs or healings.

JESUS BECAME THE TEMPLATE FOR REPAIRING OUR OWN CORE WOUNDS.

---

5 AGONIES, 5 REPAIRS

Jesus began His Passion Gift for humanity on the night of Passover, after the meal with His disciples. It completed upon His death on the Cross the next day. There were five distinct sufferings that Jesus incurred as reparations for the sins of humanity.

1. SOUL: *AGONY IN THE GARDEN*

Jesus began His reparations for humanity the night before His crucifixion in the Garden of Gethsemane.[1] The Apostle Luke, who was a medical doctor, described Jesus as sweating blood[2], as He became flooded with anxiety and soul pain as reparations for the sins against our own soul.

> *"Then Jesus came with them*
> *to a place called Gethsemane,*
> *and he said to his disciples,*
> *'Sit here while I go over there and pray.'*
> *He took along Peter and the two sons of Zebedee,[3]*
> *and began to feel sorrow and distress.*
> *Then he said to them,*
> **'My soul is sorrowful even to death***.*
> *Remain here and keep watch with me.'"*
> Matthew 26:36-38

The Torah of the Old Testament speaks of how the blood sacrifice makes atonement for our soul.

"For the life of the flesh is in the blood,
and I have given it to you on the altar
to make atonement for your souls;
for it is the blood by reason of the life
that makes atonement."
Leviticus 17:11

The antidote:

- Healing our soul wounds.
- Yoking to the Holy Spirit, the opposite of grieving or violating the Holy Spirit and God's Heart. Yoking to the Holy Spirit syncs our soul to its highest purpose and capacity; it calibrates our soul to pure Spirit.
- Cultivating the three holy virtues of faith, hope and love to strengthen and sanctify our soul, and come into union with God and Christ Jesus.

———

2. BODY: *SCOURGED AT THE PILLAR*

Jesus was flogged, "scourged at the pillar", as reparations for the sins of our flesh. It is said that the beating was so vicious that His skin was falling off of Him.

"Then Pilate took Jesus and had Him scourged."
John 19:1

This was in fulfillment of the prophecy in Isaiah 53:5, *"But He was wounded for our transgressions, He was crushed for our wickedness [our sin, our injustice, our wrongdoing]; the punishment [required] for our well-being fell on Him, and by His stripes (wounds) we are healed."* The "stripes" are the bloody whip marks on His body.

By receiving Jesus' bodily sacrifice, our own body becomes transformed.

*"Or do you not know that **your body**
is a temple of the Holy Spirit within you,
whom you have from God,
and that you are not your own?"*
1 Corinthians 6:19

The antidote:

- Cultivating the virtue of Temperance to take full dominion over our own body and to bring it into fulfillment as God's temple. The opposite of gluttony, lust, addictions and sloth.
- Cultivate other godly virtues which support us in respecting and treating our body as a temple of the Holy Spirit.

———

3. EGO: *CROWN OF THORNS*

To mock His spiritual kingship, the Romans placed a viciously painful crown of thorns on Jesus' head, and pressed it into His skull for maximum pain. This was an intentional act of denigration to humiliate him. This suffering was reparations for the sins of our ego, especially pride.

> *"And they stripped Him and put a red cloak on Him.*
> *And after twisting together a crown of thorns,*
> *they put it on His head,*
> *and put a reed in His right hand;*
> *and they knelt down before Him **and mocked Him**, saying,*
> *'Hail, King of the Jews!'*
> *And they spit on Him,*
> *and took the reed and beat Him on the head.*
> *And after they had mocked Him,*
> *they took the cloak off Him*
> *and put His own garments back on Him,*
> *and led Him away to crucify Him."*
> Matthew 27:28-31

The antidote:

- Cultivating the supreme virtue of humility.
- Cultivating godly virtues that are the opposite of arrogance, pride, hubris, vanity, narcissism and self-centeredness; such as selflessness, generosity, consideration.

———

4. CHARACTER: *CARRYING HIS OWN CROSS*

Jesus had foretold the need for His brethren to "carry their own cross" (metaphorically). This is an exhortation to deny personal desires and agendas, a call to higher character. He is also telling them that in this life they will have difficulties and trials[4], that there is a "dying to self" that is part of a relationship with Him and necessary for fulfilling our own ultimate spiritual destiny, which is union with God.

> *"Then Jesus told His disciples,*
> *'If anyone would come after me,*
> **let him deny himself**
> **and take up his cross and follow me.**
> *For whoever would save his life will lose it,*
> *but whoever loses his life for my sake will find it.*
> *For what will it profit a man*
> *if he gains the whole world and forfeits his soul?*
> *Or what shall a man give in return for his soul?'"*
> Matthew 16:24-26

After having sustained an excruciating shoulder injury and a vicious beating whereby His skin was falling off, Jesus was forced to carry His own cross up to Mount Calvary[5] for His crucifixion. This was a long uphill trek.

The antidote:

- Cultivating noble character virtues including prudence, fortitude, forbearance, self-denial and carrying your cross (tests, trials and tribulations) with dignity.
- Cultivating godly virtues that are the opposite of selfishness, narcissism, a critical or complaining spirit, a religious spirit, a controlling spirit, guile, arrogance, manipulation, craftiness, possessing hidden or selfish agendas.

———

5. WILL: *CRUCIFIXION DEATH*

In this final act of suffering a brutally painful death, Jesus expressed the perfection of personal will married to God's Will through the ultimate virtue: offering up his life for the greater good. As He exhorted in John 15:13: *"Greater love has no one than this, that a person will lay down his life for his friends."*

"After this, Jesus,
knowing that all things
had already been accomplished,
in order that the Scripture would be fulfilled, said,
'I am thirsty.'
A jar full of sour wine was standing there;
so they put a sponge full of the sour wine on a
branch of hyssop and brought it up to His mouth.
Therefore when Jesus had received the sour wine,
He said, 'It is finished!'
And He bowed His head and gave up His spirit."
John 19:28-30

. . .

The antidote:

- Dying to self, individualism, ego-centeredness.
- Living God's Will; living in God the Father's Heart.
- Cultivating the virtues of selflessness and charity (love of God).
- Cultivating godly virtues that are the opposite of willfulness, rebelliousness, pridefulness, hubris, stubbornness, narcissism, self-centeredness, selfishness, blind or personal ambition.

Now let's sanctify our soul in order to close a fundamental portal to the demonic and establish inner peace and freedom.

———

CHAPTER 19

SANCTIFYING THE SOUL

WHAT IS SOUL?

There are differing opinions and beliefs as to what is the definition of soul. In many Christian circles, "soul" is defined as mind, will and emotions. However, if this were true, the supreme Commandment would not be correct.

> *"Love the Lord your God with all your heart*
> *and with all your soul and with all your mind*
> *and with all your strength."*
> Mark 12:30

If mind is part of soul, then the Torah[1] would not have separated out the two entities. Mind is listed separately from soul. Therefore, <u>mind is not soul.</u> Soul is our spiritual nature. Soul is the spiritual component of a human being. The mind or intellect are *faculties* of the soul; but are not the soul any more than a tire is a car.

.   .   .

Soul is the spiritual component of a human being.

The soul is in relationship with the mind, will and emotions but not merely the compilation of the three. It's reasonable to propose that this limited and erroneous understanding and definition of soul can limit the spiritual experiences and growth of people who prescribe to it.

Since we were created in God's image and God IS Spirit, then our core essence is spirit. Soul is the spiritual principle of a human being. Here is a rich definition of soul:

> "The spiritual principle of human beings. The soul is the subject of human consciousness and freedom; soul and body together form one unique human nature. Each human soul is individual and immortal, immediately created by God. The soul does not die with the body, from which it is separated by death, and with which it will be reunited in the final resurrection." [2]

This understanding of soul is found in the Sacred Scriptures.

*"And do not be afraid of those who kill the body
but are unable to kill the soul;
but rather fear him who is able to
destroy both soul and body in hell."*
Matthew 10:28

With this in mind, we can understand more clearly how Jesus' agony in the Garden of Gethsemane the night before His crucifixion was the beginning of His reparations for humanity. It began with reparations for humanity's sins against their soul. How do we damage our own soul?

HOW WE CAN DAMAGE OUR SOUL

There are many ways we can damage our own soul.

- By going against what God has purposed for us.
- By going against God's Will and teachings, which are the positive ordering and expression of life.
- By rejecting His love and rejecting a relationship with Him.
- By choosing activities, relationships and behaviors that are detrimental to us.
- By neglecting our soul, our true spiritual nature and good.
- By living opposed to our true nature.

LIVING OPPOSED TO OUR TRUE NATURE DAMAGES OUR SOUL.

Their Soul Rejected My Statutes.[3]

God describes the ramifications of choosing to cut off our soul from His Heart and Will: *"If, instead, you reject My statutes, and if your soul loathes My ordinances so as not to carry out all My commandments, but rather to break My covenant ... I will set My face against you so that you will be defeated before your enemies; and those who hate you will rule over you, and you will flee when no one is pursuing you.* Leviticus 26:15 & 17

Rejecting the Holy Spirit.

Another way we damage, transgress or violate our soul is by rejecting the Holy Spirit, which is God's Spirit released to the world as the agency of His love and ways. When we block, refuse, reject God's Spirit, we reject His Heart and His love. We have blocked the source of love itself. We addressed this in Chapter 15, "Healing Soul Wounds."

When our soul is synced with God's Spirit, we are living God's purpose for our life; we are living in Truth. To seal and mark our soul for God, to sanctify our soul, we repair and strengthen our soul.

> *"Create in me a clean heart, God,*
> *And renew a steadfast spirit within me.*
> *Do not cast me away from Your presence,*
> *And do not take Your Holy Spirit from me."*
> Psalm 51:10-11

> A CLEAN HEART IS THE DOORWAY TO A TRUE RELA-
> TIONSHIP WITH THE HOLY SPIRIT & HAVING A SANC-
> TIFIED SOUL.

SANCTIFYING THE SOUL

To sanctify our soul is to restore it to God's blueprint, to purify it. It is to exercise our free will to have our soul at one with God's Spirit, to allow it to be holy as God is holy. It accompanies the healing of our soul. We see this expressed in the following Scripture.

> *"If you walk in My statutes and*
> *keep My commandments and [obediently] do them,*
> *I will make My dwelling among you,*
> *and My soul will not reject*
> *nor separate itself from you."*
> Leviticus 26:3 & 11 AMP[4]

Separation from God's soul creates tears and wounds in our own soul. Connection to God's Heart and soul is through the agency of the Holy Spirit.

> CONNECTION TO GOD'S HEART IS THROUGH THE
> AGENCY OF THE HOLY SPIRIT.

· · ·

All Your Heart and All Your Soul.

At least 20 times throughout the Sacred Scriptures is the phrase *"all my soul"* or *"all your soul."* Sanctification, setting apart dedicated to, is an all-in proposition. It is not half-hearted. But the payoff is incredible! God CAN actually remove the desire to sin from your heart. I can attest to this.

"And the Lord your God will circumcise your heart
and the hearts of your descendants [that is,
He will remove the desire to sin from your heart],
so that you will love the Lord your God
with all your heart and all your soul,
so that you may live
[as a recipient of His blessing]."
Deuteronomy 20:36

Because the Holy Spirit is the agency for connecting to God's Heart, the following protocol is designed to repair and restore our relationship with the Holy Spirit; thereby bringing our soul into oneness with God and sanctifying our soul.

HEALING OUR RELATIONSHIP WITH THE HOLY SPIRIT

[Speak this prayer protocol out loud for maximum efficacy.]

1. Preparation.

Reflect on ways that you have not accepted the agency of

God's love for you; times that you did not follow God's plan; ways that you knowingly or unknowingly went against God's moral code; times that you rejected or disrespected Him. You may want to write these down so as to remember to include them in this prayer.

2. Going Before God's Throne of Mercy and Grace.

Lord God Heavenly Father, I come before your Court of Mercy and Grace and ask that the courts be seated and the books be opened, according to Daniel 7:10. I come before You to repent for all of my violations to your Holy Spirit, which have hurt my own soul. I am truly sorry for how I have mistreated your precious gift, el Ruach HaKodesh, the Holy Spirit.

Lord God, I put on the robe of Jesus Christ's righteousness according to Isaiah 61 and I loose the Blood of Jesus over myself to enter into your Court sanctified, in praise and thanksgiving, in love and gratitude. I recognize and accept that You Lord God, have also clothed me with the garments of deliverance and covered me with the robe of acts of loving kindness according to your Word in Isaiah 61:10.

It is now clear to me how the precious gift of your Holy Spirit has been mistreated, misunderstood, disrespected, used and dishonored. I now see how these violations against the Holy Spirit are at the core of violations against my own soul and even spiritual sickness. I see how sanctifying my soul is connected to Your gift of the Holy Spirit, as 1 Thessalonians 4:7-8 shares:

"For God has not called us for impurity, but in sanctification. Therefore, the one who rejects this is not rejecting man, but the God who gives His Holy Spirit to you."

Dear Heavenly Father, please receive my sincere repentance for all the ways I have grieved the Holy Spirit; have mistreated, ignored, misunderstood, used, disrespected or dishonored the Holy Spirit. He is your precious gift to me from your heart to mine, and should be deeply cherished and guarded.

3. Renounce & Repent.

[Some of these may or may not apply to you. Only do what resonates and feels comfortable to you and add your own prayers as well.]

Lord God, I come in the name of Jesus Christ to sincerely repent and apologize for all the ways I have committed violations against your Holy Spirit. Now that my eyes are open and the veils are falling from my eyes and heart, I see just how pervasive are these violations. They are even baked into our culture. God forgive me.

I understand that *repent* means to turn away from, to change and transform my mind and way of living. It is a commitment to cease and turn away from activities and habits that are detrimental to my spirit which was made in your image.

. . .

I repent for all the times and ways You offered your helping hand through your Holy Spirit, but I rejected it and chose my own ways to my detriment. I repent for all the times and ways You brought me your offering of help, warning and protection, but I did not heed, I did not listen. I repent for all the times and ways I did not give time to You Lord God, and to having a relationship with You.

I repent for all the times and ways I sought truth, inspiration and understanding from the wrong sources and not from the source of truth which is your Holy Spirit. I repent for relying on people with their subjective opinions, beliefs and agendas, rather than taking the time and care to go into stillness and hear from your Holy Spirit. I repent for being attached to and in hubris with my own opinions and beliefs, rather than seeking to know Your Heart.

I renounce and repent for treating the Holy Spirit like a vending machine, to get the fruits of the spirit, like the gift of prophecy. The Holy Spirit is not a thing. He is not a means to a personal, self-serving end. I repent for seeking the fruits and gifts of the Holy Spirit, whilst bypassing actually cultivating a true relationship WITH your Holy Spirit. God please forgive me. I also repent for taking credit for things — revelations, foresight and ideas that actually came from the Holy Spirit.

Lord God, I repent for not believing, for denying and/or for forgetting that there IS a witness to everything I say and do in my life, and that is your Holy Spirit. When I lie to someone, I am lying to You. When I mistreat *"the least of Jesus' brothers, that I do unto Him"*. I repent for not seeing and honoring the sacredness in others, thereby dishonoring their indwelling spirit.

Ananias and Sapphira lost their lives because they lied to Peter. It was You that they actually lied to, because Peter was filled with the Holy Spirit. It was especially grievous because *"the company of believers was of one heart and soul."* I now understand from this story how vital it is to keep a clean and honest heart. I now understand that this is actually the doorway into a true relationship with the Holy Spirit. I repent for all the ways I have tested the Holy Spirit, believing I could get away with it.

Father God, I am truly sorry for all the times and ways that I rejected your love, that I rejected your guiding hand on my life and chose my own lesser and often reckless ways. I repent for not respecting and honoring my own soul, which is a precious gift from You.

[Feel free to add your own personalized prayers of repentance.]

4. Plead Guilty.

Dear Heavenly Father, for everything I have repented and renounced here, I plead guilty. I present the Blood of the Lamb of God, Jesus Christ, as atonement.

Lord God, I ask for redemption from the curse, by the Blood of Jesus, that according to Colossians 2:13-15, every case and ordinance against me has been nailed to the cross with the shed Blood of Jesus Christ Yeshua.

5. Reparations ~ Penance.

Dear Heavenly Father, please guide me to right penance and reparations for all the violations I have committed against the Holy Spirit and my own soul.

Convict me in mind and heart of right reparations to make through my actions, relationships, charity, teaching, sharing, giving, sacrifices, prayers and fasting.

6. Petitions.

Dear Father God, I want to cultivate a truly holy relationship with your Holy Spirit. In so doing, strengthen and sanctify my own heart and soul, seal them against demonic attacks, making them a worthy abode for the indwelling spirit.

These petitions are based upon your Word, which is the legal document of your Covenants with me.

The Holy Spirit Enters Through the Heart.

Dear Heavenly Father, your Word in Galatians 4:6 makes it clear You send your Spirit into our hearts — not our minds, tongues or ego: "*Because you are sons, God has sent forth the Spirit of His Son into our hearts, crying, 'Abba! Father!'*"

. . .

Dear Abba Father God, I now comprehend that one of the greatest ways I have sinned against the Holy Spirit is by not having a clean heart, a humble and contrite spirit to enter into a true and pure relationship with the Him. Truly, a clean, pure and kind heart are hallmarks of being genuinely baptized in the Holy Spirit, not merely speaking in tongues or giving prophetic utterances.

Indeed, Paul warned us in 1 Corinthians 13:1-2: *"If I speak in the tongues of men or of angels, but do not have love, I am only a resounding gong or a clanging cymbal. If I have the gift of prophecy and can fathom all mysteries and all knowledge, and if I have a faith that can move mountains, **but do not have love**, I am nothing."*

So without love in our hearts, we are nothing. Apostle Paul teaches in Romans 5:5 that God's love is actually poured into our hearts through the Holy Spirit Himself. *"And hope does not put us to shame, because God's love has been poured out into our hearts through the Holy Spirit, who has been given to us."*

Now I understand that a loving and kind heart are home to the Holy Spirit. Conversely, a stoney heart cannot house the Spirit of Holiness. It's always been about Love.

A LOVING AND KIND HEART ARE HOME TO THE HOLY SPIRIT.

. . .

Therefore Heavenly Father, I open my heart to your Holy Spirit. I give it full permission to take up residence in my heart and soul; to help me to love as You love, to see others as You see them, to possess and express patience, kindness, compassion, forgiveness and mercy as You do.

Make of Me a Clean Heart.

Hebrews 10:14-17 teaches that the Holy Spirit testifies to our sanctification in Christ Jesus: *"For He has perfected forever, in one offering, those who are being sanctified. And the Holy Spirit is testifying to us: for after it He said, 'This is the covenant which I shall make with them after these days, says the Lord: putting My Teachings upon their hearts and I shall write them upon their minds and I shall never, ever remember their sins and their iniquities.'"*

Heavenly Father, make of me a clean heart, according to Ezekiel 36:25-27: *"Cleanse me O Lord, give me a new heart and put a new Spirit within me and take away the stony heart from my flesh and give me a heart of flesh. Put your Spirit within me and cause me to walk in your statutes that I will keep and do your judgments."* I choose this because I now know that your love covers me and sustains me.

Give me anew your Spirit in my heart as a pledge, according to 2 Corinthians 1:21-22 which says: *"Who also sealed us and gave us the Spirit in our hearts as a pledge."*

. . .

"Create in me a clean heart, O God; and renew a right spirit within me. Cast me not away from thy presence; and take not thy holy spirit from me," according to Psalm 51:10-11.

The Holy Spirit Guides Me Into All Truth.

Truly Lord God, your Spirit has always been with us. It *"hovered over the deep"* in Genesis. King David spoke of Him in Psalm 51:13: *"Cast me not away from your presence and take not your Holy Spirit from me."*

Yet something changed with the advent of the New Covenant. You brought us the ability to have an intimate relationship with the Holy Spirit like never before. Now He has been made available to all of us, regardless of stature or status. This is what we have taken for granted. God please forgive me. I now realize that <u>the agency of the Holy Spirit helps my soul to connect with You</u> more deeply, and therefore, become sanctified.

John 15:26-27 describes the new, personal access to the Holy Spirit that accompanies the New Covenant: *"When the Advocate comes, whom I will send to you from the Father—the Spirit of Truth who goes out from the Father—he will testify about me. And you also must testify, for you have been with me from the beginning."* Thank you Lord God, for this profound gift of 'equal access' under the law of the New Covenant. This is the true blessing of your Holy Spirit, that <u>my own soul may grow and strengthen through a relationship with your Holy Spirit.</u>

. . .

I proclaim John 16:13-14 which describes this new experience of the Holy Spirit that accompanies the New Covenant: *But when He, the Spirit of Truth, comes, He will guide me into all the truth. He will not speak on his own; He will speak only what He hears, and He will tell me what is yet to come. He will glorify Lord Jesus because it is from him that He will receive what He will make known to me.* I now understand that <u>through the agency of the Holy Spirit, I can receive profound spiritual revelations and understanding that mature my soul</u> and bring me into deeper union with You Lord God.

Father God, make me an instrument of your Holy Spirit, that all of my thoughts, words, actions and deeds are truly one with your Spirit, your Holy Spirit. Let your Spirit guide me into all truth; so that in that truth I shall have abiding love, joy peace, strength and freedom.

Fruits of the Holy Spirit.

Dear Heavenly Father, help me to attain the fruits of the Spirit, which are actually virtues of noble character. I now understand that truly noble character must be on the foundation and soil of a clean and pure heart, that truly loves as Jesus loves, as You love us, to honor His commandment to *"love one another as I have loved you."*

Help me Lord God, to cultivate all the gifts of the Spirit, according to Galatians 5:22-23: *"But the fruit of the Spirit is love, joy, peace, patience, kindness, goodness, faithfulness, gentleness, self-control; against such things there is no law."*

. . .

I now understand Father God, that **living** the greatest Commandment is the entryway into oneness with the Holy Spirit, and therefore, sanctification of my soul. As Jesus exhorted in Luke 10:27: *"You shall love the Lord your God with all your heart, and with all your soul, and with all your strength, and with all your mind; and your neighbor as yourself."* Help me Heavenly Father, to love the way that You do. Help me Lord Jesus, to love the way that You do.

True Circumcision.

Dear Father God, please circumcise my soul, my heart, my ego and my mind; meaning, please remove anything that stands in the way of a pure relationship with You and the Holy Spirit. As Philippians 3:3 says: *"For we are the true circumcision, who worship in the Spirit of God and glory in Christ Jesus and put no confidence in the flesh."*

Heavenly Father, I give over my fleshly confidence, my confidence in my flesh mind and ego, to make room for living truth in the Holy Spirit, who leads me into ALL truth.

Circumcision requires surrender. Surrender requires humility. Humility requires recognizing my own weaknesses. Now I see how your Spirit can help me in my walk to deeper circumcision; I am not alone.

I take hold of Romans 8:26-27: *"In the same way the Spirit also helps my weakness; for I do not know how to pray as I should, but the Spirit Himself intercedes for me with groanings too deep*

*for words; and He who searches the hearts knows what the mind
of the Spirit is, because He intercedes for the saints according to
the will of God."*

Search my heart and soul Holy Spirit. Intercede for me Holy
Spirit. I trust you and want to be one with You.

God I Trust in Thee.

Dear Heavenly Father, I now realize that only to the extent
that I trust in You, do I allow the Holy Spirit into my own
heart, soul and life. This is part of true faith. I commit to
Proverbs 3:5-6 and declare: *I trust in the Lord with all my heart
and shall not lean on my own understanding. In all my ways I
will acknowledge Him, and He will make my paths straight.*

I proclaim Psalm 62:8: *I shall trust in You Lord God at all times;
I shall pour out my heart before You; You Lord God, are a refuge
for me. Selah.*

Lord God, *I draw near with a sincere heart in full assurance of
faith, having my heart sprinkled clean from an evil conscience
and my body washed with pure water,* according to Hebrews
10:22.

We Are All David.

Psalm 51 is a plaintive cry from King David after he was
severely reprimanded by the Prophet Nathan for having the
husband of his lover Bathsheeba intentionally killed on the

battlefield. After the horror of the ramifications of his crime begins to sink in, David is filled with remorse. He cries out to God, repenting for his wicked sin. He pleads with God not to take the Holy Spirit from him.

This means David has known and been in a relationship with the Holy Spirit. He recognizes the value of the Holy Spirit in his life. He also asks God to renew his own spirit.

Lord God, truly we are ALL David, sinning and believing we could get away with it. We are ALL David seeking forgiveness, mercy and reconciliation. Please receive my petitions to bring healing and restoration to my soul; and to sanctify my soul to You.

Verse 6 says: *"Behold, You desire truth in the innermost being, and in the hidden part [of my heart] You will make me know wisdom.*

I petition: Dear Lord God, I give over to You everything in me that is not truth, not from or a part of your truth. As I surrender this to You, fill me with your wisdom, your truth and your Spirit of Truth.

Verse 7 says: *"Purify me with hyssop, and I will be clean; wash me, and I will be whiter than snow."*

I petition: Dear Lord God, cleanse my heart and soul, my mind and my thoughts. Sanctify me Lord God. Make me white as snow in purity, for this is true consecration to You.

. . .

Verse 8 says: *"Make me hear joy and gladness and be satisfied; let the bones which You have broken rejoice."*

I petition: Dear Lord God, as I surrender all of me to You, I make room for peace and joy of the Lord.

Verse 9 says: *"Hide your face from my sins and blot out all my iniquities."*

I petition: Dear Lord God, thank you for blotting out my sins as I sincerely repent for my mistakes and transgressions, for my weakness of flesh and mind, for transgressions against my soul.

Verse 10 says: *"Create in me a clean heart, O God, and renew a right and steadfast spirit within me."*

I petition: Dear Lord God, I now realize that out of your mercy for me, You will create and create yet again a clean heart in me. Your mercy is truly profound. There are no words to express my gratitude for your mercy, your grace and your love.

Verse 11 says: *"Do not cast me away from your presence and do not take your Holy Spirit from me."*

I petition: Dear Lord God, in your mercy, do not let me go from You, do not allow me to be far from You ever again. Do not take your Holy Spirit from me!

Verse 12 says: *"Restore to me the joy of your salvation and sustain me with a willing spirit."*

I petition: Dear Lord God, on account of your mercy-love, after every storm, every trial, test and tribulation, there is restoration. Thank you for restoring me to joy, to the joy of salvation in You. Let your mercy-love fill me with a willing spirit that will bring me strength and perseverance to always complete the race at hand, to be victorious in You.

Verse 13 says: *"Then I will teach transgressors your ways, and sinners shall be converted and return to You."*

   I petition: Dear Lord God, this verse teaches me that I am called to pay it forward, with mercy and love. I commit to sharing the message of your mercy, the good news of salvation and reconciling love that You have given us in your Son, our Lord Jesus Christ.

7. Thanks and Gratitude.

   [Dedicate time to thank God after all of your petitions.]

- Thank you Lord God for receiving my sincere repentance and my petitions.
- Thank you for healing and sanctifying my soul.
- Thank you Heavenly Father for giving me the great gift of your Spirit of Truth, the Holy Comforter, and for helping me to cherish this gift in my heart and soul always, <u>as the agency for my soul's purification, maturation and expression</u>.
- To You alone be all the glory in Heaven and upon the Earth, forever and ever! AMEN!!!

SEALING PRAYER

For this reason I kneel before the Father,
from whom every family in heaven and on earth
derives its name.
I pray that out of His glorious riches
He may strengthen me with power
through His Spirit in my inner being,
so that Christ may dwell in my heart through faith.
And I pray that I, being rooted and established
in love, may have power,
together with all the Lord's holy people,
to grasp how wide and long and high and deep
is the love of Christ,
and to know this love that surpasses knowledge
that I may be filled to the measure of
all the fullness of God.
Ephesians 3:14-19

———

Now that we have sanctified our soul, we cultivate the three most godly virtues of faith, hope and love in order to strengthen and mature our soul. These virtues are profound inoculation against demonic powers. The more deeply these virtues are embedded into our character, the more unshakable we are, and the more unwavering is our inner peace. This is true freedom!

———

CHAPTER 20

STRENGTHENING THE SOUL

THE THREE GODLY VIRTUES

CULTIVATING the three godly virtues of faith, hope and love strengthens and sanctifies the soul, and help us come into union with God the Father, Jesus His Son and the Holy Spirit.

> *"But now faith, hope, and love remain, these three;*
> *but the greatest of these is love."*
> 1 Corinthians 13:13

Faith, Hope & Love Bring Us Into Union With God.

Faith, hope and love bring us into union with God because we are removing all that stands between us and Him and because we are taking on His attributes. This kinship brings us into union with Him.

- Faith dissolves doubt and distrust.
- Hope dissolves despair and separation.
- Love dissolves barriers and wounds.

When we are in union with the source and author of love who is God the Father; the manifest expression of love who is Jesus Christ; and the agency of love who is the Holy Spirit, then our soul is whole. Our soul is restored. <u>Our soul becomes impenetrable to forces of evil.</u>

OUR SOUL IS MADE WHOLE IN UNION WITH GOD THRU THE VIRTUES OF FAITH, HOPE & LOVE.

In Summary:

- When we have true and abiding faith in God and His Word, we come into an intimacy with Him. Faith dissolves distrust which is the barrier to intimacy.
- When we hold hope in His promises, we draw ourselves into a bond with Him.
- When we love as God loves, our heart is in union with His Heart.
- In this way, the three sublime virtues of faith, hope and love bring us into union with God. This union is our anchor in this turbulent world.

WHAT IS THE VIRTUE OF FAITH?

Faith is the substance of things not yet come to pass, but the conviction that they shall. Faith is believing in God's promises, believing that He wants the best for you, is there for you, will be there for you. Faith is truly believing you can count on God to walk with you through this life. Faith is "Jesus, I trust in you" and believing it!

> *"Now faith is the certainty of things hoped for,*
> *a proof of (conviction about) things not seen."*
> Hebrews 11:1

Trusting in someone, believing in their word, brings a deeper connection with that person. If we don't trust someone, we keep them at arm's length, at best. If we trust them, we allow ourselves to become closer to them.

Cultivating the Virtue of Faith.

Faith in God's promises brings forth God's reality as our operating system. This brings us into union with Him. The virtue of faith is <u>consciously choosing to live in faith in God's promises</u>.

THE VIRTUE OF FAITH IS CONSCIOUSLY CHOOSING TO LIVE IN GOD'S PROMISES AS OUR OPERATING SYSTEM.

WHAT IS THE VIRTUE OF HOPE?

Hope is the fruits of faith, the belief that a promise will be fulfilled. It typically contains a vision of a future state or promise. The virtue of hope is the assurance that the Kingdom of Heaven is available to us and is our destiny.

. . .

The Hebrew word for hope is *mikveh*, which means abiding. So when we hope, we are abiding — abiding in God's promises. Its root is *qavah*, which means to wait for, to eagerly await. One could say that hope, *mikveh*, is the state or way of being in eager expectation. It is not just a moment or event of waiting, but abiding in that eager expectation.

THE VIRTUE OF HOPE IS ABIDING IN EAGER EXPECTATION OF GOD'S PROMISES.

Hope is an Anchor of the Soul.

The Word describes hope as *"an anchor of the soul."* An anchor keeps the boat steady, still, intact and safe.

> *"In the same way God, desiring even more*
> *to demonstrate to the heirs of the promise*
> *the fact that His purpose is unchangeable,*
> *confirmed it with an oath,*
> *so that by two unchangeable things*
> *in which it is impossible for God to lie,*
> *we who have taken refuge would have strong encouragement to*
> *hold firmly to the hope set before us.*
> ***This hope we have as an anchor of the soul,***
> *a hope both sure and reliable*
> *and one which enters within the veil."*
> Hebrews 6:17-19

Cultivating the Virtue of Hope.

From this passage in Hebrews, we see that cultivating the virtue of hope means recognizing:

- We are heirs to a promise
- The unchanging nature of God's purpose
- His Word is true (unchangeable)
- God does not lie
- Hope is a safe harbor (we flee to take hold of it)
- Hope is an anchor for our soul
- Hope takes us *"within the veil"* to intimacy with God

"The virtue of hope... keeps man from discouragement; sustains him during times of abandonment; opens up his heart in expectation of eternal beatitude."[1]

WHAT IS THE VIRTUE OF LOVE?

The virtue of love, in God's terms, is the embodiment of the Greatest Commandment: *"And you shall love the Lord your God with all your heart and with all your soul and with all your strength."*[2] And as Jesus exhorted: *"Love one another as I have loved you"*[3], which is an unconditional, abiding, pure love.

Jesus extended God's invitation for sanctification by teaching: *"Therefore you shall be perfect, as your heavenly Father is perfect.*"[4] He was speaking of the way that we can love others, loving the way that God the Father loves.

Often we will see the word "charity" used here instead of "love." This is because in our culture love is equated with simply a personal feeling. "I love hamburgers." "I love my house." However, "love" as a godly virtue is "charity", "the theological virtue by which we love God above all things for His own sake and our neighbor as ourselves for the love of God."[5]

This is the essence of the first and supreme Commandment that God has given us, <u>to love the way He loves</u>. Charity is wishing the good for another, loving others as God loves them. It is <u>possessing the Heart of God in loving others</u>.

THE VIRTUE OF CHARITY LOVE IS POSSESSING THE HEART OF GOD IN LOVING OTHERS.

This is an unselfish love. ***It is loving the way that God loves***, an unconditional and pure love. So the virtue of love becomes both the cure for and the inoculation against demonic powers.

LOVING THE WAY THAT GOD LOVES IS THE CURE FOR
AND THE INOCULATION AGAINST DEMONIC POWERS.

In this prayer protocol, we are asking for God's help in cultivating these three most holy and soul-strengthening virtues. We are proclaiming our commitment to doing so and asking God to bear witness to our commitment.

CULTIVATING THE VIRTUES OF FAITH, HOPE & LOVE
[Speak this prayer protocol out loud.]

Coming Before Lord God Adonai
Dear Heavenly Father, I come before You today that You may bear witness to my commitment to cultivate the godly virtues of faith, hope and love; to ask for your help in doing so; in order to strengthen my soul and inoculate it against demonic powers; that I may live a truly virtuous life and be a man/woman of virtuous character; that I may be a shining example and inspiration to others as a brother/sister of Christ Jesus; that others will experience Jesus' love through me.

Lord God, I pursue these virtues to remove my own leaven, so that I may *become a partaker of the divine nature, to escape the corruption that is in this world on account of lust. And so I apply all diligence, in my faith I supply moral excellence, and in my moral excellence, knowledge, and in my knowledge, self-*

control, and in my self-control, perseverance, and in my perse-
verance, godliness, and in my godliness, brotherly kindness, and
in my brotherly kindness, love; according to 2 Peter 1:4-7.

I understand that if I lose sight of the spiritual value of these
virtues, I have surely *forgotten my purification from former sins.*
I understand, Father God, that my commitment to godly
virtues is *the entrance into the eternal kingdom of our Lord and*
Savior Jesus Christ who will be abundantly supplied to me;
according to 2 Peter 1:9 & 11.

I thank you Lord God, for this mercy and grace. Thank you for
healing, strengthening and sanctifying my soul.

1. CULTIVATING FAITH

Heavenly Father, so many righteous men and women of your
Word demonstrated that possessing the virtue of faith enabled
them to possess Herculean strength and endurance, to persevere and triumph over evil and bear witness to your Glory.

Accordingly, I take hold of Hebrews 11:33-35, to be one of the
"Righteous ones who by faith conquered kingdoms, performed
acts of righteousness, obtained promises, shut the mouths of
lions, quenched the power of fire, escaped the edge of the sword,
from weakness were made strong, became mighty in war, put
foreign armies to flight. Women received back their dead by
resurrection." I receive this Word into my very being as the soil
of my faith!

. . .

I take hold of your mighty sons' and daughters' triumphs as models of inspiration for my own commitment to embed the virtue of faith into my character. Either I believe in You and your Word of promises or not. Either I believe that I am in a true relationship with You, one that is fully honoring and loving You or I am not. Either I believe in your mercy and justice or I do not. I choose to believe You Father God. I do choose to believe You and trust in You.

Lord God, I humbly receive tests and trials, that as James 1:3 instructs, the testing of my faith shall produce perseverance. And surely perseverance is its own virtue; and I commit to pursuing perseverance as a noble character trait and habit as part of the virtue of faith.

Lord God, surely faith is an inoculation against the culture of lies and deceit in which we currently abide. I choose to so inoculate myself now by anchoring myself in your Word and binding myself to your Heart.

Father God, I commit to living by faith. I release to You all in me — habits, beliefs, fears, attachments, worries, that stand in the way of my truly and fully living by faith. *"For in it the righteousness of God is revealed from faith to faith; as it is written, 'But the righteous man shall live by faith'"*, according to Romans 1:17.

Father God, I commit to *trusting in You with all of my heart, not relying on my own understanding; and in all my ways I shall acknowledge You, that You will make my paths straight,* according to Proverbs 3:5-6.

2. CULTIVATING HOPE

Dear Heavenly Father, I come before You today that You may bear witness to my commitment to cultivate the godly virtue of hope, to be a man/woman of inner strength, honor and valor; to walk out the virtue of hope in a way that inspires and models to others your promises of eternal life.

The Keys to the Virtue of Hope.

Dear Father God, I see that the keys to cultivating the virtue of hope are found in Hebrews Chapter 10.

- **I have confidence based upon access.** *"We have confidence to enter the Most Holy Place by the Blood of Jesus."* Hebrews 10:19
- **There is a new way of access to Christ Jesus.** *"A new and living way opened for us through the curtain."* Hebrews 10:20
- **I have a great priest looking out for me.** *"We have a great priest over the house of God."* Hebrews 10:21
- **My heart draws closer to God.** *"Let us draw near to God with a sincere heart."* Hebrews 10:22
- **I have assurance that faith brings.** *"The full assurance that faith brings."* Hebrews 10:22
- **My heart is cleansed.** *"Having our hearts sprinkled to cleanse us from a guilty conscience."* Hebrews 10:22

- **My purified body.** *"Having our bodies washed with pure water."* Hebrews 10:22
- **Jesus is faithful.** *"Let us hold unswervingly to the hope we profess, for he who promised is faithful."* Hebrews 10:23

So Heavenly Father, I embrace the virtue of hope as accepting, knowing and believing in the promises of Christ Jesus; that He has made a way for me to be in union with Him and You; that I have an advocate, Jesus the High Priest; that as I cleanse my heart and purify my body and soul, I shall attain the promises of eternal life and the joys of the Kingdom of Heaven. How profound!

Beatitudes to Cultivate the Virtue of Hope.

Dear Lord Jesus, I see how the Beatitudes that You taught us are the foundation and food for cultivating the virtue of godly hope; and how You were expounding on the Law and Prophets in the Beatitudes. You unwrapped the teachings of the Old Testament (the Torah and Tanakh) and gave them to us as assurances of blessedness, which gives us hope. So I take hold of these Beatitudes as the nourishment for godly hope![6]

Matthew 5:3 teaches: *"Blessed are the poor in spirit, for theirs is the kingdom of heaven."* From Isaiah 61:1 brings the hope of miracles: *"The Spirit of the Lord God is upon me, because the Lord anointed me to bring good news to the humble; He has sent me to bind up the brokenhearted, to proclaim release to captives and freedom to prisoners."* ***I take hold of this Beatitude to transmute suffering into divine destiny, the Kingdom of Heaven.***

. . .

Matthew 5:4 says: "*Blessed are those who mourn, for they will be comforted.*" Isaiah 61:2-3 says: "*To comfort all who mourn, to grant those who mourn in Zion, giving them a garland instead of ashes, the oil of gladness instead of mourning, the cloak of praise instead of a disheartened spirit. So they will be called oaks of righteousness, the planting of the Lord, that He may be glorified.*" ***I take hold of this Beatitude to bring a higher purpose and fruits to mourning; to transmute loss, sorrow and grief, through the supernal power of hope, into shalom peace.***

Matthew 5:5 exhorts: "*Blessed are the gentle (humble), for they will inherit the earth.*" Psalm 37:11 promises: "*But the humble will inherit the land and will delight themselves in abundant prosperity.*" ***I take hold of this Beatitude that humility has its own rewards beyond the evident material world.***

Matthew 5:6 teaches: "*Blessed are those who hunger and thirst for righteousness, for they will be satisfied.*" Isaiah 55:1 proclaims: "*You there! Everyone who thirsts, come to the waters; and you who have no money come, buy and eat. Come, buy wine and milk without money and without cost.*"

Isaiah 55:3 continues: "*Incline your ear and come to Me. Listen, that you may live; and I will make an everlasting covenant with you, according to the faithful mercies shown to David.*" ***I take hold of this Beatitude that hope is deepened,*** *knowing that striving for righteousness brings its own rewards from our Father.*

Matthew 5:7 says: "*Blessed are the merciful, for they will receive mercy.*" Hebrews 4:16 says: "*Let us then with confidence draw near to the throne of grace, that we may receive mercy and find grace to help in time of need.*" Lamentations 3:22-23 says: "*The steadfast love of the Lord never ceases; His mercies never come to an end; they are new every morning; great is your faithfulness.*" **Heavenly Father, how can I not possess hope within my own soul when I hear that your mercies and love never cease?**

Matthew 5:8 says: "*Blessed are the pure in heart, for they will see God.*" Psalm 24:3-5 proclaims: "*Who may ascend onto the hill of the Lord? And who may stand in His holy place? One who has clean hands and a pure heart, who has not lifted up his soul to deceit and has not sworn deceitfully. He will receive a blessing from the Lord and righteousness from the God of his salvation.*"

Beloved Lord Jesus, how my hope deepens and matures realizing that your Beatitudes came 1000 years after Psalm 24 was written! Seeing how You perfectly aligned your Word across time and space fills my soul with glorious hope and your glory!

Matthew 5:9 continues: "*Blessed are the peacemakers, for they will be called sons of God.* Isaiah 26:1-3 presages You Jesus, as our strong city: *"We have a strong city; he sets up salvation as walls and bulwarks. Open the gates, that the righteous nation that keeps faith may enter in. You keep him in perfect peace whose mind is stayed on you, because he trusts in you."* **Thank you Jesus Christ, for giving me your perfect peace as the soil of my hope.**

John 1:12-13 affirms the promise of this Beatitude: *"But as many as received Him, to them He gave the right to become children of God, even to those who believe in His name, who were born, not of blood nor of the will of the flesh nor of the will of man, but of God."*

John 16:33 confirms that <u>my hope finds a home in your peace</u>, Lord Jesus: *"I have said these things to you, that in me you may have peace. In the world you will have tribulation. But take heart; I have overcome the world."*

How Lord God, can I not posses the virtue of hope when I receive into my heart these promises and revelations?

Dear Heavenly Father, I see how the last Beatitudes help me to <u>use difficulties as the bread of hope</u>. For Matthew 5:10 says: *"Blessed are those who have been persecuted for the sake of righteousness, for theirs is the kingdom of heaven."*

. . .

Matthew 5:11 continues: "*Blessed are you when people insult you and persecute you, and falsely say all kinds of evil against you because of Me.*" And Matthew 5:12 consoles: "*Rejoice and be glad, for your reward in heaven is great; for in this same way they persecuted the prophets who were before you.*"

1 Peter 4:13-14 inspires me to embrace, rather than fear, persecution: "*To the degree that you share the sufferings of Christ, keep on rejoicing, so that at the revelation of His glory you may also rejoice and be overjoyed. If you are insulted for the name of Christ, you are blessed, because the Spirit of glory, and of God, rests upon you.* **Lord God, I take hold of Your Spirit of glory as the agency of my virtue of hope. In this way, there is no striving; only coming into union with Your Spirit of glory as it lives godly hope through me.**

Future Glory.

Dear Jesus, You gave me hope of a glorious future of my own, because your life as Son of Man blazed a trail for my own spiritual destiny.

As You prayed in John 17:22-24: "*The glory which You have given Me I also have given to them, so that they may be one, just as We are one; I in them and You in Me, that they may be perfected in unity, so that the world may know that You sent Me, and You loved them, just as You loved Me. Father, I desire that they also, whom You have given Me, be with Me where I am, so that they may see My glory which You have given Me, for You loved Me before the foundation of the world.*"

. . .

I take hold of this Word, that I shall be with You where You are in your Heavenly abode; and this gives me the ultimate hope. In this, I have peace and faith knowing that my journey on this earth is for the purpose and destination in You and with You; and that my life is to be a celebration of this gift.

1 Peter 5:10 assures: *"And the God of all grace, who called you to His eternal glory in Christ, after you have suffered a little while, will himself restore you and make you strong, firm and steadfast."*

How can I not grow in the virtue of hope when I take hold of this beautiful promise, plant it in the garden of my heart and soul, and water it with gratitude and love?

Predestined in Christ Jesus Deepens Hope.

Dear Father God, the virtue of hope is sharpened and deepened within me, believing in your Word in Titus 3:5-7 which tells me I am an heir to eternal life. I take hold of this promise, for truly, *"He saved us, not on the basis of deeds which we did in righteousness, but in accordance with His mercy, by the washing of regeneration and renewing by the Holy Spirit, whom He richly poured out upon us through Jesus Christ our Savior, so that being justified by His grace we would be made heirs according to the hope of eternal life."*

. . .

Truly, *I celebrate in hope of the glory of God*, according to Romans 5:2. The vision of this future life, <u>embeds hope into the fabric of my being</u>. Thank you God, for this incredible spiritual destiny that I may now experience and express even here on earth.

Lord God, I take hold of Romans 8:28 as the blueprint of godly hope, knowing that as I love you and live out your purposes for my life, all will work together for your good; and this gives me a foundation of hope for my life. *"And we know that God causes all things to work together for good to those who love God, to those who are called according to His purpose."*

Romans 8:29-30 seals the deal — knowing that I am predestined in Christ Jesus, how can I not live in divine hope? *"For those whom He foreknew, He also predestined to become conformed to the image of His Son, so that He would be the first-born among many brothers and sisters; and these whom He predestined, He also called; and these whom He called, He also justified; and these whom He justified, He also glorified."*

Hope is Knowing & Believing in Spiritual Law.

Dear Father God, I now understand that living in the virtue of hope is knowing and truly believing in your spiritual laws; as Job 14:7 expresses: *"For there is hope for a tree, when it is cut down, that it will sprout again, and its shoots will not fail."*

Thank you for your law of love and your law of mercy, that are the food of my hope; as Psalm 130:7 speaks of redemption as the destination for my hope: *"For with the Lord there is mercy, and with Him is abundant redemption."*

Truly Lord God, *"You are my hope; Lord God, You are my confidence from my youth,"* according to Psalm 71:5.

3. CULTIVATING CHARITY LOVE

Dear Heavenly Father, I come before You to bear witness to my commitment to cultivate the godly virtue of love, to love as You love and as Jesus loves; <u>to know your heart which will then enable me to love and understand others as You love and understand them</u>. For truly, You teach us how to love others and ourselves in the midst of imperfections. In this way of love, we triumph!

Without Love, We are Nothing.

Dear Abba Father God, You have given us Love as the supreme commandment and virtue to possess. I now understand that if anything is conducted from a manner, emotion or agenda that contains anger, roughness, hostility, hubris, envy, jealousy, resentment or superiority, it is <u>not</u> your way or Will.

Lord God, I take hold of 1 Corinthians 13:1-3 and proclaim: *If I speak with the tongues of mankind and of angels, but do not have love, I have become a noisy gong or a clanging cymbal. If I have the gift of prophecy and know all mysteries and all knowledge, and if I have all faith so as to remove mountains, but do not have love, I am nothing. And if I give away all my possessions to charity, and if I surrender my body so that I may glory, but do not have love, it does me no good.* So I choose love as the supreme virtue!

I commit to *loving the Lord my God with all my heart, and with all my soul, and with all my mind* and *loving my neighbor (others) as myself,* according to Matthew 22:36-40.

I take hold of Ephesians 5:1-2 and commit to being an *imitator of God, as a beloved child; and walking in love, just as Christ also loves me and gave Himself up for me, an offering and a sacrifice to God as a fragrant aroma.*

Charity - Love of God for Others.

Heavenly Father, through John 15:12-13, I understand that love of others contains and calls for a selflessness, laying down my own desires, attachments, interests, agendas and ambitions to serve others: *"This is My commandment, that you love one another, just as I have loved you. Greater love has no one than this, that a person will lay down his life for his friends."*

Father God, I repent for all the times and ways I have been selfish in relationships with others, been selfish towards You; doing what I wanted instead of what would have truly served Love. I repent for callousness, pettiness or just plain self-involvement that caused me to be insensitive to others, to those who were in need and could have used a helping hand — time, energy or money that would have made a difference to them. I am truly sorry Lord God. Please forgive me.

. . .

I repent for taking for granted those close to me — a spouse, family member, a friend; and in so doing neglected to extend charity, your version of and capacity for love, towards them. I repent for my self-involvement, caught up in my own world and activities, that I lost the moment when they needed my ear or a sympathetic heart. I am truly sorry Lord God, please forgive me. Reveal to me ways that I can make it up to them, if possible. Or pay it forward to a total stranger in a random act of kindness and caring.

Charity: Love of God & Neighbor in Action.

Dear Abba Father God, your living Word, Jesus Christ, taught us in Matthew 22:36-40 that love of God and love of neighbor are the supreme laws.

Father God, I want to know your heart, I want to live as your heart here on earth. In this way, I can know and express your love for others. I can give and share your love. Only by understanding and experiencing YOUR heart, and therefore YOUR love, can I possibly love others as You and Christ Jesus love them. Make of us one heart Father God.

MAKE OF US ONE HEART FATHER GOD.

Lord God, Isaiah 54:10 expresses another way to understand your version of love, as lovingkindness, *chesed*, which is a mercy compassion in action: *"For the mountains may be removed and the hills may shake, but My lovingkindness will not be removed from you."*

Father God, I understand that this love is your version and your traits of love: steadfast, unfailing, loyal, devoted. Help me to possess these qualities as part of the virtue of charity love.

Father God, I commit to cultivating love-in-action charity and will seek out ways to extend it to others.

Lord God, crown me with lovingkindness and tender mercy, according to Psalm 103:4, that I may be these virtues of love to others, and exemplify this highest character as your son/daughter.

———

CHAPTER 21

SANCTIFYING THE BODY

"Do you not know that your bodies
are temples of the Holy Spirit, who is in you,
whom you have received from God?
You are not your own; you were bought at a price.
Therefore honor God with your bodies."
1 Corinthians 6:19-20

A FUNDAMENTAL VIRTUE TO seal our body against future violations is the virtue of temperance. This is a mindful discipline of what we do with and to our body, what food and drink we put in our body temple, what activities we engage in. Control over bodily impulses is critical for closing gateways to demonic attacks and influence.

This includes sex, porn, drugs, alcohol, cannabis, any mind-altering substance, overeating, sloth, laziness or inactivity, lack of sufficient healthy exercise, excessive or detrimental t.v. exposure, exposure to satanic entertainment (music, concerts, music videos) which contain subliminal messages and imagery for mind programming and denigration. Any of these activities can create openings for the demonic to enter in to your life.

The point of sanctifying our body is to possess full dominion over it; to possess full dominion and control over our senses, passions, inclinations, desires, cravings, attachments and addictions. In so doing, we close them off to demonic powers and agendas.

SANCTIFYING OUR BODY INOCULATES IT AGAINST DEMONIC POWERS AND AGENDAS.

To this end, we seek to cultivate the virtue of temperance.

A PRAYER FOR TEMPERANCE

[Speak this prayer protocol out loud.]

Dear Heavenly Father, I come before You today that You may bear witness to my commitment to cultivate the godly virtue of temperance; to purify my body and all impulses connected to it; to ask for your help in doing so; to inoculate my body against demonic powers and influences; that my body is a worthy temple for the Holy Spirit.

. . .

Heavenly Father, I learn from Proverbs 25:28 that self-control repels and neutralizes demonic attack: *"Like a city that is broken into and without walls, so is a person who has no self-control over his spirit."*

I understand Lord God, that lack of self-discipline and self-control, the antithesis of temperance, creates openings for demonic attack and control. Therefore, I commit to self-discipline and self-control, according to 1 Corinthians 9:27, *"I discipline my body like an athlete, training it to do what it should. Otherwise, I fear that after preaching to others I myself might be disqualified."*

Lord God, I take hold of 1 Corinthians 6:19-20 and commit to temperance, moderation and self-control in all ways and things; *for my body is a temple of the Holy Spirit within me, whom I have from God, and I am not my own. For I have been bought for a price: therefore I shall glorify God in my body.*

Dear Heavenly Father, I commit to crucifying my flesh, *as one who belongs to Christ Jesus, crucifying my flesh with its passions and desires,* according to Galatians 5:24. Help me to do so. Help me Lord God, to crucify the flesh; to only take into my body and do with it what is your will and best for me.

Lord God, I understand from your word in Galatians 5:19-21 that temperance is not only bodily, but temperance of emotions and responses to life, that when I follow the desires of my carnal nature, the results are very clear: *sexual immorality, impurity, lustful pleasures, idolatry, sorcery, hostility, quarreling, jealousy, outbursts of anger, selfish ambition, dissension, division, envy, drunkenness, wild parties, and other sins like these. I understand that anyone living that sort of life will not inherit the Kingdom of God.*

Heavenly Father, I sincerely want to inherit your Kingdom. I repent for these weaknesses and flaws and ask for your help in overcoming them for good, and replacing them with godly virtues. I ask You for grace!

Dear Heavenly Father, I commit to crucifying my flesh, as one who belongs to Christ Jesus, *crucifying my flesh with its passions and desires,* according to Galatians 5:24. Help me to do so. Jesus, help me walk in this empowerment of the Spirit.

I take hold of Romans 8:26-27 and ask for the Holy Spirit to help me to anchor into myself the virtue of temperance. *Now in the same way the Spirit also helps my weakness; for I do not know what to pray for as I should, but the Spirit Himself intercedes for me with groanings too deep for words; and He who searches my heart knows what the mind of the Spirit is, because He intercedes for the saints according to the will of God.* Intercede for me Holy Spirit! Intercede for me!

Dear Heavenly Father, I commit to honoring my body as your temple, as the abode for your indwelling spirit; to listening to what You want and need for my body and to act accordingly. I commit to fasting or abstaining your way, not what comes from my mind or other people's beliefs.

I commit to temperance in all things; *because having suffered in the flesh being like-minded with Christ, I am done with intentional sin having stopped pleasing the world, so that I no longer spend the rest of my natural life living for human appetites and desires, but live for the will and purpose of God,* according to 1 Peter 4:1-2.

Dear Heavenly Father, bless, strength and sanctify my body, so that I may experience and express the fullness of Christ Jesus in me. Amen.

———

CHAPTER 22
SANCTIFYING THE EGO

THE MOST POWERFUL way to sanctify the ego is to cultivate true humility. Numerous professional exorcists have testified that Mary, the mother of Jesus, is present at every exorcism. They say it is because she has utter and complete humility and therefore satan has absolutely no power over her. Jesus declared this for himself as well, when He told His disciples:

> *"I will not speak with you much longer,*
> *for the ruler of the world (Satan) is coming.*
> *And he has no claim on Me [no power over Me*
> *nor anything that he can use against Me]."*
> John 14:30

At the core of *"no claim"* is humility, which is the core of Jesus' teachings. He exhorted His disciples to humble themselves.

"Truly I say to you, unless you change
and become like children,
you will not enter the kingdom of heaven.
So whoever will humble himself like this child,
he is the greatest in the kingdom of heaven."
Matthew 18:3-4

HUMILITY IS KEY TO ENTERING THE KINGDOM OF
HEAVEN.

CULTIVATING HUMILITY TO SANCTIFY THE EGO

[Speak this prayer protocol out loud.]

1. Preparation.

This is constructed as a protocol going before God's
Throne of Mercy and Grace. Take time to reflect on what in
your ego requires repentance — traits, habits, flaws. Ask the
Holy Spirit to reveal to you these things beforehand.

2. Presentation of Purpose.

Heavenly Father, I come before your Throne of Mercy and
Grace to sanctify my ego. I come to repent for traits and iniquities that have kept me from true humility as part of a sanctified
ego. I ask for your support to be in true humility as the foundation of genuine strength, and to seal my ego from ungodly traits
and habits. I ask You to bear witness to my commitment to
cultivate humility as part of sanctifying my ego. Thank you for
your love, mercy and forgiveness.

.   .   .

Father God, I seek full deliverance from all curses, strongholds and spirits that are inhibiting true humility, elements that have plagued my life and lineage, and fostered traits in me that are the antithesis of humility. I have come to take full responsibility for them; and to repent and plead guilty for all of my actions that have caused, fed and perpetuated unhealthy ego expressions.

I understand that curses, strongholds and demons exist and continue to wreak havoc on account of my behavior, actions and choices; as well as those from my family lineage both living and deceased. I come before You Lord God, to seek forgiveness by the atoning Blood of Jesus Christ and on account of your love for me as your son/daughter.

I commit to turning over a new leaf, as true repentance means turning away from wrong; leaving behind wrong behavior, thinking and values; and turning towards and into your light. I am becoming a new creation in Christ Jesus, according to 2 Corinthians 5:17.

3. Renounce & Repent.

Dear Heavenly Father, I come in the name of Jesus Christ to renounce and repent of all of my ego sins, including all the times and ways I have created, perpetuated and allowed entry ways for curses, strongholds, spirits and traits having to do with pride, hubris, haughtiness, arrogance, criticism, competitiveness, judgmentalness, snobbery, arrogance, bragging, boasting, pettiness, showmanship, social status and social climbing, need for superiority and intellectualism, controlling, power hungry, ungodly ambition, holding a grudge or offense; being jealous, envious and vengeful. I hereby release and lay at the feet of Jesus Christ all of these detrimental traits, habits, curses and programs; and all of the sources and causes of them.

I repent for all my sins of the ego including pridefulness, self-centeredness, selfishness, narcissism, superiority, needing to be right or best, vengefulness, spitefulness, not turning the other cheek; and other ego traits, habits and actions that the enemy has been holding over my life that have enabled and allowed curses, strongholds and various spirits to operate in my life.

I now realize that indulging in certain character traits, flaws and habits has actually kept demonic powers activated and successful in sabotaging and damaging elements of my life. I now want to walk in my fullness as Your son/daughter and as a brother/sister of Jesus Christ, and I ask You to help me to do so.

I hereby renounce, reject, nullify, forbid and divorce all ungodly, unjust, unrighteous, anti-christ covenants, contracts, oaths, agreements, curses, strongholds, iniquities that I or anyone in my lineage has created, fed and expressed as and through ego flaws. I no longer want to carry family iniquities that express as character flaws, including flaws of the ego.

[Feel free to add your own specific repentance prayers.

Families have their own unique character/ego traits and behavior patterns.]

4. Plead Guilty.

Heavenly Father, for everything I have repented of and renounced here, I plead guilty to remove all cases that satan and his demonic powers have held against me. I present the Blood of the Lamb of God, Jesus Christ Yeshua as atonement. Lord God, I ask for redemption from all curses for which I've repented, by the shed Blood of Jesus Christ which breaks EVERY curse according to Galatians 3:13.

Lord God, let the speaking Blood of Jesus revoke, revoke, revoke every judgement against me now. Let the atoning Blood of Jesus revoke all curses, strongholds and spirits set against me. Silence the enemy from holding and bringing any cases against me because of what the Blood of Jesus speaks, because of the finished work of Jesus on the Cross.

Lord God, I come into agreement with the Blood of Jesus that cries for mercy, redemption and forgiveness. Let the Blood of Jesus Christ bring me into union with You and Jesus, one heart, one spirit; so that it is no longer I, the expression of ego, that lives, but Christ in me, according to Galatians 2:20.

5. Reparations ~ Penance.

Dear Heavenly Father, please guide me to right penance and/or reparations for all the iniquities, sins and transgressions that I have committed on account of my ego.

· · ·

Speak to me through your Holy Spirit. Convict me in mind and heart of right reparations to make through my actions, relationships, charity, teaching, sharing, giving, sacrifices, prayers and fasting.

6. Petitions and Proclamations to Cultivate True Humility.

Dear Heavenly Father, as your son/daughter and as a brother/sister of Jesus Christ, I dedicate and consecrate myself to You. I present the following petitions to remove all hindrances to my being in true humility to sanctify my ego. I present and apply Your Word as purification for my ego, *cleansed by the washing of water with the Word*, according to Ephesians 5:26.

Humility Makes Me Teachable.

Dear Heavenly Father, I understand that You desire a teachable heart. This is the way to growth and maturity. I ask You to *guide me in being humble in judgment and teach me your Way of humility*, according to Psalm 25:9.

Humbling Makes Me Stronger.

Dear Heavenly Father, being humbled is usually painful but I recognize its spiritual value. Any remaining leaven of pride, egoism, hubris, bragging, showing off, need to feel superior, narcissism, stubbornness, personal insistence, rebelliousness, laziness, inattentiveness, self-centeredness or self-absorption, I lay at the foot of the

Cross now. Let this release of remaining leaven be gentle yet thorough.

I cast my burden upon You LORD and I know that You will sustain me. You will never allow the righteous to be moved, according to Psalm 55:23.

I declare Psalm 68:20 that *I am blessed by Adonai, who daily bears burdens for me, the God of my Deliverance/Salvation. Selah.*

Humility is Bred from Weakness.

Dear Father Abba, I understand from 2 Corinthians 12:9-10 that for the power of Christ Jesus to dwell in me I must be *content with weaknesses, with insults, with distresses, with persecutions, with difficulties, for Christ's sake; for when I am weak, then I am strong.*

So I give my weaknesses to You Lord God. Instead of overcoming by my own might and power and ego, I allow for the power of Christ Jesus to dwell in me, as the better Way. Then I may not boast of my own clever overcoming, but give all glory to You Lord God.

Humility and Forgiveness Go Hand in Hand.

Dear Heavenly Father, I understand that unforgiveness is a barrier to true humility, as is victimhood. Your Word in Matthew 6:14-15 instructs me: *"For if you forgive others their trespasses [their reckless and willful sins], your heavenly Father will also forgive you. But if you do not forgive others [nurturing your hurt and anger with the result that it interferes with your relationship with God], then your Father will not forgive your trespasses.*"

I repent for all the times and ways I have withheld forgiveness. I release any unforgiveness I am still holding. Holy Spirit, reveal to me any grudges or offenses that I am still holding and help me to release them all now. God forgive me for any way that my unforgiveness has hurt others.

In purification of my heart and ego, I *put on a heart and inner thoughts of compassion, kindness, humility, gentleness, patience; bearing and forgiving others if any would have a complaint against me or I them: just as the LORD forgives me, so also I choose to forgive,* according to Colossians 3:12-13.

I commit to resisting a common reaction of the proud by *"not paying back evil against evil"*, according to Romans 12:17. Father God, I repent for any time in my past where I have done this.

Humility Deepens Compassion and Charity.

Lord God, I take hold of Jesus' teaching in Luke 14:11, where He advises His disciples to take the least of places because, *"Everyone who exalts himself will be humbled and the one who humbles himself will be exalted."* I commit to humbling myself and not exalting myself. I commit to giving all glory to God in all good things.

Dear Lord Jesus, I commit to your teaching on selfless love and service in Luke 14:13-14, *"But when you would make a banquet you must always invite poor, crippled, lame, blind: then you will be blessed because they do not have the means to repay you, for it will be repaid to you in the resurrection of the righteous."*

Dear Heavenly Father, I now see how compassion feeds humility and humility deepens compassion. Thank you for all the experiences, trials and tribulations that You have given me or allowed, that have deepened and matured my compassion for others, and brought me into deeper and true humility.

Thank you for all the ways You have been purifying, fine-tuning, maturing and growing my heart, so that I may have the heart of Christ Jesus, which is in fact, part of my original divine blueprint. Thank you for restoring my ego to factory settings, your version of my identity in Christ Jesus.

Humility Brings Unity of the Spirit.

Dear Heavenly Father, You have shared from your heart that You want us, your children, to have unity in the faith, unity of the spirit. I now understand how true humility is foundational to this unity. We can express uniqueness and enjoy the differences of others while at the same time being one in your spirit. Pride divides; humility and love unite.

. . .

I choose to *walk worthily in the calling to which I have been called, with all humility and gentleness, with patience, and bearing others in love, being diligent to keep the unity of the Spirit in the bond of peace; one body and one spirit, just as also I was called in one hope of my calling,* according to Ephesians 4:1-4.

Dear Heavenly Father, I commit to the advice of Apostle Paul in Romans 12:3, 4 & 6 to *not think too highly of myself beyond which is necessary to think, but to think to put a moderate estimate of myself, in the same manner as God divided to each a measure of faith.... I recognize that we, the many, are one body in Messiah... having different gifts according to the grace given to us.* I commit to seeing others as You seem them.

Dear Heavenly Father, I embrace your Word in Romans 12:16 to *be of the same mind with one another, not being proud but yielding to the lowly menial tasks; to not ever become wise in my own estimation.*

Humility Brings Grace.
    Dear Heavenly Father, I now understand that by emptying out my own ego and mind attachments, emptying out of beliefs and dogma, emptying out of things that feed my ego of the need to be special or superior, I am making room for more of your Spirit to take up residence within me. I am making room for more of your heart to be one with my heart. <u>I am making room for more of your qualities of love to be my own nature</u>.

· · ·

I now understand that the indwelling spirit grows as the ego "I" of me diminishes. *"He (the Lord Jesus) must increase, but I must decrease."*[1] With this infilling of your Spirit, <u>your Spirit becomes the doer of my life</u>, not my ego. Let your Holy Spirit be the doer of my life!

In this way, I open to more grace as James 4:5-6 confirms: *"Or do you think that the Scripture says to no purpose, 'He jealously desires the Spirit whom He has made to dwell in us?' But He gives a greater grace. Therefore it says, 'God is opposed to the proud, but gives grace to the humble.'"* Grace is your better way, better than anything my limited mind and ego can imagine or create. I choose your better way Father God!

I *submit therefore to You, God. I resist the devil, and he will flee from me,* according to James 4:7. I repent for all the times and ways I did NOT resist the devil, but entertained my own negative thoughts and feelings, looping in them. It's a form of idol worship, bowing to my mind and looping thoughts, rather than trusting in You.

I *choose to come close to You Lord God so that You will come close to me,* according to James 4:8. I surrender all hindrances in my ego that would compromise or block true intimacy with You. Therefore, I *humble myself in the presence of You Lord, and You will lift me up,* according to James 4:10.

· · ·

Now Lord God, 2 Chronicles 7:14 takes on deeper meaning: *"If My people who are called by My name will humble themselves and pray, and seek My face and turn from their wicked ways, then I shall hear from heaven and will forgive their sin and will heal their land."*

2 Chronicles 7:15 continues: *"Now My eyes will be open and My ears attentive to the prayer in this place, for now I have chosen and sanctified this House so My name may be there forever and My eyes and My heart will be there perpetually."*

Dear Heavenly Father, as I choose to walk in humility before You throughout my life, sanctify my home and family. Sanctify your Holy Church. Sanctify me. Sanctify my ego. Sanctify my life in joyful service to your heart.

Walk Humbly in Purity.

Dear Heavenly Father, I take hold of Micah 6:8 which says: *"He has shown you, O man, what is good. And what does the LORD require of you, but to do justice, to love lovingkindness, and to walk humbly in purity with your God."* I choose to walk humbly in purity with You Lord God.

I commit to living my life in reverence[2] of You Lord God, according to Proverbs 22:4, *"The reward of humility is reverence of the LORD, riches and honor and life."* I open to experiencing the shear awe of You! The more I empty of egoism, the more space and capacity to experience the wonders of You!

. . .

Humility is the Gateway to True Love.

Dear Heavenly Father, I now comprehend that genuine humility is the gateway to true love, to truly loving another human being as Jesus loves me and as You love me; to loving You and receiving love from You with abandon! Ego self-love overshadows and inhibits truly loving another. Unselfish love is a gateway to true joy and freedom.

I declare over myself 1 Corinthians 13:3-7 to help seed it into my very heart and soul: *"If I give away all my possessions to charity, and if I surrender my body so that I may glory, but do not have love, it does me no good. Love is patient, love is kind, it is not jealous; love does not brag, it is not arrogant.*

It does not act disgracefully, it does not seek its own benefit; it is not provoked, does not keep an account of a wrong suffered, it does not rejoice in unrighteousness, but rejoices with the truth; it keeps every confidence, it believes all things, hopes all things, endures all things."

What more, Lord God and dear Jesus Christ, could I possibly ask for? Halleluia!

7. Thanks and Gratitude.

[Let this be dedicated time to thank God after all of your petitions. You may want to play or sing praise music, or other ways that you express thanks and praise.]

- Thank you God for your compassion, mercy and love!
- Thank you God for sanctifying my ego.
- Thank you for helping me to walk and live in humility as the foundation for true strength, joy, love and freedom.
- To You alone be all the glory in Heaven and upon the Earth forever and ever! AMEN!!!

"All of you, clothe yourselves with humility
towards one another,
because God opposes the proud
but shows favor to the humble."
1 Peter 5:5

CHAPTER 23

SANCTIFYING THE CHARACTER

"And if someone likewise competes as an athlete,
he is not crowned as victor
unless he competes according to the rules."
2 Timothy 2:5

STRENGTH OF CHARACTER is a free will choice. Strong moral and ethical fiber is a personal value and choice. There is arguably little value in a secular and cynical world to possessing honor and valor. To whom should it matter? Hopefully to ourself. Surely to our Creator. It matters that we *"compete according to the rules"* in order to be crowned a victor. These are God's rules, unchanging spiritual laws.

Many people who identify as "spiritual" or "religious" tend to neglect self-examination for character weaknesses, sources of personality traits that hurt others and themselves, and causes of negative patterns in their lives. Yet sanctifying the character through self-examination is essential for spiritual growth and maturation.

. . .

Transmutation of Weaknesses to Strengths.

This book is designed to help you develop the truly empowering habit of radical self-examination and self-honesty. When it becomes habituated, it becomes a trait, a positive character trait.

With this, all kinds of flaws, bad habits and weaknesses can be overcome. Not only can they be overcome, their antitheses can be born.

Cowardice and apathy can transmute to courage and valor. Depression or laziness can transmute to inspiration and creative power. Anger and hurt can transmute to joy and compassion for others.

SELF-EXAMINATION AND SELF-ABNEGATION CAN TRANSMUTE CHARACTER FLAWS TO VIRTUES.

The prayer protocol in this chapter corresponds with Jesus' admonition to "carry our own cross" (metaphorically). Matthew 16:24-26 says: *"Then Jesus told His disciples, 'If anyone would come after me, let him deny himself and take up his cross and follow me. For whoever would save his life will lose it, but whoever loses his life for my sake will find it. For what will it profit a man if he gains the whole world and forfeits his soul? Or what shall a man give in return for his soul?'"*

. . .

Sanctifying Character Unlocks Spiritual Destiny.

Jesus is calling us to higher character, to adjust our priorities from personal desires and agendas to those that come from God's heart. Denying ourself leads to fulfilling our true spiritual destiny, which is union with God. With this union, we come into a currency of life that draws out our creative capacity and purposes in profound and very fulfilling ways.

PARADOXICALLY, RELINQUISHING PERSONAL AGENDAS UNLEASHES SPIRITUAL CREATIVITY & DESTINY. IT IS A RELEASE FROM SELF-LIMITATIONS.

Apostle Paul exhorts us to sanctifying our character:

> *"Therefore I, the prisoner of the Lord,*
> *urge you to walk in a manner worthy of*
> *the calling with which you have been called,*
> *with all humility and gentleness, with patience,*
> *bearing with one another in love,*
> *being diligent to keep*
> *the unity of the Spirit in the bond of peace."*
> Ephesians 4:1-3

SANCTIFYING THE CHARACTER

[Speak this prayer protocol out loud.]

Coming Before Lord God Adonai

Dear Heavenly Father, I come before You today to ask for your help in cultivating godly character and sanctifying my character. Please receive my petitions for grace support and bear witness to my commitment to growing in godly character in Christ Jesus.

Firstly, I renounce and repent of the seven deadly vices of pride, greed, wrath, envy, lust, gluttony and sloth; all seven being contrary to the seven godly virtues of prudence, justice, temperance, fortitude, faith, hope and charity (love).

Lord God, I take hold of 2 Peter 1:3-7 as <u>a divine template for godly character</u>, *for your divine power has granted to me everything pertaining to life and godliness, through the true knowledge of Him who called me by His own glory and excellence.*

Through these He has granted to me His precious and magnificent promises, so that by them I may become a partaker of the divine nature, having escaped the corruption that is in the world on account of lust.

Now for this very reason also, applying all diligence, in my faith, I commit to moral excellence, and in my moral excellence, knowledge, and in my knowledge, self-control, and in my self-control, perseverance, and in my perseverance, godliness, and in my godliness, brotherly kindness, and in my brotherly kindness, love.

Celebrate Tribulations.

Heavenly Father, it is clear that, *"in this world we shall have challenges,"* and that my trials and tribulations can be viewed and used as gifts and opportunities to refine my character, to develop godly virtues, and to mature emotionally, relationally and spiritually.

As such, I repent for all the times I have complained about my adversities rather than taking hold of them as a spiritual opportunity to share in Christ's sufferings and therefore unite with Him; and <u>therefore unite with Christ's virtues</u> of loving obedience to You, perseverance to fulfill my God destiny, compassion and forgiveness for those who persecute me, and love and charity.

By Romans 5:3-5 I proclaim that, *I also celebrate in my tribulations, knowing that tribulation brings about perseverance; and perseverance, proven character; and proven character, hope; and hope does not disappoint, because the love of God has been poured out within my heart through the Holy Spirit who was given to me.*

Father God, I commit to embracing tests and difficulties as an heir to inheriting your glory, and proclaim that *the Spirit*

Himself testifies with my spirit that I am a child of God, and if a child, heir also, heir of God and a fellow heir with Christ, if indeed I suffer with Him so that I may also be glorified with Him, according to Romans 8:16-17. What a profound gift!

True Character is Internal.

Heavenly Father, You shall not be mocked. True character is internal, possessing internal virtues, not ones for outer show and vainglory. Godly virtues are not for vanity and applause; but quiet, seeking no credit or spotlight. I commit to walking in godly virtues that have only You as their reward.

As Apostle Paul shares in Romans 2:29, *"Circumcision is circumcision of the heart, by the Spirit, not by the written code. Such a person's praise is not from other people, but from God."* Circumcise my heart and character, Heavenly Father.

Truly, Jesus taught in Matthew 6:3 to never boast about doing good works, but to keep it private to ourself, *"But when you give to the needy, do not let your left hand know what your right hand is doing."* Truly, bragging about good works dilutes and even nullifies the spiritual benefit of them. I repent for ever doing this.

Keep Right & Righteous Company.

Dear Lord God, it is abundantly clear from your Word that it is imperative to keep right and righteous company. Even if someone is not ill-meaning, their vices, values and lifestyle can have a damaging or dangerous affect on me. I repent for all the times and ways I have been careless or ignorant about with whom I keep company. I know it has damaged my spiritual life and other areas of my life. I commit to being vigilant and resolved in keeping only spiritually and morally compatible and uplifting company.

For Psalm 1:1-2 says: *"Blessed is the person who does not walk in the counsel of the wicked, nor stand in the path of sinners, nor sit in the seat of scoffers! But his delight is in the Law of the Lord, and on his Law he meditates day and night."*

1 Corinthians 15:33-34 convicts me: *"Do not be deceived: 'Bad company corrupts good morals.' Sober up morally and stop sinning, for some have no knowledge of God. I say this to your shame."*

Proverbs 13:20 warns: *"He who walks with wise men will be wise, but the companion of fools will suffer harm."*

Proverbs 14:7 tells me that wrong company can impair my discernment: *"Leave the presence of a fool, or you will not discern words of knowledge."*

Strive for Holiness.

Heavenly Father, repeatedly You have exhorted your people to *"Consecrate yourselves therefore, and be holy, for I am holy."* If it were not possible, You would not have asked us repeatedly! For 1 Peter 1:15 says: *"But like the Holy One who called you, be holy yourselves also in all your behavior."* This is the call to sanctify character. I commit to holiness and ask for your help in this Lord God.

Heavenly Father, I am convicted by Hebrews 12:14 which says: *"Strive for peace with everyone, and for the holiness without which no one will see the Lord."* Surely I DO want to see You Lord God!

I understand that <u>it is by the agency of the Holy Spirit that I am made holy</u>, according to 1 Thessalonians 4:7-8, *"For God has not called us for impurity, but in holiness. Therefore whoever disregards this, disregards not man but God, who gives His Holy Spirit to you."* Come! Holy Spirit come! Come into my heart! Come into my life! Make me clean and holy unto the Lord God Most High! Help me Holy Spirit!

Lord God, I proclaim Psalm 25:21, *"May integrity and uprightness preserve me, for I wait for you."*

NOBLE VIRTUES

Prudence - The wisdom to discern correctly.

Heavenly Father, I strive to possess greater prudence and ask for your help in doing so. I repent for all the times and ways I did not possess and act on correct discernment and discipline; when I did not discern your voice, the Holy Spirit, whispering right actions into my ear or directly through another person.

I repent for listening to talking heads rather than seeking your voice in the stillness, so as to cultivate true and accurate discernment and wisdom. For surely Proverbs 8:12 states: *"I, wisdom, dwell together with prudence."*

Father God, I commit to cultivating the virtue of prudence by developing greater self-control and moderation in all things; for Proverbs 14:15 states, *"The simple believe anything, but the prudent give thought to their steps."* I understand that *"giving thought to my steps"* means taking the time to check in with You first before I act, before I make decisions, be they personal or business. I repent for all the times and ways I acted rashly, impulsively, did not seek your Will, and barged ahead to my own detriment and the detriment of others. Please forgive me.

Lord God, I commit to prayerfully and carefully seeking your wisdom, your Will and your heart in every situation in my life; for Proverbs 13:16 notes that *"All who are prudent act with knowledge, but fools expose their folly."*

. . .

Justice.

Heavenly Father, God of Justice, according to Isaiah 30:18, I understand that the virtue of justice is multi-fold: seeking justice for myself, being an instrument for bringing justice on behalf of others, being an ambassador and intercessor for your justice. So many of your prophets admonished us to seek justice for those who are oppressed or down-trodden; that in seeking justice we are displaying compassion and lovingkindness, and also being an instrument of your mercy, justice and love.

Lord God, I repent for all the times and ways I have chosen laziness, apathy, fear, fear of losing social status, fear of what people will think of me and other forms of cowardice, instead of standing for justice. I realize that by not doing so when I should have, I may have contributed to the suffering of others. God forgive me. Reveal to me any penance and/or reparations to do for these transgressions of my character.

Lord God, I commit to the instructions of Isaiah 1:17 and will *learn to do good; seek justice, correct oppression; bring justice to the fatherless, plead the widow's cause.* I repent Lord God, for the times I did not take the time and care to plead and stand up for others, when I took the easy or cowardly way out. I ask You to bring me a means to make up for those mistakes and missed opportunities to help those in need by seeking justice for them.

Father God, Micah 6:8 convicts me of the importance of possessing the virtue of justice: "*He has told you, O man, what is good; and what does the Lord require of you but to do justice, and to love kindness, and to walk humbly with your God?*"

. . .

Dear Father God, I see from Proverbs 21:15 how the virtue of justice can strengthen my character and weaken the works of evildoers: *"When justice is done, it is a joy to the righteous but terror to evildoers."* Truly, justice counters evil and nullifies its intentions.

Lord God, your Word in Isaiah 61:18 comforts me and fortifies me to contend for justice: *"For I the Lord love justice; I hate robbery and wrong; I will faithfully give them their recompense, and I will make an everlasting covenant with them."*

Dear Father God, I humbly ask that your Holy Spirit fill me with greater strength, fearlessness and fortitude to contend for justice; for justice is part of the fabric of your heart and therefore meant to be a part of my own heart and character.

Proverbs 21:3 affirms the value and importance of the virtue of justice: *"To do righteousness and justice is more acceptable to the Lord than sacrifice."*

Father God, I repent for all the times and ways I have not been an adequate and acceptable ambassador of your justice, as You have called me to be. I repent for the times and ways I did not live up to the redemption privileges and salvation blessings You have bestowed upon me.

. . .

I repent for any time or way that I refused to pay attention, turned a stubborn shoulder and plugged my ears from hearing when, *"The Lord of armies has said: 'Dispense true justice and practice kindness and compassion each to his brother; and do not oppress the widow or the orphan, the stranger or the poor; and do not devise evil in your hearts against one another,'"* according to Zechariah 7:9-11. God forgive me. Bring me the opportunities to make amends and stand for the down-trodden and the persecuted.

Fortitude: Enduring Trials with Patience and Dignity.

Dear Heavenly Father, I understand that fortitude is both a cultivated virtue and a gift of the Holy Spirit. I ask for your help and grace in possessing fortitude as both a virtue and a gift; as I commit to cultivating fortitude by noble deeds and actions.

I repent for all the times and ways that I was weak, cowardly, apathetic, prejudiced, insensitive, selfish, lazy and uncaring, in my own ambitions and agendas, and so did not display fortitude in situations where I should have. I am truly sorry for that. Please forgive me Heavenly Father. Reveal to me any penance and/or reparations to do for these transgressions of my character.

Father God, I commit to the expression of fortitude that is endurance, as Apostle Paul describes in Romans 5:4, that *endurance cultivates proven character (spiritual maturity); and proven character, hope and confident assurance [of eternal salvation].*

Lord God, I now realize that I must cultivate fortitude because we are in a battle against evil on this earth. Indeed 2 Corinthians 12:12 confirms this: *"The signs that characterize the true Apostle have been done among you, accompanied by unwearied fortitude, and by tokens and marvels and displays of power."*

I commit to *"unwearied fortitude"* and understand that fortitude can be developed more deeply as a virtue, and I commit to doing so now.

Father God, I take hold of 1 Timothy 6:11 and proclaim: *I shall flee from these detrimental things; and strive for uprightness, godliness, good faith, love, fortitude, and a forgiving temper.*

Integrity.

Dear Heavenly Father, I repent for all the causes and acts in me that have taken me out of integrity. I repent for cowardice, weakness, lack of resolve, dishonesty, duplicity, guile, craftiness, deceitfulness, selfishness and selfish gain. I repent for being blinded by my own feelings and subjectivity, and for misplaced loyalties.

I repent for not standing up for You, Jesus Christ and the Holy Church, when and how I should have. Instead I thought of my own skin, protecting my own reputation or acceptance by others. God, please forgive me. I resolve to walk uprightly and with courage as your son/daughter.

Truly, Proverbs 10:9 convicts me: *"Whoever walks in integrity walks securely, but he who makes his ways crooked will be found out."*

Surely Lord God, You see all of our acts and words that are out of integrity. We only fool ourselves when we are not honorable; as Hebrews 4:12 says: *"For the word of God is living and active, sharper than any two-edged sword, piercing to the division of soul and of spirit, of joints and of marrow, and **discerning the thoughts and intentions of the heart.**"*

Colossians 3:9-10 instructs: *"Do not lie to one another, since you laid aside the old self with its evil practices, and have put on the new self who is being renewed to a true knowledge according to the image of the One who created him."*

I commit to being honest, truthful, forthright and honorable, especially in times and circumstances where it is most difficult to do so and be so.

Gentleness.

Dear Heavenly Father, I repent for all the times and ways I have been rough, arrogant, insensitive, thoughtless, cruel and hurtful in my dealings, speech and interactions with others.

The ends does not justify the means to the end. My own mood or circumstances are no excuse for cruelty or harm to others. Please forgive me.

Lord God, I commit to godly gentleness with my fellow brethren in Christ Jesus and with total strangers, as Galatians 6:1 instructs: "*Brothers and sisters, even if a person is caught in any wrongdoing, you who are spiritual are to restore such a person in a spirit of gentleness; each one looking to yourself, so that you are not tempted as well.*"

For truly, it is a spiritual loss to hurt or damage the heart of another person. For Jesus says: "*As you do to the least of my brothers, that you do unto me.*" I recognize Jesus' words as spiritual law. I harm Jesus Christ himself when I harm others. God forgive me for all the times and ways I have done so; I am truly sorry.

Ephesians 4:1-2 makes clear that gentleness is a noble virtue: "*Therefore I, the prisoner of the Lord, urge you to walk in a manner worthy of the calling with which you have been called, with all humility and gentleness, with patience, bearing with one another in love.*"

Noble Service.

Dear Heavenly Father, I repent for all the times and ways I have fallen short of noble service. Perhaps there were times You wanted me to help someone and I did not, or I did not do it to your standards of love. I am truly sorry.

. . .

Ephesians 2:10 explains, *For I am His workmanship, created in Christ Jesus for good works, which God prepared beforehand, that I should walk in them.* I commit to walking in good works!

Heavenly Father, I commit to *showing myself in all respects to be a model of good works, and in my teaching show integrity, dignity, and sound speech that cannot be condemned, so that an opponent may be put to shame, having nothing evil to say about me,* as a brother/sister of Christ Jesus, according to Titus 2:7-8.

Humility.
Dear Heavenly Father, I repent for all the times and ways I have been in hubris, arrogance, pridefulness, egoism. I repent for taken credit when I should not have and for times I just had to point out how clever I was or that I was right. Please forgive me.

Matthew 18:3 explains why humility is so vital to being able to enter your Kingdom of Heaven, that *unless I am converted and become like a child, I will not enter the kingdom of heaven.*

Isaiah 66:2 exhorts: *"All these things my hand has made, and so all these things came to be, declares the Lord. But this is the one to whom I will look: he who is humble and contrite in spirit and trembles at my word."*

. . .

Lord God, I am convicted of the supreme value of humility and ask for your help in truly living in abiding humility whilst denying myself.

Walking by the Spirit.

Father God, I repent for all the times and ways I have walked in my own ego and for my own desires and agendas, rather than what You desired for me, which was also much better for me than my own choices. I commit to choosing every day to yield to your Spirit and to walk by your Spirit, not my own ways.

Lord God, I want to be under Grace, not the Law; for it is the way of living and being under the New Covenant that Jesus bought for me with His Blood, and is the Way for me to return to being made in Your image.

Romans 8:14 establishes: *"For all who are being led by the Spirit of God, these are sons and daughters of God."* I want to be a son/daughter of YOU God, not of this world!

Not Being Conformed to This World.

Dear Heavenly Father, it is hard not to be conformed to this world. There is such a bombardment of information, views, talking heads, media prophets, telling us what to think and believe. Lord God, I surrender it all to You completely.

. . .

Wipe my hard drive clean of all false teachings, information, beliefs, programs; everything that blocks, inhibits or compromises my ability to truly know You in your fullness and to be in full union with Christ Jesus; everything that blocks my fully knowing Your heart.

I give You full permission to remove from me all manner of conformities to this world; that I may fill up with only your Truth, your Spirit of Truth and all of His agency, which includes the agency of miracles and grace!

I take hold of Romans 12:1-2 and *I present my body as a living sacrifice, holy and acceptable to You God, which is my spiritual worship. I commit to not being conformed to this world, but being transformed by the renewal of my mind, that by testing I may discern what is the will of God, what is good and acceptable and perfect.*

Lord God, I commit to *keeping myself unstained from the world*, according to James 1:27.

A Pure Heart.

Dear Heavenly Father, 1 Samuel 16:7 instructs: *"Do not look on his appearance or on the height of his stature, because I have rejected him. For the Lord sees not as man sees: man looks on the outward appearance, but <u>the Lord looks on the heart</u>."* Help me to see as YOU see Lord God, with a pure heart.

· · ·

396 MARIA T. TONELLO

Lord God, it's clear from your Word that being committed to your truth and obedience (hearing and heeding You), purifies the heart and soul, as 1 Peter 1:22 says, *"Having purified your souls by your obedience to the truth for a sincere brotherly love, love one another earnestly from a pure heart."*

Lord God, I take hold of 2 Timothy 2:22 and *I flee youthful passions and hereby pursue righteousness, faith, love, and peace, along with those who call on the Lord from a pure heart.*

Make of me a clean heart, a pure heart, Lord God. I lay at the feet of Jesus all that does not belong in my heart — envy, resentment, anger, hurt, unforgiveness, offenses, pettiness, jealousy, grudges.

Unity of the Faith.

Dear Heavenly Father, your Word in Colossians 3:12-15 tells me that love in Christ brings unity. As such, I commit to put on then, *as God's chosen, holy and beloved, a compassionate heart, kindness, humility, meekness and patience, bearing with others and forgiving others; as the Lord has forgiven me, so I also must forgive. And above all these, I commit to putting on love, which binds everything together in perfect harmony. And I let the peace of Christ rule in my heart, to which indeed I am called with my fellow brothers and sisters in Christ into one body.* Amen and thank you Lord God!

Heavenly Father, I commit to remaining rooted and unwavering in your call on my life; and therefore take hold of

Ephesians 4:11-13 which says, *"And He gave some as apostles, some as prophets, some as evangelists, some as pastors and teachers, for the equipping of the saints for the work of ministry, for the building up of the body of Christ;* **until we all attain to the unity of the faith,** *and of the knowledge of the Son of God, to a mature man, to the measure of the stature which belongs to the fullness of Christ."*

1 Thessalonians 4:9 instructs on loving: *"Now concerning brotherly love you have no need for anyone to write to you, for you yourselves have been taught by God to love one another."*

So if I *"have been taught by God to love"* others, than surely <u>You Father God, have created my heart with this capacity</u>. Remove from me everything that inhibits this capacity for love. Remove from me the spirits of strife and divisiveness, and all of their causes and effects in me.

Let your purifying Word in my petitions remove everything that has distorted your creation and purposes for my heart, character and life! Lord God, I commit to loving your other sons and daughters. In this way, I am also loving You and Christ Jesus.

Righteousness is the Roadmap to the Kingdom of Heaven.

Father God, it is clear from Matthew 5:20 that sanctifying my character, to walk in righteousness, is necessary to be able to enter the kingdom of heaven: *"For I say to you that unless your righteousness surpasses that of the scribes and Pharisees, you will not enter the kingdom of heaven."*

I ask for your grace to walk and live in righteousness, as the fruits of sanctifying my character. Amen!

SEALING PRAYER

I commit to:
ridding myself of the old self,
which was corrupted
in accordance with the lusts of deceit
and commit to being renewed
in the spirit of my mind,
and to put on the new self,
which in the likeness of God
has been created
in righteousness and holiness of the truth.
I commit to being kind to others,
compassionate, forgiving others,
just as God in Christ
also has forgiven me.
Ephesians 4:22-24, 32

———

CHAPTER 24

SANCTIFYING THE WILL

SANCTIFYING personal will is a practical antidote to the presence and influence of demonic powers. We can fortify our soul and our life by re-aligning and re-calibrating our will to God's Will. This is the response to God's invitation to *"Be ye holy as I AM holy."* It is a roadmap back to our divine blueprint.

SANCTIFYING THE WILL IS A WAY BACK TO OUR DIVINE BLUEPRINT.

Sanctifying the will is setting us apart from the paradigms and programs of this fallen world and recalibrating to God's Being, His heart and His Will. It is a re-orientation back to the operating system of the indwelling spirit, rather than the ego, mind, will, emotions and self-limiting programs and beliefs. It is being restored to factory settings to operate from our spirit, the indwelling spirit of God, which is a spiritual and supernatural anchor.

Sanctifying the will restores us to factory settings, operating from the Spirit.

Remember, we were made in God's image, as the Book of Wisdom reiterates.

> *"For God created man for incorruption[1];*
> *And made him in the image of his own eternity."*
> Book of Wisdom 2:23[2]

Now let's ask for God's help in sanctifying our will, re-calibrating it to His Will and His Heart. How amazing!

SANCTIFYING THE WILL

This is a protocol going before God's Throne of Grace to ask for God's help in sanctifying our will. Please speak this prayer protocol out loud!

1. Going Before God's Throne of Grace.

Dear Heavenly Father, I put on the robe of Jesus Christ's righteousness according to Isaiah 61 and I loose the Blood of Jesus over myself to enter into your Court of Grace sanctified, in praise and thanksgiving, in love and gratitude.

. . .

I come before your Throne of Grace to ask for your grace in sanctifying my will and recalibrating it to your Will and your Heart. I now understand that any defects, vices and leaven in me are magnets for the demonic. I also understand that *all things work together for good for those who love You and are called according to your purposes*, according to Romans 8:28.

I see that demonic attacks, trials and tribulations are a hidden grace opportunity for me to strengthen my virtues, to overcome my defects and vices and therefore realize the holiness to which You have called me. In this way, I am no longer a victim but a conqueror in Christ Jesus.

Dear Heavenly Father, I ask for your grace help in fully realizing holiness as my highest God destiny. In this way, my will is sanctified, consecrated to You. You have exhorted this invitation to, *"Be ye holy as I AM holy,"* throughout your Word, and I now realize this is the way to be truly inoculated against demonic powers. Not only to be inoculated, but to utterly conquer and vanquish them. Halleluia!

2. Petitions for Sanctifying the Will.

Dear Heavenly Father, I stand before You and ask You to bear witness to my commitment to sanctifying my will in order to be inoculated against demonic powers and become one with your Will and your Heart.

The Galatians Roadmap for Sanctifying the Will.

Heavenly Father, I see how Galatians 5:13-26 is actually a

roadmap for sanctifying the will. I take hold of it now and ask You to bear witness to my proclamations.

I Shall Use My Freedom for Good.

Galatians 5:13 says: *"For you were called to freedom, brothers and sisters; only do not turn your freedom into an opportunity for the flesh, but serve one another through love."*

Dear Heavenly Father, as I am called to freedom, I commit to using my God-given freedom to serve You through serving others, to choosing your desires for my life and body rather than my own flesh desires. Even though I have been stubborn in my own will, I am willing now to let You be in the driver's seat.

I Shall Love as God Loves, True Charity.

Galatians 5:14 says: *"For the whole Law is fulfilled in one word, in the statement, "You shall love your neighbor as yourself."*

Dear Heavenly Father, I now understand that charity, "love of neighbor", is love in action, not just an emotion or feeling or words.

Heavenly Father, fill me with your version of love for your sons and daughters, for the unloveable, for those who oppose me and test me. <u>Give me your compassion and mercy, to see others as You see them, and love them as You love them.</u>

. . .

I no longer want to live, love and feel from my personal, and therefore very limited, will. I want to love in a way that has me living from an unbounded, unlimited spirit of love, that is a replica of your Spirit of love.

I Shall Not be Consumed by Resentments.

Galatians 5:15 warns: *"But if you bite and devour one another, take care that you are not consumed by one another."*

Dear Heavenly Father, I repent for holding on to resentments and offenses. These are bitter seeds of the ego-mind. I reject them now. If they come calling, I shall rebuke them as spirits that are lies from the enemy. I now realize this is how the adversary has torn apart relationships. Please heal and remove from me now the source and cause of these tendencies and impulses.

I Shall Walk by the Spirit.

Galatians 5:16 exhorts: *"But I say, walk by the Spirit, and you will not carry out the desire of the flesh."*

Dear Heavenly Father, I choose to walk by the Spirit, over carrying out my desires of the flesh. I commit to choosing daily, hourly, each and every moment, what are YOUR desires for me, for my body and for my life. Help me to hear from You and follow your promptings in my spirit.

I Shall Live in the Spirit.

Galatians 5:17 explains: *"For the desire of the flesh is*

against the Spirit, and the Spirit against the flesh; for these are in opposition to one another, in order to keep you from doing whatever you want. But if you are led by the Spirit, you are not under the Law."

Dear Father God, I want to live by the Spirit, your Holy Spirit. I now understand that this is true freedom. Help me to do so now! I choose to live in the Spirit of God, not the spirit of man. I choose true freedom! I commit to yielding to your Spirit every day.

My Commitments to Sanctifying My Will.

Dear Heavenly Father, I commit to the following to sanctify my will.

I Choose the Fruits of the Spirit.

Dear Father God, I choose the fruits of your Spirit, which are *"Love, joy, peace, patience, kindness, goodness, faithfulness, gentleness, self-control; against such things there is no law,"* according to Galatians 5:22-23.

When the mind and will are in captivity, law is needed to control their passions. When they are liberated in Christ Jesus, they are free in the Spirit which by its nature, is self-regulated to righteousness. I choose living in the Spirit that I may possess these fruits of the Spirit.

I Am One With the Spirit.

Dear Heavenly Father, I want to be one with the Spirit, your Holy Spirit. I now realize that *if I live by the Spirit, I shall follow the Spirit as well*, according to Galatians 5:25.

I Shall Stay Focused on Pleasing God.

Dear Heavenly Father, I commit to *not being boastful, challenging others, envying others*, according to Galatians 5:26. Rather I yoke to your heart and allow love to override ego.

I Throw Off All Hindrances.

Dear Heavenly Father, I commit to Hebrews 12:1-2, that since I am *surrounded by such a great cloud of witnesses, I am throwing off everything that hinders me and the sin that has so easily entangled me. I shall run with perseverance the race marked out for me, fixing my eyes on Jesus, the pioneer and perfecter of my faith.* Jesus Christ, perfect my faith!

I now understand that faith is an unwavering strength and certainty that comes from being rooted in the Spirit of God, the indwelling spirit. It is not merely "mind over matter", but being grounded in the Spirit, which then <u>steers the ship of my soul and will</u>. Holy Spirit, steer the ship of my soul and will!

I Replace Vices with Virtues.

Dear Heavenly Father, I take hold of Ephesians 4:31-32 and I *put away all bitterness and wrath and anger and clamor and slander from me, along with all malice. I commit to being kind, tenderhearted, forgiving of others, as God in Christ forgave me.* In so doing, I replace my vices with virtues.

. . .

I Have Victory in Christ Jesus.

Dear Heavenly Father, your Son Jesus made a way for me to overcome this world and embody holiness as He did. I take hold of His victory as the promise of my own victory.

For John 16:33 says: "*I have said these things to you, that in me you may have peace. In the world you will have tribulation. But take heart; I have overcome the world.*" This tells me that tho I may have challenges, so long as I am anchored in the indwelling spirit of God, I will always be victorious. The slings and arrows of this world will not faze me.

Revelation 3:12 promises: "*The one who conquers, I will make him a pillar in the temple of my God. Never shall he go out of it, and I will write on him the name of my God, and the name of the city of my God, the new Jerusalem, which comes down from my God out of heaven, and my own new name.*" Thank you Father God, for this promise that strengthens my faith and hope. I have victory in Christ Jesus!

I Choose YOUR World Lord God.

Dear Heavenly Father, 1 John 2:16 declares: "*For all that is in the world—the desires of the flesh and the desires of the eyes and pride of life—is not from the Father but is from the world.*"

Dear Heavenly Father, I choose YOUR world over the standards and norms of this fallen world; and proclaim

Romans 12:1-2, *I present my body as a living sacrifice, holy and acceptable to You Lord God, which is my spiritual worship. I shall no longer be conformed to this world, but be transformed by the renewal of my mind, that by testing I may discern what is the will of God, what is good and acceptable and perfect.*

Selflessness Leads to Holiness.

Dear Heavenly Father, I plant the holy seeds of Philippians 2:3-7 into my heart and commit to watering them with love and devotion to You. *I shall do nothing from selfish ambition or conceit, but in humility count others more significant than myself. I shall look not only to my own interests, but also to the interests of others.*

Father God, I commit to emulating Christ Jesus, by continually emptying myself and taking the form of a servant, as Jesus himself did.

I Shall Serve Others Through Love.

Dear Heavenly Father, Galatians 5:6, 13 & 14 sum up the totality of Jesus' teachings: *"For in Christ Jesus neither circumcision nor uncircumcision means anything, but faith working through love. Serve one another through love. For the whole Law is fulfilled in one word, in the statement, 'You shall love your neighbor as yourself.'"*

Heavenly Father, I understand that this is not human love with its conditions and limitations. This is loving as YOU love. Put

<u>your Heart in mine</u>, that I may love others as You love them, and see them the way that You see them.

Then I will understand and experience your depths of compassion and mercy, forgiveness and forbearance. Then I will take nothing personally, as Christ Jesus lives in me, and your love in me and for me are the only truth that matter. In your truth is true and everlasting freedom. <u>Your Truth in me sanctifies my will!</u>

A Guide for Sanctified Will.

Dear Heavenly Father, You rewarded King David's right-eousness because he kept your ways. The following passage from 2 Samuel Chapter 22 is <u>a guide for sanctified will:</u>

- Keep your ways
- Do not turn from You
- Do not turn from your decrees
- Remain blameless, without sin
- Remain faithful to You
- Possess purity of heart and actions
- Keep You as my lamp, the light of my soul

I pray <u>King David's song of gratitude</u> to You from 2 Samuel 22:21-30, to edify my spirit and sanctify my will:

"The Lord has dealt with me according to my righteousness; according to the cleanness of my hands he has rewarded me. For

I have kept the ways of the Lord; I am not guilty of turning from my God.

All His laws are before me; I have not turned away from His decrees. I have been blameless before him and have kept myself from sin.

The Lord has rewarded me according to my righteousness, according to my cleanness in His sight. To the faithful you show yourself faithful, to the blameless you show yourself blameless, to the pure you show yourself pure, but to the devious you show yourself shrewd.

You save the humble, but your eyes are on the haughty to bring them low. You, Lord, are my lamp; the Lord turns my darkness into light. With your help I can advance against a troop; with my God I can scale a wall."

3. Thanks and Gratitude.

- Thank you Abba Father for receiving me before your Throne of Grace for sanctifying my will.
- Thank you for bringing my will into oneness with your Divine Will, that I may operate fully from my indwelling spirit.
- To You alone be all the glory in Heaven and Earth forever and ever! Amen!

SEALING PRAYER

For I am called to freedom,
only I shall not turn my freedom
into an opportunity for the flesh,
but to serve others through love.
For the whole Law is fulfilled in one word,
'You shall love your neighbor as yourself.'
I shall walk by the Spirit
and not carry out desires of the flesh.
If I am led by the Spirit,
I am not under the law of the flesh.[3]
If I live by the Spirit,
I shall follow the Spirit as well.
Whoever sows to please their flesh,
from the flesh will reap destruction;
whoever sows to please the Spirit,
from the Spirit will reap eternal life.
Galatians 5:13-15, 16, 18, 25, 6:8

———

CHAPTER 25

LIVING IN DIVINE WILL

"I delight to do your will, O my God;
your Law is within my heart."
Psalm 40:8

LIVING in God's Divine Will is the means to and the goal of sanctification, which 1 Thessalonians 4:3 perfectly sums up: *"For this is the will of God, your sanctification."* Living in Divine Will means we are synced up to God's perfect way of being, His best solutions, the highest, best ways and purposes for our own gifts to creatively express in the world.

LIVING IN DIVINE WILL ACTIVATES THE HIGHEST CREATIVE EXPRESSION OF OUR GIFTS & LIFE PURPOSE.

THE BENEFITS OF LIVING IN DIVINE WILL

- Our acts have deeper merit.
- We grow in holiness and sanctification.
- We are restored to *"made in His image."*
- All of our works are assured to be fruitful.
- We live fully in God's current and currency.
- Our virtues have their center in God's Divine Will.
- Our godly virtues will grow, strengthen and deepen.
- Our virtues will be used of God only for His purposes.
- Our innate (God-given) creative capacity and purposes take on their highest expression and fulfillment.
- We abide in God's protection and provision in spite of outer circumstances.

JESUS AS DIVINE WILL INCARNATE

While Jesus as Son of Man was given free will, He demonstrated Divine Will Incarnate by choosing to give His free will entirely to God His Father. Jesus was one with His Father and only did His Father's Will.[1] He proved that we also can live as Divine Will Incarnate.

He did this as love, for love. He lived as Divine Will Incarnate to help us do the same, to return to the fullness of love, Divine Love. *"If you love me, you will keep my commandments."*[2] So Divine Love and Divine Will are enjoined and beat as one eternal heart.

Love of God and will of God beat as one
eternal heart.

Jesus Lived Out the 3 Keys to Living in Divine Will.

3 KEYS TO LIVING IN DIVINE WILL

1. **EMPTY** the soul, the mind, the will of all personal beliefs, attachments, agendas, insistences and programs.
2. **SURRENDER** personal agendas. Human purposes do not produce spiritual growth. Only actions and virtues that are in the Divine Will support fulfillment of spiritual destiny.
3. **COMMIT** in your heart to being fully in the Divine Will.

Love causes us to want to do God's Divine Will. Doing God's Will fulfills love and perfects love. In this way, we become *"perfect as our Father in Heaven is perfect,"* as Jesus exhorts in Matthew 5:48.

So becoming "perfect" is not an act of personal will. It is just the opposite. It is giving over personal will, emptying out of it, and surrendering to God's Divine Will. It is the opposite of efforting.

> DIVINE WILL IS THE MANIFEST EXPRESSION
> OF DIVINE LOVE.

The Sacred Scriptures invariably provide clues for how to return to our divine blueprint. Since Jesus is Divine Will Incarnate, we find three times (the number for confirmation) where God declared Jesus as His Beloved Son in a very public way, so that others would bear witness to Him as Divine Will Incarnate.

3 SACRAMENTS TO CULTIVATE DIVINE WILL

Three times was the voice of God audibly heard by people who were with Jesus. Three times God recognized His Son in the company of others, acknowledging Jesus as the Incarnation of His Divine Will.

These three times reveal three sacraments or ways that Divine Will is cultivated in our soul. Again, Jesus provides the blueprint for restoration of our own soul. These three are sanctification, transformation and self-abnegation (denying oneself).

> JESUS PROVIDES THE BLUEPRINT FOR RESTORATION
> OF OUR SOUL.

1. Sanctification ~ Baptism.

The first time God's voice is audibly heard by the masses acknowledging His Son Jesus is in Matthew 3:16-17.

> *"After He was baptized,*
> *Jesus came up immediately from the water;*
> *and behold, the heavens were opened,*
> *and he saw the Spirit of God*
> *descending as a dove*
> *and settling on Him, and behold,*
> *a voice from the heavens said,*
> ***'This is My beloved Son,***
> ***with whom I am well pleased.'"***
> Matthew 3:16-17

In this profound act of baptism inaugurating His ministry of Reconciliation, Jesus brought sanctifying grace to earth for all of humanity. That is, a kind of grace that marks us as God's child. Baptism is the primordial gateway into living in Divine Will.[3]

2. Transfiguration ~ Transformation.

The second time God's voice is heard declaring Jesus as His Son, Jesus has taken His three closest disciples, Peter, James and John, with him up Mount Tabor. In their presence, Jesus transfigures into radiant light.

As if that weren't enough, Moses representing the Torah (God's teachings), and Elijah representing the Prophets, appear beside

Jesus and carry on a conversation with Him. The totality of the Word (Torah, Prophets and the Living Word) convene together. As Matthew 17:2-3 describes:

> *"And He was transfigured before them;*
> *and His face shone like the sun,*
> *and His garments became as white as light.*
> *And behold, Moses and Elijah appeared to them,*
> *talking with Him."*
> Matthew 17:2-3

Peter goes into flesh mind mode, wanting to make tabernacles (booths) for each of the three men of God. God intervenes.

> *"He was still speaking when, behold,*
> *a bright cloud overshadowed them,*
> *and a voice from the cloud said,*
> ***'This is my beloved Son,***
> ***with whom I am well pleased;***
> ***listen to him.'"***
> Matthew 17:5

Needless to say, the three disciples freak out. This time God makes a point of saying: *"Listen to him."* If they had any doubt as to the divinity of Jesus Christ, it must have been wiped out in that instant.

.   .   .

One could say that this event presaged the transfiguration that these disciples would experience at Pentecost when their character, will and hearts were transformed by the descent of the Holy Spirit unto them.[4] They went from fearful to fearless, competitive and jealous to one in the spirit.

This was a profound sacrament into Divine Will. This sacrament is available to all of us.[5] It brings a profound anointing to fulfill God destiny.

3. Self-abnegation ~ Self-denial.

The third time God's voice is audibly heard by others is when Jesus is preparing for His passion sacrifice on behalf of humanity. In John 12:27-28, Jesus says:

> *"Now My soul has become troubled;*
> *and what am I to say?*
> *'Father, save Me from this hour?'*
> *But for this purpose I came to this hour.*
> *Father, glorify your name.*
> *Then a voice came out of heaven:*
> ***'I have both glorified it,***
> ***and will glorify it again.'"***
> John 12:27-28

This is a sacrament of dying to self to glorify God. Ironically, it is in dying to self, that we are truly born to our spiritual self. This is because we are releasing a self that by its very nature is limited. It is limited to time and space, programs and beliefs, personal identity and experiences.

Our spiritual self is of God, and there is no limit to how God may express with and through us as divine creation, divine will in expression, when we are born of spirit. Jesus speaks of this spiritual rebirth:

> *"Truly, truly, I say to you,*
> *unless someone is born of water and the Spirit,*
> *he cannot enter the kingdom of God.*
> *That which has been born of the flesh is flesh,*
> *and that which has been born of the Spirit is spirit."*
> John 3:5-6

THERE IS NO LIMIT TO HOW GOD CAN EXPRESS THROUGH US AS DIVINE CREATION.

BORN OF THE SPIRIT

What is truly remarkable is that Jesus elaborates by equating people *"born of the Spirit"* as being like the wind:

> *"The wind blows where it wishes,*
> *and you hear the sound of it, but you do not know*
> *where it is coming from and where it is going;*
> *so is everyone who has been born of the Spirit."*
> John 3:8

. . .

Jesus is saying that people born of the Spirit are moving in this world, but are not of it. They are physically present — you hear the sound of the wind, but you don't know where it is coming from or going to. That is, there is an element that is transcendent to this physical world and senses and the carnal/flesh mind.

Now we can more deeply appreciate 2 Corinthians 5:17, *"Therefore if anyone is in Christ, this person is a new creation; the old things passed away; behold, new things have come."*

Dying to self and self-will makes way for re-birth into spiritual life living in the Divine Will. What an extraordinary sacrament! In this sacrament of self-abnegation, dying to self, we are "glorifying His name."

Then comes the ultimate gift of choosing to sacrifice self in order to live in Divine Will: passing out of death into eternal life. What greater freedom can there possibly be?

"Truly, truly, I say to you,
the one who hears My word,
and believes Him who sent Me,
has eternal life,
and does not come into judgment,
but has passed out of death into life."
John 5:24

. . .

ETERNAL LIFE IS THE ULTIMATE FREEDOM.

In John 17:3, Jesus describes what is eternal life when praying to His Father the night before His crucifixion: *"And this is eternal life, that they may know You, the only true God, and Jesus Christ whom You have sent."* This knowing is spirit to Spirit. It is experiential, not merely mental. It is a knowing that comes from union.

This final prayer protocol is designed to help you live in Divine Will. It seals this deep and sacred journey. May God richly bless you for your courage, dedication and determination!

PRAYER TO LIVE IN DIVINE WILL

[Please speak this prayer protocol out loud!]

Coming Before Lord God Adonai

Dear Heavenly Father, I come before You today that You may bear witness to my commitment to live in your Divine Will. In this way, I shall become truly united with You and Jesus Christ, in fulfillment of John Chapter 17:21: *"Just as You, Father, are in Me and I in You, that they also may be in Us."* I understand that to be living in and as your Divine Will, I choose to empty of my own will and all of its expressions, habits and contents.

Jesus lived as the complete and perfect embodiment of your Divine Will. Three times your audible voice was heard by the people whilst in the company of Jesus, acknowledging Him as yours. These three times express three sacraments for coming to live in your Divine Will: sanctification, transfiguration and self-abnegation. I lay my proclamations and commitments before You accordingly.

Sanctification to You Lord God.

Heavenly Father, the purpose of living a consecrated, sanctified life is to be in complete union with You and the Chief Shepherd, Jesus Christ Yeshua. Accordingly, I commit to being, as 2 Timothy 2:21 puts it, *"An implement for honor, sanctified, useful to the Master, prepared for every good work."*

Lord God, as part of consecrating myself to You, I take hold of Isaiah 1:16-17 and I commit to *washing myself, making myself clean; removing the evil of my own deeds from before your eyes; ceasing to do evil, learning to do good; seeking justice, correcting oppression; bringing justice to the fatherless, pleading the widow's cause.*

Beloved Abba, *be gracious to me, according to your faithfulness; according to the greatness of your compassion, wipe out my wrongdoings. Wash me thoroughly from my guilt and cleanse me from my sin*; according to Psalm 51:1-2, that I am sanctified and purified for You, for a consecrated life in You.

Lord God, I declare that *the old in me has passed away and the new has come*, according to 2 Corinthians 5:17. Receive me Holy Father as a new creation in Christ Jesus, with a circumcised heart, a purified mind, heart, soul and body; fully living in your Divine Will.

Transfiguration.

Teach me to do your Divine Will, for You are my God. *Let your good Spirit lead me on level ground*, according to Psalm 143:10.

I proclaim Philippians 2:13 that *it is not by my strength, but it is YOU God who is effectively at work in me, both to will and to work, that is, strengthening, energizing, and creating in me the longing and the ability to fulfill my purpose for YOUR good pleasure.*"[6]

Lord God, *fill me with the knowledge of your Divine Will in all spiritual wisdom and understanding*, according to Colossians 1:9.

Lord God, You have not only raised up Lord Jesus, but *will also raise me up through your power*, according to 1 Corinthians 6:14.

· · ·

I proclaim John 4:34 as my own, that *my food is to do your Will Father God, and to accomplish your work.*

Heavenly Father, I proclaim 1 Peter 4:2, *so as to live the rest of the time in the flesh no longer for the lusts of men, but for the Will of God.*

Lord God, I take hold of 1 Thessalonians 5:16-18, where You have provided a guideline for being in your Will: *I rejoice always and delight in my faith; shall be unceasing and persistent in prayer; in every situation, no matter what the circumstances, shall be thankful and continually give thanks to You God; for this is the Will of God for me in Christ Jesus.*

Heavenly Father, I proclaim John 7:17-18 that *if anyone is willing to do Your Will, and I am Lord God, then I shall know about the teaching, whether it is of God, or I am speaking from myself. The one who speaks from himself seeks his own glory; but the one who seeks the glory of the One who sent him, he or she is true, and there is no unrighteousness in them.*

Empty me Lord God, of any and all unrighteousness!

I seek your Glory Lord God. I want to glorify You, not my own views, opinions, beliefs and accomplishments. You Lord God and Jesus must increase, but I must decrease according to John 3:30.

. . .

Self-abnegation.

Heavenly Father, "*I have been crucified with Christ; and it is no longer I who live, but Christ lives in me; and the life which I now live in the flesh I live by faith in the Son of God, who loved me and gave Himself up for me,*" according to Galatians 2:20.

I *therefore consider the members of my earthly body as dead to immorality, impurity, passion, evil desire, and greed, which amounts to idolatry,* according to Colossians 3:5.

Lord God, I choose to die to myself and I pray Luke 9:23, that I *come after and seek union with Jesus Christ, I deny myself, take up my cross daily and follow Christ Jesus.*

Heavenly Father, for the purpose of living in your Divine Will, I separate myself from all that stands between You and me; including lures and lies of the adversary about what is important and a priority above You. I give You full permission to separate me from all that stands between You and me, and my ability to live your Heart's desires in and through me.

I separate myself from all habits, foods, activities, entertainment, attachments, addictions and relationships that allow principalities of this world, such as leviathan and jezebel, to get a foothold into my psyche and life.

I declare and take hold of your instruction in 2 Corinthians 6:17-18, that I shall therefore, *come out from their midst and be separate, and shall not touch what is unclean; and I pray Lord God that You will welcome me. And You will be a Father to me, and I shall be your son/daughter.*

Consecrate Me Lord God.

Heavenly Father God, *purify me with hyssop, and I will be clean; cleanse me, and I will be whiter than snow. Let me hear joy and gladness, let the bones You have broken rejoice. Hide your face from my sins and wipe out all my guilty deeds. Create in me a clean heart, O God, and renew a right spirit within me,* according to Psalm 51:7-10.

May the God of peace Himself sanctify me completely, and may my whole spirit and soul and body be kept blameless at the coming of our Lord Jesus Christ, according to 1 Thessalonians 5:23.

Consecrate me Abba Father, for *You have not called me for impurity, but in sanctification,* according to 1 Thessalonians 4:7.

My Consecration to You Lord God.

Dear Heavenly Father Abba, I give over to You ALL parts and expressions of my personal will — my thoughts, words and deeds, my works, my ego needs and aspirations, my schedule and time, my relationships and family, my body, heart and soul. Help and guide me to release and relinquish ALL that stands in the way of living in Your Divine Will.

. . .

I declare Psalm 40:7-8, *"Behold, I have come; it is written of me in the scroll of the book. I delight to do your Will, my God; your Law is within my heart."* I do indeed Lord God, delight to do your will!

I consecrate myself now, so that tomorrow You Lord God will do wonders amongst us, and in and through me, according to Joshua 3:5.

Heavenly Father, I consecrate myself to you according to Colossians 3:12-17, *so, as those who have been chosen of God, holy and beloved, I put on a heart of compassion, kindness, humility, gentleness, and patience; bearing others, and forgiving others, whoever has a complaint against anyone; just as the Lord forgave me, so must I do also.*

In addition to all these things I put on love, which is the perfect bond of unity. I let the peace of Christ, to which I am indeed called in one body, rule in my heart; and be thankful.

I let the word of Christ richly dwell within me, with all wisdom teaching and admonishing one another with psalms, hymns, and spiritual songs, singing with thankfulness in my heart to God.

Whatever I do in word or deed, I commit to doing everything in the name of the Lord Jesus, giving thanks through Him to God the Father. Amen.

SEALING PRAYER

Let Us Love One Another - Divine Will in Action

I choose to... *love others, for love is from God,*
and whoever loves has been born of God and knows God.
Anyone who does not love does not know God,
because God is love.
In this the love of God was made manifest among us,
that God sent His only Son into the world,
so that I might live through him.
In this is love, not that I have loved God
but that He loves me and sent His Son
to be the propitiation for my sins.
If God so loves me,
I also ought to love others.
No one has ever seen God;
if I love others,
God abides in me
and His love is perfected in me.
1 John 4:7-12

———

EPILOGUE
STAND FIRM

"But the one who stands firm to the end will be saved."
Matthew 24:13

PERSEVERE!

I want to encourage you to keep persevering with these prayer protocols. Do them again from time to time. We are in a fallen world in which layer upon layer of programs, powers and traumas have encased us.

It is impossible to know all that shrouds our heart, to hide our true nature made in God's image, to make us forget and even abandon our true identity and destiny in Christ Jesus. The casing shell did not happen in a day and will not likely come off in a day. Habits can take awhile to break.

So persevere! You WILL experience breakthroughs and transformational growth if you so choose.

YOU ARE IN GOOD COMPANY

Apostle Paul frequently spoke of the importance of pressing on, persevering in the face of trials and tribulations. Perseverance produces character and character produces hope.

"And hope does not put us to shame,
because God's love has been poured out
into our hearts
through the Holy Spirit,
who has been given to us."
Romans 5:4-5

Hope brings a new sense of life. Hope can resurrect buried dreams. Hope gives us a vision of new possibilities. Hope can heal bitterness and wipe away cynicism. Hope restores dreams and heals the heart.

Proclaim: "God's love has been poured into my heart through the Holy Spirit! And I receive! I receive! I receive!"

God wants you to be happy. God wants you to fulfill your destiny, the purpose for which He created you.

"Your eyes have seen my unformed substance;
and in your book were all written the days
that were appointed for me,
when as yet there was not one of them."
Psalm 139:16

. . .

It's never too late to heal and be free. It's never too late to receive the love of God and the gift of new life in Christ Jesus. It's never too late to love and be loved. It's never too late to be happy.

Proclaim: "Abba Father God, I shall fulfill the book you wrote of my life! Thank you for this precious gift of life! Thank you for restoring my joy, my hope and my life!"

GOD'S LOVE HAS BEEN POURED INTO YOUR HEART

When calcification around the heart is removed, when wounds have been healed, when traumas have been dissolved, when defenses have melted, when demonic powers have been put down, we are able to receive and give so much more love.

We are able to love others better. We are able to forgive more and to experience greater compassion. We are able to receive more of God's love and grace. The rich in Christ Jesus get richer. *"I have come to give you life and life more abundantly."*[1]

The love that has always been available to us from God and loved ones, finds a deeper home in our heart. It is a profound experience to truly feel the love that God has for you. So much healing can come by being able to receive love and acceptance. I pray you will allow God's love for you fully into your whole heart and being.

"There is no fear in love.
But perfect love drives out fear,
because fear involves punishment,
so the one who is afraid
is not perfected in love
[has not grown into sufficient understanding
of God's love]."
1 John 4:18

Proclaim: "Lord Jesus Christ, fill me with your unconditional love! Fill me with your forgiveness. Touch my heart and heal my wounds. Fill me with your love and compassion. Help me to love the way that You love."

LOVE HEALS ALL WOUNDS

Jesus Christ came as the embodiment of pure love, perfect love. Jesus healed all who were oppressed of the devil, of demonic powers. He gave His disciples a commandment at the Last Supper before He gave His life for humanity: *"This I tell you, love one another as I have loved you."*[2]

He was telling His disciples that they too were capable of perfect love. That is, an unconditional love that comes from who we are in Christ Jesus. He demonstrated that love heals all wounds. He walked as perfect love and cast out fear, demons and diseases.

. . .

Jesus Christ came to heal the broken-hearted. He came to set the captives free. The Prophet Isaiah spoke of Messiah Jesus Yeshua hundreds of years before He came. He prophesied in detail the trials and sufferings that Jesus would experience out of His love for us.

> *"Surely He has borne our sicknesses, our pains*
> *But He was wounded because of our transgressions,*
> *bruised because of our iniquities,*
> *the chastisement for our peace fell upon Him,*
> *and by His stripes (wounds) we are healed."*
> Isaiah 53:4-5

Proclaim: "Thank you Jesus, for your profound act of love; being brutally wounded and giving your own life for my mistakes and transgressions, for taking the hit for me, so that I may receive grace, mercy and freedom. By your wounds at the Cross, I am healed! Halleluia!

YOUR LIGHT WILL BREAK OUT LIKE THE DAWN

> *"Then your light will break out like the dawn,*
> *your healing (restoration, new life).*
> *will quickly spring forth;*
> *your righteousness will go before you*
> *[leading you to peace and prosperity],*
> *the glory of the Lord will be your rear guard."*
> Isaiah 58:8

Proclaim: "My light has broken out like the dawn! My healing has quickly sprung forth! My righteousness goes before me, leading me into peace and prosperity, for the Glory of the Lord is with me and in me! Halleluia!"

YOU ARE DESTINED TO BE ENTHRONED WITH GOD

The Hebrew word for enthroned is *yashab*[3] and it means to sit, to dwell, to remain, to inhabit. We are destined to dwell with God. Our true home is with God and in God. It is the most intimate place of Covenant relationship with God. Keep your eyes on the prize! If you are ever feeling discouraged, recite these Scriptures to proclaim your destiny in God.

"He does not withdraw His eyes from the righteous
[those in right standing with Him];
But with kings upon the throne
He has seated them forever,
and they are exalted."
Job 36:7

Proclaim: "Abba Father, do not withdraw your eyes from me, as I am in right standing with you. As a king on the throne, You have seated me forever with You and I thank You Heavenly Father! Halleluia!"

Approximately 2000 years after Job, Apostle Paul speaks of us being enthroned with God. See how God speaks to you across and beyond time and space! <u>Our spirit is seated with His Spirit even as we are here on earth</u>.

> *"And He raised us up together with Him,*
> *and seated (enthroned) us with Him*
> *in the heavenly places,*
> *in Christ Jesus."*
> Ephesians 2:6

Proclaim: "I am abiding with Christ Jesus in God's Heavenly abode! Halleluia!"

This supernatural enthronement is also a <u>spiritual place of protection</u> expressed in Psalm 91.

> *"When I sit enthroned*
> *under the shadow of El Shaddai,*
> *I am hidden in the strength of God Most High."*
> Psalm 91:1

Proclaim: "I am abiding in the secret place of stillness where I find You and hear from You Lord God, and You give me strength, peace and protection. Thank you Heavenly Father! Halleluia!"

SEALING PRAYER

I was *taught to put away my former way of life,*
my old self, corrupt and deluded by its lusts,
and to be renewed in the spirit of my mind,
and to clothe myself with the new self,
created according to the likeness of God
in true righteousness and holiness.
Ephesians 4:22-24[4]

———

NOTES

PREFACE

1. *Operating in the Courts of Heaven*, Robert Henderson, Robert Henderson Ministries, USA, 2014.

   Issuing Divine Restraining Orders from the Courts of Heaven, Dr. Francis Myles with Robert Henderson, Destiny Image Publishers Inc., Shippensburg, PA, 2019.

   The Battle of Altars: Spiritual Technology for Divine Encounters, Dr. Francis Myles, Published by Dr. Francis Myles and Francis Myles International, Stockbridge, GA, 2020.

   I Speak to the Earth: Release Prosperity, Dr. Francis Myles, Published by Dr. Francis Myles and Francis Myles International, Scottsdale, AZ, 2017.

1. LET'S BEGIN!

1. "The proof of the pudding is in the eating of it."
2. *"For this reason God highly exalted him and gave him the name that is above every name."* Philippians 2:9.

   Jesus' name in Hebrew is *Y'shua* which means 'to deliver, 'save'. See the Glossary of the *One New Man Bible,* "Y'shua" entry on page 1817 for more details.
3. "In the name of Jesus".... Whatever is the pronunciation of His name in that person's language... Jesu, Yesu, Yeshua, Jesus. God knows the heart.
4. See www.roman-catholic-saints.com/incorruptible-saints.html
5. From the Prophet Isaiah 61:1, prophesied 700 years before the birth of Jesus Christ: *"He has sent me to bind up the broken-hearted, to proclaim liberty to the captives, and opening of eyes for those who are bound."*

2. WHAT ARE DEMONIC POWERS?

1. *Catechism of the Catholic Church*, Ascension Edition, Ascension Publishing Group, West Chester PA, 2022; Catechism (CCC) 2853

3. WAITING ON THE LORD

1. Romans 5:20
2. CCC 1848

4. THE COURTS OF HEAVEN

1. **Sin vs. Iniquity vs. Transgression**

    The Sacred Scriptures contains many different references to sins, iniquities and transgressions. They are different from each other and therefore are addressed differently. In the Hebrew language, sin is *chattah* (ḥaṭṭāṭ) and infers 'missing the mark'; iniquity is *awon/avon* or *avayah* in Aramaic (found in Daniel); and transgression is *pesha*, which means rebellion or rebellious act. Sin 'misses the mark' of righteousness or righteous action. *Awon* or iniquity refers to inner character, character flaws. *Pesha* or transgression is a willful rebellion.

    Psalm 32:5 covers all the bases: "*I acknowledged my sin to you and did not cover up my iniquity. I said, 'I will confess my transgressions to the LORD.'*"

2. **Sin:** An action or inaction that displays inner nature or character.

    • **Sin Lists:** Rom. 1:29-30, 1 Cor. 5:11; 6:9-10; 2 Tim. 3:2-4, Col. 3:5-9, Gal. 5:19-23.

    • **Sins of deception, sins of ignorance.** If you do something you did not know was morally wrong, it is a sin of ignorance.

    • **Everyone sins.** Romans 3:23 – "*For all have sinned and fall short of the glory of God.*" 1 John 5:17 – "*All unrighteousness is sin.*" Isaiah 53:6 – "*We all, like sheep, have gone astray, each of us has turned to his own way.*"

    • **Sins of omission**. Sin is not only doing what God forbids; but also the failure to do what God requires. James 4:17 – "*Anyone, then, who knows the good he ought to do and doesn't do it, sins.*"

3. **Iniquity**: Inner character flaws, deviation from right moral standards, a pattern of behavior that is not righteous, e.g. adultery, addictions, criminal inclinations, habitual lying. These character tendencies can run through a bloodline.

    • **Inherited proclivity**, tendency, to transgress and sin in a particular way.

    • **Guilt.** From the Hebrew, *awon*.

    • God forgives iniquity, as He does any type of sin when we repent. (Jeremiah 33:8; Hebrews 8:12).

    • **Twistedness.** (As found in the Hebrew Psalm 51.) A twistedness in our nature or character. Versions of twistedness are expressed in the principalities who embody them.

• **No fear of God.** Iniquity left unchecked leads to a state of willful sin with no fear of God.

• **Unnatural affections** come from continued iniquity. Romans 1:28–32 - *"And just as they did not see fit to acknowledge God, God gave them up to a depraved mind, to do those things that are not proper."* The sons of Eli are examples of reprobates God judged for their iniquities (1 Samuel 3:13–14).

• **Penance for iniquities** from Daniel 4:27 (NASB) *"Therefore, O king, may my advice be pleasing to you: wipe away your sin by doing righteousness, and your wrongdoings* (iniquities in the Hebrew) *by showing mercy to the poor, in case there may be a prolonging of your prosperity."*

4. **Transgressions:** Rebellion, rebellious acts.

• **Willful wrong action**. Knowing there is a moral standard but choosing your own desires anyway.

• **Rebelliousness.** Violating a law, rebelliousness. It can transpire in the heart. So the person can be thinking about or looking for the opportunity to sin.

• **Intentional.** Intentionally choose to disobey. Samson intentionally broke his Nazirite vow by touching a dead lion (Numbers 6:1–5; Judges 14:8–9) and allowing his hair to be cut (Judges 16:17); in doing so he was committing transgressions.

• **Sin of Presumption.** If you know full well and do it anyway, it is transgression.

• **Failure to act rightly.** Also, failing to do something you should have done, failing to do your duty. Isaiah 57:4 says: *"Are you not children of transgression, offspring of falsehood."* (NRSV) The NASB translation is: *"Are you not children of rebellion, offspring of deceit?"*

• **God hands us over to our transgressions.** Lamentations 1:14 says: *"The yoke of my wrongdoings* (transgressions, pesha) *is bound; by His hand they are woven together. They have come upon my neck; He has made my strength fail. The Lord has handed me over to those against whom I am not able to stand."*

• **Choosing our desire nature.** The previous verse tells us we are handed over to our desire nature, a desire to do what we want which is the exercise of our free will. This is how character flaws and vices feed the beast of its corresponding principality. This is why we trace our sins and transgressions back to their causal source in iniquity, our own and our family bloodline's iniquities.

5. The Courts of Heaven is a gift God has given us in this age for clearing spiritual inheritances from our ancestral lineage. This includes curses, addictions, behavior patterns, temperament; and other causes and sources of learned/inherited character flaws and detrimental traits.

The Sacrament of Reconciliation is for personal sins, wrong actions, inactions, negative traits, bad habits and faults. Many of these are the fruits of what we have learned or inherited through our lineage.

For example, a critical spirit runs through a family bloodline. Within the family culture, members of that family cultivate the habit or what can be considered a character flaw or trait, of being habitually critical of others. Going to Confession, the Sacrament of Reconciliation, can cleanse from a specific act of criticism. However, if the root cause is not removed, the critical spirit remains. The character flaw of being critical remains. Either pop the head of the dandelion or pull up the weed at its root and be fully rid of it. Your choice!

The Sacrament of Reconciliation is different from the Courts of Heaven or just repenting to God directly because in this Sacrament, *we are also reconciling with the Church*, the Body of Christ against whom we have transgressed. It also gives sanctifying grace. Both have their spiritual value and work together to bring full metanoia, transformation.

What is NOT for the Sacrament of Reconciliation is anything outside of our own personal actions or choices. It is only for personal sins, iniquities, flaws; where we have personally fallen short.

6. Vindicate: to clear, as from an accusation, imputation, suspicion, or the like. Dictionary.com
7. *"Give thanks to the Lord of lords* (Adonai ha'adonim), *for His faithfulness is everlasting."* Psalm 136:3
8. 'ă-ḏō-nāy
9. James 4:2

5. 5 KEYS TO PURIFICATION

1. We will cover this in detail in Chapters 16 and 17.
2. CCC 1431
3. Lamentations 5:21
4. John 19:37; Zechariah 12:10
5. CCC 1432
6. 1 Peter 4:8

7. 9 STEPS TO PETITIONING

1. https://biblehub.com/greek/3341.htm
2. "Atonement: The theological meaning 'reconciliation' (of man with God through the life, passion, and death of Christ) is from 1520s; that of 'satisfaction or reparation for wrong or injury, propitiation of an offended party' is from 1610s." Source: https://www.etymonline.com/word/atonement

3. "Be in harmony, agree, be in accordance," from adverbial phrase *atonen* (c. 1300) "in accord," literally "at one," a contraction of at and one. It retains the older pronunciation of *one*. The meaning "make up (for errors or deficiencies)" is from 1660s; that of "make reparations" is from 1680s.

"To bring *at one*, to reconcile, and thence to suffer the pains of whatever sacrifice is necessary to bring about a reconciliation. [Hensleigh Wedgwood, *A Dictionary of English Etymology*, 1859] The phrase perhaps is modeled on Latin *adunare* 'unite,' from *ad* 'to, at' (see ad-) + *unum* 'one.'" Source: https://www.etymonline.com/word/atonement

8. THE SUPERNATURAL BLOOD AND NAME OF JESUS

1. Ron Wyatt is credited with making a number of biblical discoveries including the chariot parts in the Gulf of Aqaba (from Pharaoh's army destroyed in the Red Sea, chasing after Moses and the departing Israelites); the destroyed cities of Sodom and Gomorrah; the true Mount Sinai in Saudi Arabia, and others. See ronwyatt.com for documented articles.

2. The Ark of the Covenant is first described in Exodus Chapter 25, where God provides the exact instructions for how to build it. His directive begins in Exodus 25:8-9: *"Have them build a sanctuary for Me, so that I may dwell among them. You shall construct it in accordance with everything that I am going to show you, as the pattern of the tabernacle and the pattern of all its furniture."*

   The Ark of the Covenant contains the two tablets of the 10 Commandments, i.e., God's Torah (Teaching/Laws); Manna (the bread that came down from Heaven); and the sprouting Rod of Aaron the high priest and brother of Moses.

   Jesus would come as the fulfillment of the Ark of the Covenant. He is the Torah.

   He is the Bread that came down from Heaven. *"I am the true bread that came down from heaven. Anyone who eats this bread will not die as your ancestors did (even though they ate the manna) but will live forever."* John 6:58

   He is the High Priest and Ruler of God's Kingdom. *"The kingdom of the world has become the kingdom of our Lord and of His Christ; and He will reign forever and ever."* Revelations 11:15

   Hebrews 9:4 also describes the contents of the Ark of the Covenant.

3. The Book of 2 Maccabees 2:4-8 tells how the Prophet Jeremiah took and hid the Ark of the Covenant from the impending invaders: *"The same document also tells how the prophet, in virtue of an oracle, ordered that the tent and the ark should accompany him, and how he went to the very mountain that Moses climbed to behold God's inheritance. When Jeremiah*

arrived there, he found a chamber in a cave in which he put the tent, the ark, and the altar of incense; then he sealed the entrance. Some of those who followed him came up intending to mark the path, but they could not find it. When Jeremiah heard of this, he reproved them: "The place is to remain unknown until God gathers his people together again and shows them mercy. Then the Lord will disclose these things, and the glory of the Lord and the cloud will be seen, just as they appeared in the time of Moses and of Solomon when he prayed that the place might be greatly sanctified." NABRE

This of course begs the question how does one reconcile this Scripture with Ron Wyatt's discovery? This author does not have the answers. However, Ron Wyatt established a credible track record, working with the Holy Spirit, discovering many biblical artifacts and sites. His account of discovering the Ark of the Covenant and this Maccabees passage are not necessarily conflicting. Nobody else has been allowed to find the Ark where Ron discovered it. God is full of mysteries!

4. "In humans, each cell normally contains 23 pairs of chromosomes, for a total of 46. Twenty-two of these pairs, called autosomes, look the same in both males and females. The 23rd pair, the sex chromosomes, differ between males and females. Females have two copies of the X chromosome, while males have one X and one Y chromosome." Source: medlineplus.gov

5. *"But when he had thought this over, behold, an angel of the Lord appeared to him in a dream, saying, 'Joseph, son of David, do not be afraid to take Mary as your wife; for the Child who has been conceived in her is of the Holy Spirit.'"* Matthew 1:20

6. 2 Samuel 6:1-7 and 1 Chronicles 13:9-12.

7. CCC 670, Matthew 26:28

8. "Law" capitalized indicates Torah in Hebrew, meaning teaching. Torah refers to the first five books of the Bible. So it is moral statutes or guidelines provided by God for His people to live by. Here "Law" is not what we think as societal protection or security, but rather moral living in order to bring us into union, right relationship, with God. The core issue is in translations from Hebrew and Greek to English "law" which has a different connotation, as enforcement-enforcer, rather than moral actions and guidelines that keep or restore us to right relationship with God. Torah conveys love; law infers punishment.

9. *"And when the headwaiter tasted the water that had become wine, without knowing where it came from (although the servers who had drawn the water knew), the headwaiter called the bridegroom and said to him, 'Everyone serves good wine first, and then when people have drunk freely, an inferior one; but you have kept the good wine until now.'"* John 2:9-10 NABRE

10. The Eucharistic host is the bread host used in Holy Communion.
11. Examples of a "desecrated host" include it being mishandled in some way, falling on the floor, given to someone not in the sacrament to receive it properly.

    Here is one detailed account of blood appearing on a consecrated host in Buenos Aires, Argentina, 1996. "The priest opened the tabernacle and found the host appeared to be a bloody substance. On October 5, 1999, in the presence of the Cardinal's representatives, scientist Dr. Ricardo Castañón Gómez took a sample of the bloody fragment and sent it to New York for analysis. One of these scientists was Dr. Frederic Zugiba, the well-known cardiologist and forensic pathologist. He determined that the analyzed substance was real flesh and blood containing human DNA. Zugiba testified that 'the analyzed material is a fragment of the heart muscle found in the wall of the left ventricle close to the valves. This muscle is responsible for the contraction of the heart. It should be borne in mind that the left cardiac ventricle pumps blood to all parts of the body. The heart muscle is in an inflammatory condition and contains a large number of white blood cells. This indicates that the heart was alive at the time the sample was taken. It is my contention that the heart was alive, since white blood cells die outside a living organism. They require a living organism to sustain them. Thus, their presence indicates that *the heart was alive* when the sample was taken. What is more, these white blood cells had penetrated the tissue, which further indicates that the heart had been under severe stress, as if the owner had been beaten severely about the chest.'" Ref: https://aleteia.org/2017/06/15/4-incredible-eucharistic-miracles-that-defy-scientific-explanation/
12. There are 158 documented and verified Eucharistic miracles that have occurred over the past several centuries and been approved by the Catholic Church. This author could not find any such miracles by any other Christian denomination regarding the Holy Eucharist. They may exist but have not been found by this author.

    From the most famous Eucharistic miracle, the Eucharistic miracle of Lanciano, Italy: "At the initiative of the Archbishop of Lanciano and with authorization from Rome, the Franciscans of Lanciano decided, in 1970, to have the relics examined scientifically.

    "Doctor Odoardo Linoli, head of the laboratory of clinical analysis and pathological anatomy of the hospital of Arezzo, was entrusted with the study. After careful and rigorous examinations, Linoli presented his findings on March 4, 1971.

    "Serafini explained the many steps of Linoli's studies, 'First of all, he demonstrated that the flesh is myocardial tissue; it is a fragment of the heart. Second, the blood is true blood. And third, the flesh and blood are human. Fourth, the blood type he discovered separately in flesh and blood is the AB blood type, the rarest in humans. And then also, fifth, the presence of the proteins with an electrophoretic ratio that is similar to that of fresh blood. And six, the presence of minerals in the blood.'" (Source: https://www.ewtnvatican.com/articles/miracle-hunter-a-cardiologists-journey-into-eucharistic-miracles-1802)

From an approved Eucharistic miracle in Legnica, Poland, 2013: "In February 2014, a tiny red fragment of the host was separated and put on a corporal. The Commission ordered to take samples in order to conduct the thorough tests by the relevant research institutes. After the investigations, the Department of Forensic Medicine stated: In the Histopathological image, the fragments of tissue have been found containing the fragmented parts of the cross striated muscle. (...) The whole (...) is most similar to the heart muscle with alterations that often appear during the agony. The genetic researches indicate the human origin of the tissue."

13. Another approved Eucharistic Miracle occurred in Tixtla, Mexico in 2006. The scientific research conducted between October 2009 and October 2012 released the following statement:

"The reddish substance analyzed corresponds to blood in which there are hemoglobin and DNA of human origin. Two studies conducted by eminent forensic experts with different methodologies have shown that the substance originates from the interior, excluding the hypothesis that someone could have placed it from the exterior.

"The blood type is AB, similar to the one found in the Host of Lanciano and in the Holy Shroud of Turin. A microscopic analysis of magnification and penetration reveals that the superior part of the blood has been coagulated since October 2006. Moreover, the underlying internal layers reveal, in February 2010, the presence of fresh blood. The event does not have a natural explanation." Source: https://aleteia.org/2017/06/15/4-incredible-eucharistic-miracles-that-defy-scientific-explanation/

Controversy around the Shroud of Turin arose from faulty sampling in the original study in 1987. Ensuing studies and sampling have met higher ethical scientific standards and confirm more recent findings.

14. Also found in Romans 10:13, Acts 2:21.

15. Y'shua or Yeshua is from the Hebrew root word Y-Sh-A which means to deliver from, to save.

16. The Word of God is Jesus Christ Incarnate. He "assumed our humanity" by coming as the Son of Man.

17. CCC 2666

18. CCC 2664

9. THE SUPERPOWER PRAYER OF GRATITUDE

1. Many Catholic Churches or chapels offer Adoration during specific times. The Adoration is of a sanctified Host, the spiritual Body of Christ Jesus, held in a monstrance on the altar. Many miracles and benefits have been recorded from this practice.
2. CCC 2628
3. Daniel 10:13
4. 1 Thessalonians 2:18

10. DELIVERANCE FROM THE LEVIATHAN SPIRIT

1. 1 John 2:16
2. CCC 2540
3. This includes New Age dogma, which can be very ego-I-me centered, thinly veiling narcissism.
4. John 14:16: *"He shall give you another Comforter (Parakletos), that he may abide with you."*

   1 John 2:1: *"If any man sin, we have an advocate with the Father, Jesus."*

   Also:

   Strong's #3875: parakletos (pronounced par-ak'-lay-tos): an intercessor, consoler, advocate, comforter.

   Thayer's Greek Lexicon: paraklētos

   1) summoned, called to one's side, especially called to one's aid

   1a) one who pleads another's cause before a judge, a pleader, counsel for defense, legal assistant, an advocate

   1b) one who pleads another's cause with one, an intercessor

   Source: https://www.bibletools.org/index.cfm/fuseaction/Lexicon.show/ID/G3875/parakletos.htm
5. *"I will rejoice greatly in the Lord, my soul will exult in my God; for He has clothed me with garments of salvation, He has wrapped me with a robe of righteousness."* Isaiah 61:10.

   "Let your priests be clothed with righteousness, and let your godly ones sing for joy." Psalm 132:9
6. *"Adonai"* is one of the names for God the Father. It conveys His absolute sovereignty and lordship. He is sovereign and Just Judge.
7. **Scriptures that demonstrate God's Angels assisting in emancipation, justice and enforcement of God's judgements:**

   "But during the night an angel of the Lord opened the gates of the prison, and taking them out he said..." Acts 5:19

   "And behold, an angel of the Lord suddenly appeared and a light shone

in the cell; and he struck Peter's side and woke him up, saying, "Get up quickly." And his chains fell off his hands. And the angel said to him, "Gird yourself and put on your sandals." And he did so. And he said to him, "Wrap your cloak around you and follow me." And he went out and continued to follow, and he did not know that what was being done by the angel was real, but thought he was seeing a vision." Acts 12:7-10

"*When Peter came to himself, he said, 'Now I know for sure that the Lord has sent forth His angel and rescued me from the hand of Herod and from all that the Jewish people were expecting.'*" Acts 12:11

"*And immediately an angel of the Lord struck him because he did not give God the glory, and he was eaten by worms and died.*" Acts 12:23

8. Hebrews 12:24 speaks of this voice of the Blood of Jesus: "*And to Jesus, the Mediator of a New Covenant, and to the sprinkled blood, which speaks better than the blood of Abel.*"

9. This is the last word that Jesus uttered on the cross before He gave up His last breath. It is Aramaic and has been translated "It is finished"; also "paid in full". His sacrificed death for humanity paid the ransom for our sins.

11. DELIVERANCE FROM THE JEZEBEL SPIRIT

1. 1 Kings 18-21

12. DELIVERANCE FROM THE MAMMON SPIRIT

1. 1 Timothy 6:10
2. 1 Timothy 6:6
3. 1 Timothy 6:11-12
4. Found several places throughout the Holy Scriptures, including Matthew 19:26, Luke 1:37 & 18:27, Jeremiah 32:17 & 32:27, Job 42:2.
5. See the Glossary of the *One New Man Bible*, entry "Mammon", pg. 1758.
6. From *The American Heritage® Dictionary of the English Language*, 5th Edition, HarperCollins, 2015.
7. CCC 301
8. CCC 27
9. Matthew 5:48
10. CCC 396
11. We have intentionally chosen to use colloquial grammar at times, because it is more natural to the reader and therefore likely to be more easily and quickly understood.
12. 2 Peter 3:23
13. "*Because you did not serve the Lord your God joyfully and gladly in the time of prosperity, therefore in hunger and thirst, in nakedness and dire*

poverty, you will serve the enemies the Lord sends against you. He will put an iron yoke on your neck until He has destroyed you." Deuteronomy 28:47-48

14. Numbers 23:19

13. DELIVERANCE FROM THE PYTHON SPIRIT

1. Reiki is a "healing" modality that comes out of Japan and involves various symbols and mantras released over the body of the client/subject. It is known to be from the astral realm. It is not from God. This author has received Master certification in three types of Reiki and feels qualified to speak on it. A recipient can feel relief from symptoms from it, but it does **not** heal at a causal level. It can involve or summon demons and is not recommended for anyone on a path with the One True God and Jesus Christ. It opens doors to the demonic realm and can create hooks and cords to that realm. One young practitioner had an old woman show up at all of her sessions. The practitioner, in her mid-20's at the time, began to age visibly and very quickly. Once she stopped and cut cords, her youthfulness restored. Stay away from Reiki!

2. Acts 16:16 *"It happened that as we were on our way to the place of prayer, we were met by a slave-girl who had a spirit of divination [that is, a demonic spirit claiming to foretell the future and discover hidden knowledge], and she brought her owners a good profit by fortune-telling."*

   The spirit in this passage is a python spirit. In Greek mythology, python, the earth-dragon serpent goddess, was associated with the oracle at Delphi. In the Greek translation, "a spirit (pneuma) of clairvoyance (Pythōna)." So the "spirit of divination" is the spirit of python.

3. Practices can include healing and occult spiritual practices and traditions.

4. So-called channelers are usually channeling demons, various fallen angels, part of the 1/3 angels that chose to leave their heavenly positions, along with satan. Angels, including fallen angels, possess a much higher intelligence than humans and therefore can be very attractive to humans in their channeled messages. They can also pose or present themselves as extra-terrestrials. Beware of channeling and channelers. "Test the spirit." New Agers, Christians and others participate in this deception.

5. There are many "Christians" engaging in the witchcraft of fortune-telling, passing it off as if it were coming from the Holy Spirit. They also present themselves as being Holy Spirit-filled, but are actually working with, and being given information about others, from familiar spirits. This is unfortunately pretty common. Look at the heart of the person to know the truth. Someone filled with the Holy Spirit will also have a loving heart.

6. Sexual content in lyrics and other media can draw in sex-related demons that can attack you in your sleep. Sexualized music etc. is not innocent entertainment. It provides entry ways for numerous kinds of demons

which can and do influence behavior, thoughts and impulses, including addictions. Knowledge is power.

14. DELIVERANCE FROM THE BAAL SPIRIT

1. Their practices have also morphed into the consumption of children and infant blood, blood products and flesh, especially their heart and kidney organs.

   Satanist groups in the U.S. have gone to court to appeal stricter abortion laws citing these laws would deny them their religious rights, as the abortions are regarded as ritual sacrifice. No joke.

   Please note: This does NOT mean or infer that people who get an abortion are knowingly or intentionally a part of this practice. There ARE however, groups/cults who HAVE admitted publicly and even in testimony that they are using babies for ritual sacrifice.
2. 1 Kings 18:16-45
3. DEW (directed-energy-weaponry)
4. Genetically-modified organisms (GMO) aka genetically engineered.
5. 1 Kings 18:19
6. While the Israelites' leader Moses was on the mountaintop receiving the Torah (10 Commandments Teachings) from God, the people became impatient and decided to take matters into their own hands and create their own god. *"And when the people saw that Moses delayed coming down from the mountain, the people gathered themselves together to Aaron [their priest] and said to him, "Get up! Make gods for us that will go before us, for this Moses, the man who brought us up out of the land of Egypt, we do not know what has happened to him." Exodus 32:1*

   This is a classic example of human folly. Impatience with or disloyalty to the One True God; creating our own 'gods' to live by; living by self-made rules of morality and ethics, beholden to no one for virtues or character; ungrateful for what has been given (emancipation from the bondage of Egypt); believing our own creations will satisfy us and set us free, tho ultimately they never do.
7. As of the publication of this book, the state of Minnesota allows and has an average of 5-6 post-birth murders of infants, aka infanticide, per year. What have we become? Those babies could be adopted.

16. FILL WITH THE GOOD

1. *"But you, beloved, building yourselves up on your most holy faith, praying in the Holy Spirit."* Jude 1:20

17. SANCTIFICATION

1. There are various words or terms used to refer to God's Torah (teachings). These include commandments, statutes, laws, commands, precepts, testimonies, decrees, teachings. The most accurate translation for Torah is teachings. See "Torah" entry in the Glossary of the One New Man Bible.

2. Several verses including Leviticus 11:44 & 45, Leviticus 20:7.

3. A whole book could be dedicated to the marvels of Psalm 119. In addition to it being structured as an acrostic (each first letter taken in order creates a word), and being organized in 22 stanzas corresponding to the 22 Hebrew letters, each stanza contains eight verse sets.

    Eight here is believed to correspond to the eight different words for the Scriptures: law (*torah*), testimony, precept, statute, commandment, judgment ("a rule for living"), Word of God, and promise. (Ref: Warren Wiersbe, BE Bible Study Series.)

    Eight is also the biblical number for new beginnings and 888 is the gematria for Jesus. The "Day of Salvation" is considered the eighth day, the day after the Sabbath (seven); as Jesus rose from the dead on the day after the Sabbath (Matthew 28:1-3). So eight is associated with Salvation.

    One could say that Psalm 119 expresses the fullness of ways that we can connect with God for our salvation.

18. 5 AGONIES, 5 REPAIRS

1. Gethsemane was a garden at the foot of the Mount of Olives in East Jerusalem. It means "oil press." Jesus was commencing His Passion Gift by being the oil press for humanity's sins.

2. This can be possible with the condition called *hematidrosis*, which can occur when someone is in extreme anxiety or stress.

3. The two sons of Zebedee are the Apostles John the Beloved and James aka Jacob. They were also called the "sons of Thunder."

4. *"These things I have spoken to you so that in Me you may have peace. In the world you have tribulation, but take courage; I have overcome the world."* John 16:33

5. Also known as Golgatha. Both names mean "place of skull." Golgatha is recognized as a conflation of "Goliath of Gath." After David (the future King) slayed the giant Goliath, David took his head to Jerusalem to the highest point, which is Golgatha or Mount Calvary, to display his victory over evil. This is a profound presaging of the ultimate victory over evil that was to take place on that same ground by David's descendant Jesus Christ.

19. SANCTIFYING THE SOUL

1. Also found in Deuteronomy 6:5-6: "*And you shall love the Lord your God with all your heart and with all your soul and with all your strength. These words, which I am commanding you today, shall be on your heart.*"
2. Glossary definition of 'soul', *Catechism of the Catholic Church*, Ascension Edition, 2022.
3. Leviticus 26:43
4. The *One New Man Bible*'s translation of Leviticus 26:11 is: "*And I will set My Tabernacle among you, and My very being will not abhor you.*" God's "*very being*" can imply the deepest spiritual core of God. "*Will not abhor*" is akin to "will not reject."

20. STRENGTHENING THE SOUL

1. CCC 1818
2. Deuteronomy 6:5
3. John 13:34
4. Matthew 5:48
5. CCC 1822
6. "The Beatitudes reveal the goal of human existence, the ultimate end of human acts: God calls us to His own beatitude. This vocation is addressed to each individual personally, but also to the Church as a whole, a new people made up of those who have accepted the promise and live from it in faith." CCC 1719

22. SANCTIFYING THE EGO

1. John 3:30
2. The Hebrew translation of reverence is 'awe'.

24. SANCTIFYING THE WILL

1. There are hundreds of Christian saints whose bodies are incorruptible. Saint Cecilia's is known to be the oldest on record and is over 1900 years old. The most recent is a millennial, Blessed Carlos Acutis, who died at 15 years of age in 2006. His incorruptible body is on display in Italy. It is believed that the incorruptible body is indicative of having overcome Original Sin which introduced disease, decay and death to the human body.
2. Also called "Wisdom of Solomon". This verse translation is from the Revised Standard Version of the Bible—Second Catholic Edition

(Ignatius Edition), copyright © 2006 National Council of the Churches of Christ in the United States of America. Used by permission. All rights reserved.

3. The word "law" in the Scriptures can have different meanings in different contexts and depending on the translation. "Law" has been translated from "Torah" which means God's teachings or commandments. Usually lower-case "law" refers to man's laws, inferring the need to have man-made structures where an internal compass of righteous and moral character is lacking.

When "Law" is capitalized it refers to God's Torah, the 10 Commandments and especially the Law of Love. See Jeremiah 31:33, "*I will put My law within them and on their heart I will write it; and I will be their God, and they shall be My people.*"

Approximately 350 years prior to Jeremiah giving this Word, King and Psalmist David said: "*I delight to do your will, O my God; your Law is within my heart.*" Psalm 40:8

25. LIVING IN DIVINE WILL

1. "*For I have come down from heaven, not to do My own will, but the will of Him who sent Me.*" John 6:38
2. John 14:15
3. Baptism is a precious sacrament that initiates spiritual rebirth into the Way of Christ Jesus. It brings sanctifying grace. That is, the grace of being sanctified/set apart/marked as God's own.

A Christian baptism will use water to baptize and contain the same words that Jesus instructed His disciples in Matthew 28:18-20, "*And Jesus came up and spoke to them, saying, 'All authority in heaven and on earth has been given to Me. Go, therefore, and make disciples of all the nations, **baptizing them in the name of the Father and the Son and the Holy Spirit**, teaching them to follow all that I commanded you; and behold, I am with you always, to the end of the age.'*"
4. "*When the day of Pentecost had come, they were all together in one place. And suddenly a noise like a violent rushing wind came from heaven, and it filled the whole house where they were sitting. And tongues that looked like fire appeared to them, distributing themselves, and a tongue rested on each one of them. And they were all filled with the Holy Spirit and began to speak with different tongues, as the Spirit was giving them the ability to speak out.*" Acts 2:1-4
5. The Catholic Sacrament of Confirmation brings a profound infilling of the Holy Spirit.
6. Gleaned from the AMP translation.

EPILOGUE

1. John 10:10
2. John 13:34, John 13:35, John 15:12, John 15:17
3. Also yō-šêḇ.
4. New Revised Standard Version, Anglicised (NRSVA), National Council of the Churches of Christ in the USA, 2021.

ABOUT THE AUTHOR

Maria T. Tonello has been teaching, leading and supporting prayer intercessors nationally and internationally for the past several years. The prayer protocols in this book come from that ministry and have many testimonials testifying to their transformational effects.

Maria is also the author of <u>The Eucharist Trilogy</u>, celebrating the gift of Christ Jesus as Eucharistic Lord.

Maria has been a management consultant, corporate trainer, public speaker and teacher. She holds two Masters of Science degrees, an M.S. in O.D. (Applied Behavioral Sciences) and an M.S. in Psychology; but considers her most valuable education learning to listen to, heed and serve the Father's heart.

You can do what God is calling YOU to do! Jesus' Apostles were simple men and women whose hearts were open to serving Him through the indwelling Spirit of God.

"I can do ALL things through Christ who strengthens me."
Philippians 4:13

a

www.ingramcontent.com/pod-product-compliance
Lightning Source LLC
Chambersburg PA
CBHW062040080426
42734CB00012B/2510